-Hear the Challenge-

-Kyle S. Rohrig-

Introduction

If you have even remotely considered hiking the length of the nearly 2,200-mile Appalachian Trail, then you've "heard the challenge." The question now is...will you answer it? If you have been on the fence about doing a thru-hike, the job of this book is to gently nudge, possibly even shove you off that fence, into the direction of the Appalachian Trail. But, if your mind is already made up to embark on this once in a lifetime adventure, then prepare to have your confidence elevated to new heights. Knowledge is power and information is currency; I intend to make you powerfully rich, in regards to the Appalachian Trail, as you read through the contents of this book.

The subjects of this work include, but are far from limited to...

-**Preparing your life for a thru-hike**

-**Financial preparation**

-**Mental preparation (what you bring within yourself is far more important than what you put in your pack).**

-**Physical preparation (I've been a strength and conditioning specialist for nearly a decade).**

-**Hiking with a dog (I've done the whole trail with one)**

-**Insights and information into nearly every aspect of thru-hiking, as well as life on trail and much, much more.**

-**Extensive information regarding gear and itemized lists of what this journey requires.**

-**Insights into each state, as well as noteworthy regions and the obstacles/highlights they present.**

This book is not designed nor intended to be a "how to" or a "guidebook." It is simply designed to present you with information while simultaneously inspiring the confidence to use that information in making decisions that are perfect for you. Dive in, the water is fine as it will ever be...

Table of Contents

Chapter 1: What is the Appalachian Trail?............7

Chapter 2: Preparing your life for an Appalachian Trail thru-hike……………………………………………......10

Chapter 3: Mental Preparation ………………………..21

Chapter 4: Physical Preparation……………………….34

Chapter 5: Tips, Tricks, What to Expect, and Other Insights……………………………………………………….38

Chapter 6: Gear Accumulation/Information……120

Chapter 7: Appalachian Trail Thru-Hiker Slang/Jargon……………………………………………….175

Chapter 8: Topographical - State and Regional Insight………………………………………………………182

Dedication

This book is dedicated to "Baltimore Jack" Tarlin and the restless spirit he brought to the Appalachian Trail, as well as all who knew him. You are truly a legend whose presence and mark will never be forgotten. Two paths diverged in the woods; he took the one with white blazes...

"Those who would understand-know a ship at harbor is safe, yet that is not what ships are for…"

J.A. Shedd

-Kyle S. Rohrig-

Hear the Challenge...
Answer the Call

(Hike the Appalachian Trail)

    Who are you? Think about it. This is quite possibly mankind's oldest self-reflective question. "Who am I, really?" Perhaps you already know the answer, or freely acknowledge you don't. Maybe you think you know, or maybe you're actively seeking that answer. This question, "Who am I?" is an inquiry some people spend their entire lives seeking and possibly never discovering the answer to, or perhaps thinking they already know. It's more than just your name, your parents, when and where you were born, or where you grew up; that's your driver's license, your calling card... it's not who you are. Those are simply a small fraction of the equation that equals the sum total of your complete being. So where is the rest of the equation, and how do you add it all up to make sense? There is an answer to that, albeit not a specific one. Even still, once you have the answer to the whole equation, it isn't one that can be spoken, or even understood by others. It's a feeling, a knowing; a subtle but strong cocoon of inner confidence, understanding, honesty, and trusting with and of one's self. You can't speak of it to others in any language they'll understand, but they can see and sense it for themselves in other individuals, interpreting it as they may.

    The answer to where the other pieces of the whole equation are is simple, yet complex. They're out there, but also within you. Sometimes one must journey outward in order to journey inward. To truly know WHO YOU ARE, you have to be tested. You have to test yourself, or through no designs of your own, be tested by outside events/forces. You have to be stripped to the barest of essentials, pushed to the very edge of your emotional threshold, and beaten down to the point that you give serious consideration to not getting back up again. This is when and where you will discover who you truly are... or are not. When it comes to learning and finding answers, particularly to the questions pertaining to self - there is no better teacher than life, firsthand experiences, and especially Mother Nature. Believe me when I say, "You'll find plenty of all three on the Appalachian Trail..."

Who am I? The answer to that question is ever changing and evolving; but my driver's license says I'm Kyle Rohrig. Out on the trails and within small circles I'm known as "The Mayor," or simply "Mayor." That is my trail name, and I received it because like all Mayors (I hope), I take care of my people. Who are my people? Plainly put, you are my people. Whoever is around me at any given time are "my people," and I will do anything to help, motivate, or make life easier for you in any way I can. I am an Appalachian Trail thru-hiker, as well as Pacific Crest Trail thru-hiker; with hopefully many more to come. In another life (before the trails), I was an athletic trainer, professional fisherman, and entrepreneur who wondered the same things many people wonder these days. "Who am I? What am I doing? Am I truly, honestly where I want to be - doing what I want to do? Am I happy? Am I leading a fulfilling life? What else could I be doing?"

These were all questions I asked myself before hiking the Appalachian Trail. I didn't know the answers back then, but I thought I might find some of them if I found myself wandering the wilds of the Appalachian Mountains. In the end, I got a lot more than I bargained for when I went out there. I went in search of adventure, answers, a sense of self... and what I found changed my life. It changed the direction of my life, as well as my views of people, the universe, and what life and living is all about... for me. However, I didn't write this book to tell you about me or my adventure. No, I wrote this book so you might find the confidence, inspiration, and "know how" to seek your own journey and find your own answers. If you can summon the courage to embark on a great adventure such as hiking more than 2,000 miles over mountains and through wilderness, while braving any obstacles you might encounter along the way; I promise you will find what you seek. It may very well be something you didn't know you were even looking for...

Again, the goal of this book is not to be an "end all - be all," or "this is how you do it guide/authority" on hiking the Appalachian Trail. No one, and no one thing can ever meet that demand. I do not have all the answers, and neither does this book. The true purpose of this book is to give you (the reader) a boost of confidence, as well as inspiration when it comes to deciding, planning, preparing, and ultimately pulling the trigger on an adventure such as thru-hiking the legendary Appalachian Trail; to ultimately lessen the learning curve and provide insights to the undertaking of this epic endeavor. I want to arm you with information, and give you the confidence to use it however you wish. I remember how exciting yet daunting the research preparation was for this adventure, so everything I've put into this book is what I wish I could have known/found out before I embarked on this journey. Of course, one of the greatest aspects of fun on any journey is learning things for yourself, sometimes the hard way if need be. Nevertheless, the people who adhere to that strict "going in blind" philosophy may not choose to read a book such as this one. So, seeing as how you are reading these words, I can safely assume you have questions, apprehensions, and possibly even some misgivings; I hope to ease your mind. I have consolidated many, many months of research and information gathering (not to mention learning the hard way - first hand) into one source. Whatever isn't included in this book, I have tried to make easier to find elsewhere, while attempting to give better direction to research, so you can learn more on your own. You won't find all the answers here, but you will find more than enough to empower you to take those first steps down a path that will forever leave its mark on you; possibly even changing the very direction and purpose of your life...

Chapter 1

What is the Appalachian Trail?

The Appalachian Trail is many different things to many different people. It's the best and worst thing you'll ever do in your life. It's the most fun, as well as the most misery you'll ever experience at the same time. It's the greatest or worst time you'll ever have. Ultimately, it's a nearly 2,200-mile foot path that stretches from Springer Mountain in Amicalola State Park-Georgia, to Mount Katahdin in Baxter State Park-Maine, while passing through fourteen of some of the country's oldest states.

The Appalachian Trail was first envisioned in 1921 by a man named Benton MacKaye. He claimed the idea came to him while sitting in a tree atop Vermont's Mount Stratton (yes, the AT does cross over this mountain). Benton proposed his idea for the "super trail" in the October 1921 issue of "The Journal of the American Institute of Architects." He presented the idea of the AT as a "utopian refuge from urban life," and while it was originally his project, Benton never played much of a role in the overall construction.

By March 1925 Mr. MacKaye had gathered enough of the support needed to make his vision a reality, and the Appalachian Trail Conference (ATC) was born in order to manage and present more detailed plans. Though progress was slow in the beginning, with countless obstacles to overcome, all the individual trails being blazed throughout the different states were eventually connected in August of 1937. The United States officially had a continuous, unbroken trail that stretched for more than 2,000 miles across the eastern side of the country.

While the completed Appalachian Trail came into existence in 1937, nobody would ever successfully attempt to walk its entire length until 1948. Earl Shaffer is credited as the "original thru-hiker." Earl was a World War II veteran from Pennsylvania who decided the trail would be ideal for "walking the army out of my system." In addition to his original thru-hike completed in 1948, he would go on to complete the trail two more times in 1965, and again in 1998, at the age of 79. In order to earn the true label of "thru-hiker," a thru-hike is officially described as finishing the entire trail within the year the hike was started. Doesn't matter how you finish it, so long as you hike every mile within the same year.

The thought of walking over 2,000 miles through wilderness while living outside for months on end is a very romanticized thought to many who contemplate attempting it. I believe the word "walk" conjures up a false sense of ease in most people's minds. You think to yourself, "Oh, a 2,000 mile walk in the woods sounds exactly like something I would enjoy, filled with wonderful sights, experiences, and people; I go on walks around my neighborhood and the local trails every day, so this will be right up my alley!" I'll be the first to admit this was my original impression of hiking the Appalachian Trail when first contemplating it (throw in a little wilderness survival, as well as living off the land for good measure). It was a romantic idea that didn't account for many of the factors that go into completing this hike. Now having completed the entire trail, I'll also be the first to tell you that hiking the AT is not a walk, it's a grind. You grind out the miles, you grind out the days-that turn into weeks-that turn into months; you grind out the mountains, grind through the unrelenting, unmerciful elements, and some days... you grind out each and every step.

Flat sections throughout the trail are nearly nonexistent. Sure, there are a few good stretches and small sections of level ground thrown in here and there, but for the most part, you're either going up or coming down for more than 2,000 miles. The tallest peak on the AT only tops out at 6,643 feet above sea level, and belongs to Clingmans Dome of the Smoky Mountains National Park. While this is not very tall compared to other mountains in the West/Midwestern part of the United States, what the Appalachian Trail lacks in altitude, it makes up for in frequency. Due to the constant ascents and descents, a traverse of the entire AT will equate to climbing the 29,035-foot Mount Everest approximately sixteen times. I'll be honest with you, when you finish, it feels like you did a hell of a lot more than that. The total elevation you'll gain and lose throughout the entire journey is 515,000 feet. This is over 100,000 more feet than the next closest long distance trail in regards to elevation gain/loss; the Continental Divide Trail (CDT). The CDT is close to 1,000 miles longer than the AT, yet has more than 100,000 fewer feet in elevation gain/loss. The AT is truly a monster among trails...

Every year (more in recent years), on average, several thousand hikers attempt to complete the entire trail. Most start in Georgia during the spring time and head north, but some start in Maine during the early summer and head south. Regardless of when and where they start, more than 80% of them won't make it, and a good percentage of those who do, will not have done so without skipping some small or major sections of the trail. There are many reasons why people don't make it, and we'll touch on most of them a little further on.

You may find this easy or hard to believe, but past thru-hikers take a somewhat dark pleasure in the high attrition rate when it comes to other people finishing the AT. We want to see people finish it and discover all these new things about themselves, and feel the accomplishment, but on the other hand, we know not everyone can accomplish this endeavor, and deep down we don't want just anyone and everyone to be able to do it. This wouldn't be the great challenge it is if anyone could do it; so we finishers take a certain pride in the fact that there are more people who can't do this, than people who can. You and I won't be better than other people for having done it, or even for having tried; we're better for what we've asked of ourselves, whether we make it or not.

Chapter 2

Preparing Your Life for an Appalachian Trail Thru-Hike

How do you get your life organized in order to take 4 to 7 months off to live in the wilderness? The answer is different for everyone, as well as the degree of difficulty in achieving the preparedness necessary to take a months' long vacation with no income. Fortunately, there are many strategies to make this happen. Unfortunately, some people will be dug in a hole so deep, bogged down by so much responsibility, it will be nearly impossible to make a thru-hike happen. Ultimately, if you want to thru-hike, you'll find a way to thru-hike; if not, you'll find an excuse.

Money

Money, the root of all evil is unfortunately a critical part of a thru-hike. One of the major reasons for people not completing a thru-hike is running out of cash. How much is enough? That answer varies for everyone. How do you know how much is enough for you? This is usually something you can't possibly know for sure until you get boots on the trail and some miles under your feet. Typically, the cost of a thru-hike is completely dependent on your self-control, as well as your comfort levels. People have completed a thru-hike of the AT for as much as $15,000 and as little as $600. The universal average that people will normally spout off is $1.50 per mile. This equates to about $3,000 for a thru-hike of the entire trail. To your average individual, I would recommend taking no less than $3,000 with you, more if you can.

On top of the "how much money" question, people also tend to ask, "What's the least amount of money I can bring, but still enjoy myself while doing everything I want to do?" Again, that answer is going to vary from person to person based on their wants and desires. My own personal recommendation for someone who wants to go out there and be able to do the things they want to do without feeling like they're having to restrict themselves would be $3,000 bare minimum, $5,000 to be safely comfortable. I spent slightly over 5k on my thru-hike, and I can honestly say I wanted for nothing, and did pretty much everything I wanted to do over the course of 195 days. By no means let these numbers scare you if they feel a little beyond your reach at the moment; keep reading.

This is how you should try to view money prior-to and during the hike (that is if money is even a factor for you). In theory, when you're out on trail, the only thing you need money for is food. If you've done your math, have all your gear, and have the money to pay for any and all expenses you might have back home, then all you need money on trail for is food, maybe some gear replacements, and maybe transportation; that's it. You have shelter and warmth in your backpack, so you really don't "need" to spend money to stay anywhere else but the woods; however, that's in a perfect world. Undoubtedly, you're going to spend extra money on things you don't absolutely need. Things like alcohol, hotels, hostels, haircuts, massages, restaurants, cigarettes, and any extracurricular activities or side trips, whatever they may be. These are things people spend money on, that they don't NEED to spend money on; things that don't directly contribute to the finishing of their hike. However, all the things mentioned above will contribute to your happiness, overall adventure, new experiences, new friendships, perceptions, etc.; which is ultimately what hiking the AT is all about. That is unless it's a purely physical endeavor that you simply want to say "I did it!" without the extra personal growth and experiences that comes from taking your time and soaking up the entire trail and everything around it for all it's worth. If you can view your money as being directly related to food; and food in your belly being directly related to finishing the hike, you'll be ok. Money = Food = Completed Thru-hike; while no money = No food = Go home, make more money, try again later.

So how do you save for a thru-hike of the Appalachian Trail? Well, for some people, money will not be a factor. If money is not a factor for you completing the AT, then you can skip this entire section on money.

Saving for an Appalachian thru-hike is no different than saving for anything else; you have to put money away. Do you have trouble NOT spending your money? If the answer is yes, then this might be difficult for you. The best way to save (and also prepare yourself for trail life) is to simplify. You need to start saving money in every aspect of your life. This means you need to drive less to save on gas. Only drive to work, or to places you absolutely need to go. Stop eating out (it will blow your mind how much money this will save you). All those little stops for fast food and coffee add up quick when you do it every day or even multiple times a day. Stop going out, stop buying alcohol, or stop indulging yourself with things you don't really need. If it's not food, a bill expense, or something that contributes to your income, then chances are you don't really need it, and can do without it while you buckle down and save for the adventure of a lifetime. Whatever it is you have to do, I promise it will be worth it (No, do not rob bank).

An easy way to help save money is to apply the "out of sight, out of mind" principle. Money is easier to spend when it's in your purse, back pocket, or plastic debit/credit card. You need to keep your money somewhere you can't spend it (this works wonderfully for me). Aside from a savings account, keep only what you need in your bank account to buy gas/food, or pay bills. Keep almost no cash on you. Take all the money you're saving and put it somewhere safe inside your home. It's there in case you need it, but you can't spend it. It's not on your card for online shopping, and it's not on your person for those impulse buys that hit you while you're out and about. You pretty much put yourself in a position not to be able to spend money even if you wanted to, because you can't spend what you don't have (unless you have a credit card, but that's a different story). The objective here is to be mindful of not spending what's on your debit card because you know you left yourself with just enough to pay the bills, drive to work, and buy groceries. This trick works for me, but you might be able to save money just fine without withholding and hiding it from yourself. These are simply a few suggestions that I personally found helpful.

You should have a financial fall back plan. Do you own a credit card? Have you ever owned a credit card? If you are truly worried about running out of money while you're out there, then you might want to come up with a financial fall back plan. Apply for credit cards (with no intention of using them besides in an emergency on your hike). Hold onto these credit cards, but do not use them. When you're on the trail and realize that your "real" money is beginning to run too low to finish the hike, then it's time to make a decision. Your options are to go home, or tap into the credit cards and worry about paying them off later. In my opinion, the reward of completing a thru-hike outweighs the price of paying off some small credit card debt. Start using the credit cards for resupplies and save the "real" money you have left to make minimum payments on the credit cards for the remainder of whatever time you have left on your hike. This is something I did for my hike that really helped me out during the last month I was out there, and I planned it ahead of time. Maybe your plan is to put the entire hike on a credit card and pay it off later. If that's the only way you can do it, or that's how you'd prefer to do it, then I say go for it. In my humble opinion, the reward outweighs the cost many times over.

You could also buy food and pre-package it to be sent out to you at different post offices and businesses along the trail. In all honesty, if the shipping is coming out of your own pocket, then getting food this way is actually more expensive than simply buying it in most towns. The only way to make this cost effective is to have a support system back home, willing to periodically mail food out to your location. Plus, when you pre-package food months in advance, you can't predict what you're going to be craving once it's eventually sent out to you. I've seen many a hiker give or throw away all or most of their resupply packages because they simply had no stomach for what they thought they'd want months down the road. On the flip side, some people freeze dry, or dehydrate dozens and dozens of meals before they leave, then have those shipped out. The quality and tastiness of these types of meals will outweigh the cost of having them shipped, in my opinion.

Cutting Costs While on Trail

As mentioned above, there are many different price ranges for completing a thru-hike. There are tricks, tips, and strategies you can employ out there in order to not spend everything you have. There are quite a few people who run out of money and have to go home when they had more than enough money to complete their hike in the first place. This is usually a result of frivolous mishandling of their trail expenses. It's really not their fault, because it's extremely difficult not to spend extra money while you're out there. Also, the more money you spend during your hike usually equates to more experiences, sights, people, and time on trail.

Another strategy is to only spend as much money as the miles you've hiked since your last re-supply. For example, if you've hiked fifty miles since your last re-supply and spend only forty bucks on your new re-supply, then you're way ahead of the game... that is if you don't spend any extra money on things like restaurants, hotels, etc. If you were to apply this strategy flawlessly, then you could probably do a thru-hike for just over two thousand dollars or less.

There is a saying, "time is money." This is very true, especially on the trail. The more time it takes you to hike the entire thing, the more it's going to cost you. Every day that you're out there is a day's worth of food you're paying for and eating. The more days it takes you to complete, the more money you're going to spend. Basically, if you hike faster, take less days off, and spend as little time in towns as possible, you can save yourself some serious bucks. Of course, you can alternately take your time, enjoy yourself immensely, and still save some serious bucks, but as mentioned earlier – it requires discipline. These are all things you will understand and grow comfortable with once you get out there.

For the person who wants to do this hike for as little as humanly possible... there is a way. It will take a tremendous amount of self-control, but if you've got what it takes, it can be done. You can hike the trail for less than a thousand bucks if you follow these guidelines. First of all, you need to limit yourself to only hiking and eating. This means no hotels, hostels, restaurants, indulgences, etc. Money should be limited to food, maybe some transportation to get to that food, and any minor gear replacements that you might need. Now, let's talk about the foods, because food can get expensive. You're going to have to limit the types of food you can eat. Those types of food should be grains, starches, and legumes/lentils. For example; rice, couscous, grits, oatmeal, pasta, beans, quinoa, ramen, instant mash potatoes, and maybe some junk food thrown in there. These are the cheapest, most calorie dense, most filling foods you can get almost anywhere. Individual meal packets for these foods can be found at just about any store, for a dollar each or much, much less. Granted, these are going to get extremely boring, but that's where creativity and determination kicks in. It has been done, but it's not done very often. You won't be able to make many friends, because this type of hike will require you to constantly be moving, not staying in towns, or taking days off. As a consequence, you won't find many people willing, or even able to match this hiking style... no matter how interesting you may be.

Time

It takes time to do a thru-hike. On average it will take you 4 to 7 months to complete the entire trail; in some cases faster, longer in others. It all depends on you. When should you start preparing for a thru-hike? The sooner the better. Some people plan years in advance, some people plan months in advance, and yet some people pick up and leave right away on a whim. Figure out what kind of time frame you want/need to leave by, then start planning and saving accordingly.

Responsibility

Ah, responsibilities... the little and not so little commitments we have made throughout the course of our lives. They come in many different forms, as well as many varying degrees of importance. Some can be neglected or dropped with little to no consequence, but others can be nearly impossible to work around. The number one reason people DON'T hike the Appalachian Trail... being bogged down and/or burdened by responsibility. Responsibilities like: having a reliable job, owning a home, having a mortgage, being married, having children, having car payments or various other debts. The list goes on and on, but the aforementioned are the most common and major ones. In most cases, for most people, there is no way around these responsibilities. However, where there's a will, there's a way. Someone with most, if not all those responsibilities, will more than likely never hike the trail... or never attempt it until they are retired, their debts are paid off, the kids are in college, or the spouse can come with them.

In some unique circumstances, depending on how many of these are holding you back, you can still make a run at the trail. You could sublease your house (this may provide some income), sell your house, quit your job, take your spouse with you, take your kids with you, have your spouse watch the kids and everything else (granted financials are still in order), sell your car, file bankruptcy, or if you have deep pockets and/or a large nest egg... simply quit your job and pay for everything back home while you're gone. These are obviously very extreme examples, but people have done them. I've seen families hiking the trail, couples hiking the trail, people who sold nearly everything they owned to hike the trail, people who turned their lives upside down to hike the trail (I'm one of them), and of course nearly everyone had to take a leave of absence or quit their job in order to get out there. What it comes down to is... you have this one life, and time is your most precious, nonrenewable resource during this one life. Do you really want to spend the majority of that time doing things you don't really want to do? Or better yet...NOT doing the things you'd really rather do? Think about it.

In the case that your life might be somewhat simpler than all the scenarios mentioned above, i.e. you don't own a home, don't have kids, minimal to no debt, etc.; then there are plenty of ways to cut costs back home when you decide to escape to the trail. Once again, if you own or rent a home, sub-lease/sublet it. Car insurance? Cancel it. Cell phone? Cancel it or get the simplest plan possible. Married? Take them with you or have them watch over the affairs (if plausible). Debts? Well, you need to factor those in when you save up, but you can always make payments on a credit card while you pay the minimum balance while you're gone. All you have to do is simply look at every outside expense in your life, then figure out how to eliminate it completely, or cut it back as much as you can. It takes courage, it takes determination, and it takes faith and confidence in yourself. Nothing risked, nothing gained, right?

Scheduling

One of the greatest aspects of hiking the trail is not feeling like you're on a schedule. You're out there, you're living on a whim, you've got nowhere to be (for the most part), and nobody is telling you what to do. This doesn't stop some people from trying to regiment their hike, or needing to keep to a certain schedule while they're out there. Perhaps your only chance to hike the trail is right after college... or in the summertime. Maybe you are dead set on doing it a certain year because the stars have aligned just right, except you won't have the finances or be completely free to leave until later in the year. Maybe you have to be done by a certain time to start school, a job, or perhaps your significant other has simply given you a deadline to get back home.

There is a window of opportunity in which elemental conditions are ideal for you to thru-hike the entire trail in one, or several different ways. You can go northbound, starting in Georgia and hike north to Maine. You could go southbound, starting in Maine and hike south to Georgia. Also, you have the option to flip flop, which usually means you start somewhere in the middle, hike north to Maine, then flip flop back to where you started and hike south to Georgia. I'll get into the time frames and starting dates for all these options, this way you can figure out which might be best for you based on your own personal circumstances/preferences.

Northbound

Northbound is the most popular way of thru-hiking the trail; beginning in Georgia and hiking north to Maine. The most preferred starting months are March and April, but the majority of folks will start throughout March. Given the average time it takes to hike the trail, these starting dates will put you finishing sometime in the late summer to early fall. Granted, some people start earlier than March, or as late as June. When it comes to starting earlier than March, it's important to consider the types of weather conditions and temperatures you're comfortable with. Anything in early March or earlier is guaranteed to have some freezing temperatures and possibly snow, especially in the Smoky Mountains. If you're planning to start in May or June, then you have to be fairly confident in your abilities to finish quick enough that you beat winter and the cold temperatures up north; or that you're comfortable hiking in northern winter conditions. No matter how comfortable you are with hiking in winter conditions, there is always the chance that Baxter State Park (the last section of the trail up north) closes Mt. Katahdin due to weather conditions, preventing you from summiting the final mountain. All of these are factors to consider.

Southbound

Thru-hiking the Appalachian Trail with a southbound approach of going from Maine to Georgia is the less popular option. Most southbound hikers will start in Baxter State Park at the very beginning of June, when Maine's harsh winter and cold spring is over, finishing anywhere from late September to November. They will summit Mt. Katahdin, climb back down and begin hiking south. Some people start in late June or even July, but those people need to be prepared for fall and winter conditions further south if they don't plan to hike fast. If you start earlier than June, then there is a good chance access to Katahdin will still be closed, forcing you to skip it and hike south from the base. Believe me when I say, "You don't want to miss climbing Katahdin."

Beginning a southbound hike is far more challenging than a northbound hike, especially for a novice. This is because directly after you leave Baxter State Park, you'll have a 100 mile stretch of wilderness aptly named, "The 100 Mile Wilderness," before you reach the first town for a resupply. Many people take longer than they planned, subsequently running out of food and turning up in the first Maine town of Monson quite hungry and miserable. Besides having that hundred-mile stretch to contend with, the terrain and climbs of southern Maine as well as all of New Hampshire are the toughest of the entire trail. Confronting that type of terrain before you've had the chance to let your body fully adapt is a huge challenge. Plenty of novices make it, but these are facts to consider.

South bounders tend to naturally hike the trail faster than north bounders because there are fewer distractions and less favorable weather conditions. Since there aren't as many people going south, the potential to make friends and stay in towns is considerably less. Since most will be hiking into the fall, conditions will be cooler and popular spots that were fun for "killing time" during the warm summer days will no longer be as appealing. The summit of mountains will lose their warm summer breezes that afforded hours of comfortable down time to relax and soak in the views. Swimming holes will get colder, no longer possessing their allure to dive in and cool off from the hot temperatures that no longer exist. The once lush forests will lose their leaves, turning to skeleton forests, no longer offering irresistibly beautiful locations to stop early for the day, or distract you from hiking. Yes, in my opinion, the southbound hike is a completely different experience from the northbound hike.

Flip Flop

Some people plan to do a flip flop, while others end up doing it out of necessity later on in their hike. If you're a slow hiker, or can't start until later in the year (or both), flip flopping might be the best option for you. Your typical flip flop normally entails starting at Harpers Ferry, West Virginia (the unofficial halfway point of the trail), although technically a flip flop can start anywhere. The entire point of a flip flop is to avoid the cooler months in the northern sections of the trail. Since it gets colder up north earlier than it does in the south, some people will try and finish the northern section during the warmer months, then hike the sections to the south during the cooler months when it's not nearly as cold as it is up north.

Many flip floppers start in Harpers Ferry, hike north to Katahdin in Maine, then flip flop back to Harpers Ferry and hike south to Springer Mountain in Georgia. This strategy takes care of the northern section right off the bat, then allows you to hike the southern section without worrying about conditions getting too cold to continue (ideally). On the flip side, some people will hike from Georgia up to Harpers Ferry, then flip flop up to Maine and hike back down to Harpers Ferry, finishing there. One other method would be to start in Maine, hike south to Harpers Ferry, then flip flop down to Georgia and hike north. While this last one does count as a flip flop, it tends to defeat the purpose of beating cooler weather since the final leg of the journey involves hiking north towards cooler temperatures. The basic gist is that a flip flop hike can be whatever you want it to be, starting and ending from wherever you choose. However, the ultimate goal is usually to do it in such a way that you avoid hiking in the cooler temperatures of the northern parts of the trail.

Some hikers may end up doing a flip flop when they originally had no intention of doing one. This normally happens when a north bounder realizes their pace is too slow to finish the trail before it gets too cold for their comfort, or too snowy and icy for Katahdin to remain open. When the northbound hiker realizes they probably won't reach Maine before freezing temperatures set in, they flip flop from wherever they are, up to Maine, then hike south to finish wherever they flipped from. You can make a flip flop work however needed. You can flip and flop multiple times to different sections if you want, but as long as you finish the entire trail within the same year, you still meet the criteria of "thru-hiker."

Chapter 3

Mental Preparation

Completing an Appalachian Trail thru-hike, any major hike, or any major undertaking in life whatsoever, will usually be about 10% physical and 90% mental. This percentage holds especially true for finishing the entire Appalachian Trail in one go. You've got the gear, you've got the money, but do you have the mental toughness/strength and tenacity needed to achieve your goal? Once you get out there you can be sure to expect pain, misery, discomfort, and suffering within a wide range of varying degrees (do not let this scare or intimidate you). Some of your gear, as well as how much money you brought will sometimes play a part in how little or how much of this you endure (in some areas). In other areas, nothing will save you from some of the more unpleasant experiences of the Appalachian Trail. When these unpleasant experiences occur, what will you do? Will you break and quit? Or will you rise to the occasion, bend with your circumstances and adapt accordingly to any and all obstacles as you encounter them? Yes, your mind, attitude, and outlook will be the deciding factor on whether you complete your epic endeavor or not.

Mental Toughness

"Mental Toughness" is something you're going to need a great deal of when it comes to completing your thru-hike. In its most basic definition, mental toughness is the voice in the back of your head that tells you "keep going, don't give up, you can't quit now." While out on the trail, you're going to have A LOT of internal dialogue with yourself, possibly more than you've ever had in your entire life. The big question is... what will the tone of that internal dialogue be? Will it be mostly negative or positive? Will you be trying to talk yourself "into quitting" or "out of quitting?" Will you be counting the reasons to "stay on" trail, or reasons to "get off" trail? Your internal dialogue will play a huge part in your mental state out there; in turn, directly influencing your chances of victory.

Besides the internal dialogue that you will be having with yourself nearly every solitary second spent out there, you will have a plethora of other factors that will evoke responses from your mental/emotional state. One of the greatest markers of mental toughness is the ability to control your emotions. Not "control" so much in the sense of repressing them, but in understanding them. If you're not in control of your emotions, then they're in control of you. Being able to realize and understand why you feel a certain way, but still be able to make rational decisions despite how you may feel is HUGE. I cannot emphasize that point enough. So many people make snap/impulse decisions based on how they feel at the present moment; they seldom stop to think, "Why do I really feel this way?" or "Is this really the best thing to do at this exact moment?"

This sort of mental toughness comes into play when you're thinking about quitting. There are many things that will make you question your decision to thru-hike and possibly consider quitting; things like physical pain, misery, suffering brought on by the elements, missing home, missing loved ones, missed expectations, becoming bored, or thoughts of, "I'll never make it." Thoughts are strong, but feelings are stronger. Your feelings of discomfort, boredom, or pain in the present moment can mislead your thoughts into making irrational decisions that have long term consequences/effects. You can lie to yourself with your thoughts, but your feelings will always be true, yet less in your control. This is why being able to understand and control your feelings to a certain extent is so important. You need to be able to use your thoughts clearly when your temporary feelings of the present moment may be clouding your judgment. To put it in better perspective; pain, misery, depression, discomfort, etc. are all "feelings" that can very rapidly lead to low morale and the decision to quit. There's no getting around the fact that you will experience these feelings at some point during your journey, if not many times throughout. Once these feelings arise, they're going to be accompanied by thoughts - the voice inside your head that interprets those feelings. Are your thoughts going to feed into the negative aspects of your feelings, subsequently initiating a downward spiral? Or will you keep a focused, level headed handle on your thoughts... understand and accept your feelings for whatever they may be, then use them to get through whatever outward or inward obstacle you may be facing? Don't let your thoughts defeat you on account of your feelings. Pain, misery, bad weather, tough terrain; none of it lasts forever - so don't make a decision that does. Remember, "This too shall pass."

When you've gone out there to attempt a thru-hike, it's safe to say that you "wanted it" pretty badly. At some point in your life you decided you wanted to hike over 2,000 miles and accomplish one of the great feats and adventures our planet has to offer. However, in order to seize that goal, you'll have to want it more than anything else in the world, before and during the endeavor. You know that deep inside yourself, completing the Appalachian Trail is what you want. This feeling, this desire to hike the entire trail is what brought you out there in the first place. This desire is the everlasting feeling that underlies all other fleeting emotions you'll experience throughout your journey; try to recognize and remember that. So, what is the only thing (besides injury and running out of money) that can possibly stop you from achieving your desire of a completed thru-hike? The answer is YOU. You are the only one who can stop yourself from reaching your goal. Completing an Appalachian Trail thru-hike is as simple as not quitting. Don't quit, no matter what, and your dream is as good as realized.

So, let us delve deeper into things that make people quit, as well as why someone would make the decision to quit. The most blatant explanation for quitting in almost any circumstance would undoubtedly be "rationalization." We humans are rational creatures, and we can rationalize just about anything in order to make it make sense to us, or seem like the right thing to do. You can rationalize positive things, as well as negative things. If you put your mind to it, you can rationalize pretty much any decision you could ever make to seem like the right or wrong decision. It all depends on whichever one you "feel" is more beneficial to you at the present moment. Pain and suffering (feelings!) do funny things to the human brain. It can cause you to rationalize decisions you "think" you really want to make, when in fact you really don't. Rationalization is so powerful that when you're under stress and pain, you can actually convince yourself that finishing your Appalachian thru-hike is something you never truly wanted. Maybe this is true, but more often than not, you're only fooling yourself. You don't decide to hike over 2,000 miles and not have really wanted it at some point. When do most people realize they rationalized a lie to themselves when they decided quitting was the best decision to make (at whatever time they decided to make it)? That moment of regret is when they realize they deceived themselves. They made a decision in the heat of the moment that they didn't actually believe in, and then regretted it very shortly afterward. Once they're away from the pain and suffering of the moment, and able to think clearly, they realize, "What was I thinking? I really did want to complete this adventure! Why did I talk myself out of it and quit!?" Mental toughness will help you to avoid rationalizing "heat of the moment" decisions you will later regret. It is the ability to look past your present suffering to realize you will most likely regret any decisions to quit, thus deterring you from quitting; this ability is part of what demonstrates an aspect of your mental toughness.

Earlier I stated some of the major reasons/factors that cause people to quit, as well as how they come to arrive at their decision to quit. Now let's go over those factors in a little more detail, but focus more on what helps you NOT quit.

Physical pain; something you may be a stranger to, or very familiar with. If you're a stranger to it, you won't be any longer after completing the Appalachian Trail. There is plenty of physical pain to be found and had out there. Having said this, there are two types of physical pain you will encounter while out on the trail. The first type falls into the category most of us lump all pain into, the <u>hurting</u> kind. Many people cannot distinguish between <u>good pain</u> and <u>bad pain</u>, because all pain seems like bad pain to them. This is where mental toughness/mental maturity play a huge part once again.

Let's examine good pain. This is the type of pain you're going to experience in great abundance towards the beginning of your journey. You're going to experience it so much in fact, that it's going to trick you into thinking it's bad pain. Good pain during physical activity is what we trainers like to refer to as "the burn," or "the pump." You're going to feel this pain in your quads, your calves, your feet, your back, and other areas not accustomed to carrying or bearing weight as you go up and down the inclines and declines of the trail; all day, every day. As you might expect, these pains will be at their most intense during the beginning of the journey, as your body adapts to the new stresses and challenges you confront. If you weren't hiking up and down mountains carrying a backpack every day before you decided to thru-hike the Appalachian Trail, then it's safe to assume that at some point during the beginning of your trek, the muscles of your body are going to burn and hurt to a certain degree. Some will view this as "bad pain" right off the bat, quitting in the beginning because they can't handle the constant burning pain. I urge you not to be that person. This type of pain will be very commonplace for the first four to six weeks; sometimes shorter, sometimes a little bit longer (along with other pains we will get into shortly). It all depends on the individual, as well as what they were doing prior to the trail. The average break-in time for our bodies out there is four to six weeks. After that initial four to six weeks, your body has realized, "Hey! It looks like my job is climbing mountains while carrying weight on my back! I guess I'll just devote myself to being really good at this!" Our bodies are incredible machines in the sense that they will adapt to whatever you throw at them. If you sit on the couch at home, or in a chair at work all day, not doing anything, you can bet your bottom dollar that your body is going to adapt to be good at it, and not much else. If you walk up and down mountains carrying a backpack every day, you can also bet that your body will adapt to become very good at that too. Knowing this information is the ability to realize that the initial pain of trying something new won't last forever. Your body will adapt (after considerable burning and pain), then you won't even notice it, even coming to enjoy the burning feelings derived from challenging and exerting yourself.

There is a second type of good pain that walks a very fine line with bad pain. It can sometimes be difficult to discern, even for some of the most seasoned athletes, hikers, and people with active lifestyles. The type of pain I'm talking about is "aching pain," or soreness. This is pain you will experience while you're hiking, but will continue (possibly getting worse) after you've stopped for the day, and even while you're sleeping. You're going feel this pain in your feet, various joints, and possibly your back. You may feel it in one of these areas, a couple of them, or all of them. This type of pain can cause people to rationalize that they're "injured," then quit; OR, they simply can't handle it and quit, thinking the aching pain will go on forever, get worse, or develop into a severe lifelong injury. I'll be honest with you, when you're out there, it seems like these types of pains will go on forever, but they usually don't; they are temporary. Temporary in the sense that they'll go away, or you'll become accustomed to the point that they won't bother you further down the trail. Your knees are going to ache, your ankles and feet are going to throb and have shooting pains, and your back is going to feel tight and stiff. Some people will interpret these pains as "injuries," and quit right away, for fear of them becoming worse. This is where these pains walk a fine line with "good pain" and "bad pain." I'll let you in on a little secret; pretty much EVERYONE experiences these types of pains to a certain degree while out on the trail. They are perfectly normal, and part of the adaptation process of your body. You can push through these pains (don't overdo it too much in the beginning; listen to your body) and still manage to cover good distances on a daily basis. If you are genuinely injured, then you will physically be unable to perform certain actions. When it's just an ache, then only your mind will inhibit you. As I mentioned previously, it's tough to discern an ache from an injury sometimes, especially if you're unfamiliar with both. Nevertheless, if you maintain a positive outlook, as well as a "can do" attitude, you'll know which one it is and react appropriately.

This brings me to our final type of physical pain - bad pain. This is the type of pain related to injury in all of its major and minor forms. From blisters, cuts, scrapes, bruises, bug bites, and stings; all the way to tears, strains, fractures, and breaks. These are the types of "bad pain" that can frequently be encountered out on the trail. Like anything in life, you and only you can decide how you're going to react to each and every thing that happens to you. I can almost guarantee that you're going to get blisters, cuts, scrapes, bruises, bug bites, and stings at one point or another during your 2,200-mile adventure, maybe throw in some poison ivy (I got it) for good measure. I can't guarantee that you'll experience tears and strains due to ankle rolls, missteps, and falls; or that you'll experience a broken or fractured bone, but they are very real possibilities, and not all of them are necessarily "hike ending." People have rolled, torn, fractured, and broken their bones, ligaments, and tendons out there, and still completed their hike (I'm one of them). Your mental toughness is going to be pushed to the limit if you are forced to endure anything like this. When it comes to torn ligaments or broken bones, the severity of the injury will most likely determine whether you grit it out or go home; you may not even have a choice in the matter. It may be so bad that you physically cannot continue, even though the mind and spirit are willing. This is something out of your hands that will require considerable thought, if encountered. Weigh the consequences of continuing and pushing through the pain (if possible) or going home. Try to remember (this helped me): The harder the struggle, the sweeter the victory. The more obstacles you overcome will make the feelings of your final summit day on the trail that much more momentous. Keep in mind, when things are at their most painful or uncomfortable; whatever negativity you might be feeling, those feelings will be multiplied positively when you finally reach your goal.

Getting through the smaller pains like blisters, cuts, and bugs is a grind. The best way to get through them is to view them as a positive, strength and character building experience. As the good pains burn and ultimately sculpt you into a physically stronger human being, you can view the bad pains as sculpting you into tougher, more resilient human being. They are building/molding a strength that comes from within; a strength that can't be achieved simply through physical efforts. These are the sort of experiences that build mental toughness. You can use these experiences in the future when confronted with similar situations. You'll look back and remember "Hey, I've been through something like this before; I overcame it then, I'll overcome it now." This is called confidence, and it's something that overcoming painful obstacles will give you. You simply have to see and realize the future pay-off to enduring the pain "now" - that way it won't seem as bad when encountered again at a later date. See the bigger picture that is "your suffering," and view it as something which can only make you stronger, instead of something to whine about or make you quit. There is a famous Latin quote that goes hand in hand with this viewpoint. "Perfer et obdura, dolor hic tibi proderit olim." It means, "Be patient and tough; someday this pain will be useful to you." This train of thought can be applied to almost any aspect of pain and suffering on the trail, as well as in life. Still, let us delve deeper into the other factors that cause people to end their hike...

Misery and suffering brought on by the elements, as well as terrain, are two more of the biggest obstacles that cause people to quit. Rest assured, if you go out there for the long haul, you are almost guaranteed at some point to encounter torrential rain, gale force winds, sweltering heat, freezing cold, hale, ice, and in some cases (depending on when you start) snow. Terrain wise, if you're doing the entire trail, you WILL encounter, rocks, boulder fields, mud, river crossings, creek crossings, hand over hand climbs, washed out root beds, overgrown vegetation, poison ivy, and not to mention uphill/downhill climbs and descents of every angle imaginable. Sometimes you're going to encounter horrible elements while simultaneously traversing terrible terrain. How is one to take all of this in stride while keeping up morale and not losing hope? The answer is simple; maintain your sense of humor, stay goal oriented, and keep a positive outlook at all times. Out of those three things, keeping your sense of humor is without a doubt the most important. If you can laugh at yourself, as well as all the bad things that befall you, then you're already 75% of the way to your positive attitude. If you can maintain the clarity of mind to laugh and stay positive, then focusing on the end goal will be easy.

Before you can maintain a sense of humor in the face of pain, misery, and discomfort, you first have to acquire something that I consider invaluable to any human being; something that can keep you alive and comfortable in the face of any adversity, obstacle, or situation. That something is "adaptability." The ability to change your outlook, your attitude, your routine, your strategy, your thought process, your gear, or your tactics - in order to meet the challenges of ever changing situations and environments. People that possess the ability to adapt don't let their circumstances break them. Adaptable people bend with their circumstances, making their weaknesses their strengths and allowing whatever adversity they're facing to work for them, even if it's only in their mind. In short, adaptability is synonymous with flexibility; be flexible, not rigid. Adaptability isn't something you can wake up and possess one morning. It's an art in its own right, and one of the pinnacles of mental strength.

The first step to honing your adaptability is realizing how closely intertwined it is with your positive outlook, sense of humor, and goal orientation. People who despair easily are usually not adaptable. Where does despairing, feeling sorry for yourself, and negative thoughts/internal dialogue get you? The answer is nowhere, or at least nowhere you want to be. When you encounter terrain, weather, or temperatures that don't agree with you (and I assure you that you will), the first and foremost thing you need to do is... accept them. Once you've accepted your predicament and come to terms with the fact that whatever's happening to you, couldn't have happened any other way, and that you can't change or affect any of it through any power of your own; you've just taken the first step towards adaptability. You have made the conscious decision to not waste energy on second guessing your situation, or wishing something was different or not happening to you at the moment. There is a saying I'm quite fond of... "Wish in one hand, shit in the other; see which fills up first." Wishing gets us nowhere, action does. So, now that you've accepted whatever it is that's happening to you, you can do the next best thing to ignoring it; you can embrace it. Embrace the suck. Embrace it by laughing at it, as well as finding the humor in whatever it is that's happening. This can sometimes be hard to do, if not impossible, but so long as you make the effort, you're not doing the worst thing you can do, which is to despair, or nothing.

There is a quote by Aristotle that greatly helped me through some tough times out there. It's a quote that might help put into perspective the frame of mind that's required on a journey of this magnitude. Aristotle said, "Suffering becomes beautiful when anyone bears calamities with cheerfulness, not through insensibility, but through greatness of mind." That statement sums up the frame of mind you have to adopt in order to complete the AT without quitting or having a terrible time. You have to let yourself go slightly crazy in order to laugh at your own pain or discomfort, but it's worth it. People will indeed view it as crazy or "insensible," but this is because they don't understand. If you let every single obstacle get you down, then you're not going to get very far. Laugh at them all, and view them as nothing more than events that will shape you into a stronger, more resilient human being in the long run.

In the event that you're not very moved by quotes, or perhaps don't draw any kind of strength or inspiration from them, I offer a different perspective. How do you eat an elephant? The answer is one bite at a time. The Appalachian Trail, like an elephant, is massive. The task seems impossible and overwhelming when you look at either of them as a whole. Do not look at them in their entirety, instead take them one bite, one step at a time. Keep chipping away, doing what you can, focusing only on what's directly in front of you, and eventually... there will be nothing left.

I'm going to wrap the final reasons for why people quit into a single group, because they are purely psychological and have absolutely nothing to do with the Appalachian Trail itself. Many people quit the trail due to missing home, missing loved ones, pressure from loved ones, missed expectations, or becoming bored. First off, if you have obligations back home pertaining to family, financial, pets, or whatever; then nothing I can say will influence the likelihood of you getting off trail to take care of those obligations (which you should, although they should've already been taken care of before you went out there). Albeit, shit happens, and everything is not under our control. Having said that, depending on who you are, you will probably become homesick at some point (maybe). Depending on your relationship or marital status, you will begin to miss your loved ones, or they may begin pressuring you to come home or "hurry up!" These are natural emotions and urges that can dominate your thought process, especially when all you have is time on your hands to think. There is only one weapon to combat homesickness and the beckoning call of loved ones. That weapon is "foresight." The foresight to know that if you let yourself rationalize going home due to homesickness or a loved one's call... you're going to regret it. Home will always be there waiting for you, understand and accept that. Unless someone is sick or in absolute dire need of your presence back home, then there is no reason for them to cause you to abandon your hike. If they truly love you, they will understand and trust your need to go out and attempt something of this magnitude. Hiking the Appalachian Trail isn't something you want to do; it's something you NEED to do. It calls to you, and you can feel it in your bones. Don't let anyone tell you that you're being selfish by going out and attempting to complete it; after all, it's your life, and your happiness. Realize that before you make your final decision...

Of course, there are special circumstances to every personal situation that involve emotions, feelings, and love, and I'm not going to dish out relationship or marital advice in this book; "It's a fool who looks for logic in the chambers of the human heart." What I've said above is as much as I'll say on the topics of missing home and loved ones. Whatever you do, should the debacle of going home due to those two reasons arise... it should feel completely right in your own heart; and I hope that you never regret it, regardless of your choices.

Something you wouldn't think would happen on the trail, but strangely enough does, is boredom. You will get so bored out of your mind at certain points, you'll hardly believe it's possible. When out walking in the woods all day, every day, not every single one of those days will be filled with breath taking views, life altering revelations, or exciting occurrences. At some point, you're probably going to run out of things to think about (besides how bored you are), as everything begins to look the same. "Oh, look a tree, another tree, another tree, a rock, more rocks, now I'm going uphill, now I'm going downhill..." so on and so forth. Keeping yourself and your mind occupied is sometimes easier said than done. For me, I had three ways I combated boredom. One, I would pick problems with the world, or my own life, then attempt to solve them; sometimes in a serious manner, sometimes in a joking, but as close to serious manner as I could. Two, walking and conversing with other people; you will never have more meaningful conversations with other individuals than you will while hiking, or sitting around campfires. With no distractions, nowhere to be, and all day to have them, "conversations" take on a whole new meaning out there. Take advantage of every single second you have to be able to talk to people like this. I promise this will be one of the major aspects of trail life you miss most after you're done. Three, fantasizing about food; this doesn't sound so great right now, but after you've been out in the woods for any length of time, food and hunger are going to dominate your thoughts.

Thinking about the foods I was going to track down and eat in the next town always helped to motivate me. On the flip side, this can be absolute torture and sometimes depressing once you realize that several days' worth of hiking may be separating you from your favorite meal craving. Nevertheless, it's something tangible that you can set your energy towards.

Lastly, many people quit the trail due to "missed expectations." This means they went out there with a certain experience in mind, but they're not getting it. It can also simply mean that trail life isn't what they thought it would be. Low morale or depression due to missed expectations is hard factor to overcome. If you're out there and truly not enjoying yourself, then it's safe to say you're probably wasting your time. Having said that, don't give up due to perceived missed expectations right away, especially if it's at the beginning of your journey. Give the adventure and yourself time to evolve and mature into something more "in-line" with what you want/enjoy. This adventure is purely what you make of it, so make the effort to exceed your own expectations. If you've been out there for months, and haven't enjoyed yourself for the majority of that time, then you can probably go home without too much regret; the experience will still have been incredible.

So now we've covered all major factors that contribute to people quitting, or not completing their Appalachian endeavor. We've examined the mental game, as well as how to develop and apply it to a myriad of situations. All techniques for dealing with the various obstacles are interchangeable and can work; you simply have to remember and practice them. In concluding this section, I will impart a final mental trick you can use/remember in any situation you encounter out there. Focus on the end goal and remember "WHY" you came out there. Find that reason that prompted you to set foot on the Appalachian Trail in the first place; find it, grab onto it, never let it go, and never forget it, whatever it may be. Good or bad, every single thing that happens is contributing to the overall experience, while adding to that final feeling of "I DID IT!" when you take your last steps (wherever they may be) in completing the trail. When you're in "the shit," feeling down and miserable, simply think of how absolutely tremendous the feeling is going to be when you achieve what you set out there to do, look back on everything you overcame and realize... none of it stopped me.

Chapter 4:

Physical Preparation

Many people begin and complete an Appalachian Trail thru-hike with little to no prior hiking experience, as well as little to no physical preparation. It can be done, and you will suffer more in the beginning, but if you're mentally tough, no amount of physical suffering will stop you from achieving what you set out to do. All that said, there are steps you can take to ease some of that suffering by getting yourself physically prepared for a 2,000 plus mile hike. As with anything, the best way to prepare for something is to do the closest thing to it - "Practice like you play." If you want to get good at pushups, you don't do bench press, you do pushups. If you want to get good at hiking, the best thing to do is hike. Obviously, nothing will completely prepare you for hiking over 2,000 miles without actually hiking that far first. So, you have to start out slow, getting your body prepared for some of the challenges it will meet on the trail. Something important to remember about the AT; for pretty much the entire 2,190 miles, it's either going up, or going down. If you don't have any mountains or steep inclines near you, then it's going to be difficult to give your body a dose of what to expect. Luckily, there are ways to prepare at home or in the gym in order to soften the initial shock to your body when you finally begin trekking across the Appalachian terrain.

As mentioned earlier, I'm an experienced strength and conditioning specialist, who has completed the trail and encountered all the physical hardships it has to offer. In doing so, I can better prescribe the exercises you would need to do in order to lessen the initial pain when you get out there. If you live near mountains, the first thing I'm going to tell you to do is HIKE; throw on a pack and start hiking. Doing this ahead of time will afford you the luxury of building yourself up in regards to the distances you have to do, as well as the weight in your pack. If you have no prior hiking experience, then make sure you start out easy. Acclimate yourself to walking with weight on your back, then slowly increase your distances and pack weight. As with anything, the greatest changes and bodily adaptations are going to come from pushing yourself. At some point, you're going to have to leave your comfort zone, and make it hurt; that's the only way you'll make progress. Hike just a little bit further each time, even though you want to turn back. Keep going up that incline even though you want to rest for a minute because your muscles are burning. Add that little bit of extra weight to your pack, because the last time it felt too easy. Little things like those will go a long way in helping you get stronger. Since I don't know you personally, the best advice I can give you is to be smart about it. You know yourself best, so push your limits, but don't get crazy and overdo it.

For those of you who live in an area without mountains (like me), you can still take steps to strengthen and prepare your body before you go out there. Those of you who do live in or around mountains can still take notes from the following advice; there is no harm in doing extra to prepare. As I mentioned before, the main muscles that are going to hurt and burn when you first get out there will be your feet, calves, quads, and back. There will be plenty of other aches and pains, but these are the main ones you can prepare for on the very first day. When you look at the physical actions of hiking the Appalachian Trail, you will notice there is a TON of repetition. There is a lot of stepping, striding, and pushing; done over, and over, and over again, all day long, every day. The best way to prepare for that is to try and simulate it as closely as possible at the gym, or in your home. Most people who try to prepare at home or in the gym will do so by walking on a treadmill that has been set to full incline, for as long as they can. This helps, and it's much better than nothing, but I'll tell you right now, the number of steep, smooth inclines you'll encounter on the AT can be counted on all your fingers and toes. Most of the hiking out there will be more akin to doing "step-ups." Stepping up onto rocks, ledges, fallen trees, roots, more rocks, you name it. You can help prepare yourself for this by simulating those steps on a stair stepper machine. Even better than using a machine; practice doing lunges, body weight squats, calf raises, and step ups on risers, chairs, boxes, stairs, or benches. As always, gradually up the intensity of these exercises. Raise the level of intensity by adding weight, reps, and time to them. Every so often, take yourself to muscular failure while performing a certain exercise. This means you do a specific motion or exercise until you cannot physically do it any longer. You will reach muscle failure many times when you first start on the trail, so this will prepare you to deal with that mentally and physically. It will also help push back/postpone the point in time in which you do reach muscle failure, due to your extra strength from preconditioning. As always, do these exercises within reason. Again, I do not know you personally, so I cannot account for any past injuries, or proneness to injury that you may have. Of course, you should always check with your family doctor before partaking in any kind of intense physical activity/challenge.

Some other exercises that will be invaluable to preparing you for physical demands on the trail will be exercises that help strengthen your core. You need to go out there with a strong back, as well as a strong abdomen to reinforce and support that strong back. The two simplest/best exercises to help achieve this (on your own without the help or guidance of a trainer) are body planks and supermans (prone back extensions). You can look up either of these two exercises online and be able to safely perform them on your own just by looking at them. You can perform both of them to failure, but when first starting out, take it easy and don't overdo it. They will be invaluable in helping to strengthen your core and getting you ready to tote a heavy pack around all day. It would be irresponsible of me to tell you to do all of these things without adding that you shouldn't neglect your other muscle groups. Without turning this into a sermon about working out, or a book on fitness, just make sure you don't forget to engage and exercise all other muscle groups of your body. If you need any more guidance, then I suggest you buy a book specifically on the subject, hire a trainer, or consult a friend who knows about these things (hopefully).

Aside from building up your strength and endurance, you should also spend some time improving your flexibility. Join a yoga class, or research some unassisted stretches online. Increased flexibility, as well as joint mobility will go a VERY, VERY long way in preventing injury. Stretch everything, but put extra emphasis on your hamstrings, hips, and other muscles/joints of the lower extremities.

I have one last piece of advice when it comes to physically preparing yourself for a long-distance hike. This advice may be slightly controversial, but it's completely optional and could help you out in the long run. Your feet are going to take a beating out there. You're very likely going to get blisters, and you're going to develop calluses on the bottoms of your feet, as well as your toes. The road to developing these calluses, which in the end protect your feet and skin from blisters, can be a painful one. If there is one thing I would have done in hindsight to prepare my feet, it would have been walking around barefoot more, while back home. This way I could have toughened up the pads of my feet, easing some of my future suffering when I got on the trail. Again, do this within reason. Don't go crazy and get nails, glass, and dangerous substances stuck all over the bottom of your feet. Maybe go check your mail barefoot, or walk around your back yard, driveway, and sidewalk without shoes on; make sure you check for any hazardous items that are going to wind up embedded in your foot. This trick won't completely save your feet from the rigors of the trail, but it will certainly add a buffer. That being said, there are always those individuals who are exceptions to the rule, who make it through the entire trail without a single foot issue. These people are either very experienced with maintaining their foot health and choosing footwear, or sometimes just damn lucky. On the Pacific Crest Trail, my second thru-hike, I wore trail runners for the entire hike and got thru nearly 2,700 miles with only one blister and several hot spots. This was because I knew my feet, and chose the perfect footwear for me specifically.

Chapter 5

Tips, Tricks, What to Expect, and Other Insights

The best advice I could give you is to expect the unexpected. You really never know what you'll get out there on a daily basis, and every single person's experience is unique. I will say that for most people, the trail is never what you thought it was going to be, but almost always exceeds any expectations or preconceived notions you may have had. There are some things I can give you a heads up on, but for the most part, every day will be a mystery and adventure in its own right. In no particular order, I've dedicated this chapter to describing, explaining, and bringing to light certain facts, realities, techniques, and aspects of an Appalachian thru-hike.

Animal Encounters

One of the first things that might cross one's mind when thinking about spending a prolonged period of time in the wilderness is scary animal encounters. Yes, lions and tigers and bears, OH MY! While there are very few lions (mountain lions), no tigers, and more bears than you can shake a stick at, not every single day is filled with close encounters of the animal kind. While I myself was fortunate enough to see more than twenty bears, two moose, and a multitude of other animals; I met plenty of hikers that didn't see any bears, moose, or other impressive wildlife. On the flip side, I met people who claimed to have seen mountain lions and had other wild encounters that I only wished I could have had.

When it comes to the wildlife aspect of hiking the Appalachian Trail, you're guaranteed to see some things, but your guess is as good as mine as to what you'll see and how much of it. If you want to keep your wildlife encounters and sightings to a maximum, the best thing to do is pay attention and be in tune with your surroundings. I can't tell you how many people hike with headphones on, listening to music as they go. Probably 75% of the wildlife I witnessed was first brought to my attention by the noise it was making. Whether it was making vocalizations, or trying to distance itself from me, I almost always heard the wildlife before I saw it. If you're wearing headphones all the time, you're going to miss out, plain and simple.

So, what types of wildlife are most common out there? If you're anything like Indiana Jones, then you're going to hate what I'm about to say. Besides bugs, birds, chipmunks, and other small rodents, the one type of animal you will probably encounter the most out there will be snakes. I saw hundreds of snakes during my thru-hike. Most of them will be Black Rat Snakes and Garter Snakes, but there are plenty of Rattlesnakes (I encountered five), Copperheads, Brown Water Snakes, and a few other less common species. Everyone you meet out there will have at least one snake story... or ten.

After snakes, the next major animal encounters would be deer, bear, skunk, porcupine, ground hog, tortoises, whippoorwills, moose, wild hog, coyote, raccoon, possum, and very, very, rarely...mountain lions. Bear, deer, skunk, ground hog, coyote, raccoon, and possum can be found throughout the entire trail, but I found the ground hogs to be more prevalent in the south. The majority of bears are in the Smokey Mountains, Shenandoah National Park, and New Jersey. Wild hogs and whippoorwills are most common in the south, although you're more likely to hear them than see them. Tortoises are more prevalent in the south. Porcupines begin to become more common in Pennsylvania, and your chances for encounters will increase further north, peaking in the Vermont sections. Moose will become a possibility for encountering once you reach Vermont, but their numbers and presence visibly increase the further north you go into New Hampshire and Maine. Mountain Lions are something most people will say do not exist on the eastern side of the country, but I was shown pictures from locals and heard firsthand accounts from other hikers who saw them. While incredibly rare, I believe they do exist around the trail. Wolves are another mammal that are said not to be near the trail, but locals will disagree, and there is certainly no denying the hybrid "Coywolf" presence is alive and strong.

Most people's fear of the forest stems from being afraid of scary or deadly animal encounters. Allow me to lay these fears to rest. First of all, there are no grizzly bears on the Appalachian Trail, only black bears.

While very, very rarely will any animals ever take a personal interest in you, even when hiking at night; it's even rarer when they actually do something. Simply reading this won't ease any animal hang-ups you might have, but after you've spent some time on the trail, you'll realize that 99% of the wildlife either doesn't care about you, or wants to get away from you as fast as it can. What I'm trying to say is...don't be afraid of the animals - even the bears. Moose and Rattlesnakes pose a greater threat, and even they are nothing to lose sleep over, so long as you are mindful of your surroundings. Also, keep in mind, at night, eyes that shine green belong to harmless animals, while eyes that shine yellow belong to predatory animals.

Bears

I'm devoting a little extra attention to bears in this short section. For the sake of accuracy, the term "bear" as it's used in this book will always refer to "black bears," since they are the only species of bear to be found on the Appalachian Trail. The Appalachian Trail passes through some of the most densely populated bear areas of the entire country. As I said above, the most bears reside in the Smoky Mountains National Park in Tennessee and North Carolina, Shenandoah National Park in Virginia, and the state of New Jersey. Shenandoah National Park has the most bears per square mile out of any other area in the country, but New Jersey has the most bears per square mile out of any other state. Regardless of where you are on the trail, bears are a possibility along the entire way. They should be respected, but not feared.

While you're almost certainly guaranteed to see at least one or more bears during your thru-hike, 99.99% of the time they will run or walk away, or simply stand/sit there and watch you go by. What about mothers with cubs? I ran into three different sets of mothers with cubs; all of them ran away or climbed trees. I even came within ten feet of two cubs who ran across the trail in front of me, and the mother never batted an eye. Black bears are generally just not aggressive bears and would rather steer clear of humans at all costs. On the flip side, there was a black bear related fatality in New Jersey while I was hiking the trail, however it wasn't a thru-hiker, or even on the Appalachian Trail. The bear killed a foreign exchange student who was hiking with some friends. The bear was found hanging around the body of the individual when officials finally arrived and was subsequently put down.

On the rare chance that you are confronted with a curious bear taking an interest in you, there are several things you can do. Keep eye contact with the bear (DO NOT do this with a grizzly however), make yourself appear larger; then sternly and loudly tell the bear to leave WITHOUT making "bear like" noises at it (growling, snarling), and DO NOT run. If the bear does attack you, then DO NOT play dead, fight back (DO play dead if it's a grizzly). A black bear, even a small one, is much stronger than you, but nowhere near as strong as a grizzly (a grizzly is more inclined to kill you if you do fight, and fighting back won't do much good). It is not usually in a black bear's nature to attack people, so if one does, it either means serious business, or it feels threatened and thinks the only way out of the situation is a confrontation with you. Chances are the bear really doesn't want to fight you. So, in the case of a confrontation, give it every reason to believe it's made the wrong decision. A bear that feels scared, threatened, or on the verge of getting aggressive will click its jaws, hiss, or stand its ground in an intimidating fashion.

If you are still absolutely terrified of a bear encounter, there are ways to make sure you don't see one, or at the very least surprise one you're going to see anyway. While hiking at night or anywhere known to have a dense population of bears, simply make your presence known by making a little bit of noise. You can play music while you hike, whistle, sing, wear bear bells, clap your hands to some imaginary beat, whatever. This will let any bears within earshot know you're coming; thus, scaring them away, or at the very least keeping them from being surprised when you come around the corner. You can also carry Bear Mace if you really, really want to, but that will be a very unnecessary weight for the most part.

Realistically, you should hope for as many bear sightings as possible, because they are beautiful, amazing creatures; every experience I've had with them has been surreal and magical in its own way. I hope your bear encounters are plentiful and peaceful.

Whippoorwills

Whippoorwills, also known as demon birds, are a common avian throughout the southern portions of the trail. I'm giving them their own personal mention because they undoubtedly deserve one due to the impact they have on some people. They're not dangerous, they're not destructive, and you probably won't even see one the entire time you're out there…but you will hear them. A Whippoorwill gets its name from the sound it makes; which is a rapid succession of whistles that sound like: "WHIPPOORWILL-WHIPPOORWILL-WHIPPOORWILL, so on and so forth, etc., etc., over and over again. If you want to know what one sounds like, you can look it up easily enough online, or try to whistle the tune yourself. Simply try and whistle "whip-poor-will" as clearly as you can; once you get those three syllables mastered, whistle it as fast as you can, for as long as you can. Congratulations, you're a Whippoorwill. The reason these birds are so uniquely annoying is because they tend to sing their incessant tune only in the early evening, the middle of the night, or the very early morning; basically, all the times when an individual would be asleep, or trying to be asleep.

You can potentially get one or several of them all whistling at the same time while you're trying to sleep. The first time you hear one will most likely be a wonderfully unique and magical experience no doubt; but then it will continue, and continue still, and continue yet longer, never stopping. These little demons of the dark will perch next to your camp in a nearby tree and whistle intermittently, non-stop, for the better portion of an entire night sometimes. You can tune out one, maybe two of them and fall asleep, but if you get a crowd of them, it's gonna be a long night. Now having read this, once you hear one, you'll know exactly what it is. Good luck.

Ruffed Grouse

I feel like the Ruffed Grouse is worth mentioning on its own because of the great mystery it presented me for over a month when I first got on the trail. It's a small to medium sized bird that doesn't look all too different from a chicken. The reason I want to mention them is because of the sound they make. You may or may not ever see one of these birds, but you'll definitely hear them on a daily or semi-daily basis throughout the entire trail. If you don't know what one sounds like already, or if someone doesn't tell you; you'll never know it was a bird you were hearing, especially what kind. The Ruffed Grouse will stand on a log, rock, or whatever object and beat its wings faster and faster for several seconds. The resulting sound is of a very low frequency that you can feel just as much as you can hear it. The violent flapping creates vibrations in the air that can be heard and felt for great distances. I can only liken the sound to that of a generator trying to start up; "thump….thump…thump..thump.thump thumpthumpthump," faster and faster before cutting off altogether. I've found that not everyone can hear the low frequency of the thumping, making you feel even crazier when you ask someone, "Hey, what's that sound?" and they reply, "What sound?" So, when you hear a low thumping sound and can't place where it came from…now you know.

Bugs

Bugs are something you must quickly come to terms with on the trail. You'll get use to them crawling and buzzing around you at all hours of the day and night, eventually learning to tune them out. Unfortunately, in some areas they'll be so thick, it'll be impossible to ignore, or even keep them away from you. You'll encounter spiders, flies, mosquitoes, wasps, millipedes, ants, beetles, flying insects, biting insects, etc. The entire trail has bugs, but they'll be at their worst during the summer months, as well as at the lowest elevations, and the areas with the most standing water or moisture.

Ticks

If you're hiking through Virginia, Pennsylvania, New Jersey, and New York during the late spring and summer months, you're going to encounter a lot of ticks. I noticed the most in Virginia, and cumulatively I probably brushed off close to a couple hundred ticks before they attached. On the flip side, I had more than a dozen attach to me in various places, but I was able to remove them without incident or contracting Lyme Disease. I found them attached to my upper thighs, my calves, my stomach, in between my fingers, and buried in my beard on my jaw line. I'll go over prevention and detection of ticks in the "Lyme disease" section a little further on. Remember, deer ticks are the main carriers of Lyme disease and are characterized by their smaller size in comparison to other ticks; sometimes as small as a fleck of pepper.

Trail Names

Nobody calls you by your real name out on the trail. This is because you'll get a trail name given to you. A trail name is nothing but a nickname, and the process of getting one can be fairly exciting. Some people name themselves, but this is secretly frowned upon within the thru-hiking community. The only way to get a true-blue trail name is to earn it. As you might guess, there are many ways in which to earn a trail name. You can earn it through the things you commonly say or do, or by things that happen to you. Sometimes you may even be named after the way you look or things you wear (red headed people beware). After you've earned your trail name, that's what people will call you, and that's how you will introduce yourself, even to people in towns (unless they ask you otherwise). Your trail name may be such a perfect fit that your friends and family may end up using it for the better part of the rest of your life.

Hitch Hiking

Hitchhiking can be a touchy subject for some people. Good people who wind up hitchhiking are plagued by visions of being abducted and/or murdered by the people who pick them up. On the other hand, the good people who normally don't pick up hitchhikers are plagued by visions of hitchhikers robbing and/or murdering them. Everything you learn growing up tells you not to hitchhike and not to pick up hitchhikers.

Subsequently, the number of people out there hitchhiking is fairly small, while the number of people who pick them up is even smaller. HOWEVER, there is an exception on the roads that bisect the Appalachian Trail. The people who live in the small towns along the trail are very familiar with the yearly migration of hikers, and as a result many of them are usually quite inclined to pick them up...usually.

Despite the likelihood of people picking you up, there is still a fine art to hitchhiking that I like to think I have mastered over the course of my great journey. It is a subtle art that requires more psychology than you might think. Prepare to be amazed at the amount of thought that goes into hitchhiking and the different situations that require different tactics. If you are an attractive female, then you can pretty much disregard everything you're about to read because your good looks alone will land you a ride in almost any situation. Attractive females defy the universal laws of hitchhiking.

The first rule is to pick out a suitable spot in which to hitchhike. The most important thing is visibility. Your potential ride needs to be able to see you from a good distance away. This is so they have time to slow down, and more importantly, give them time to judge your appearance and make up their mind on whether they want to stop or not.

The next important rule of hitchhiking is accessibility. You have to make sure that now that people can see you, you are also in a suitable spot for your potential ride to pull over. This means that if you're trying to hitch east, then you can't be standing on the westward traveling side of traffic. That only works if you're on a remote road in the back woods, or a road with very little traffic that your potential ride would have no problem pulling across to get to you. There is only one other time that you would stand on the opposite side of the road from the direction you are trying to go. You would only do that if there is literally nowhere for a vehicle to pull over safely, or nowhere for you to safely stand. In these cases, you have to hope for a break in traffic at the moment your potential ride sees you; or pray they are charitable enough (and not so much in a hurry) that after they pass you, they turn around, pick you up, turn around again and continue in your desired direction as well as their original direction. It's not rocket science.

The third rule and major factor you have to worry about is appearance. This is where most people mess up. If you're a hiker, then you already look homeless and unapproachable. The main goal is to make it very clear that you ARE a hiker. Make sure your backpack is visible on your back or at your feet. Homeless people have backpacks too, so make sure you have your trekking poles out as well, because homeless people don't carry trekking poles. If you have a wooden staff like me, then you're already half way screwed.

You must look approachable. Make sure you smile at the passing cars while you stick your thumb out. Don't be lazy and only half stick it out or rest your arm on your side. Achieve a 90- degree angle between your arm and torso; get that baby out there loud and proud! Make sure you wave at the cars that don't slow down or stop. This makes you look friendly as well as understanding, and sometimes people will turn around to come back and get you. Sometimes the people behind them will see your friendliness and stop instead. On some occasions, you may have people competing to give you a ride. Make sure you comb your hair and your beard; that is if you have hair, a beard, or a comb.

Let us delve further into appearances and focus a little bit on strategy. Sometimes when you're a big intimidating guy (with a beard and filthy clothes) standing on the side of the road by yourself trying to look friendly, you won't be able to get a ride to save your life. A tactic that will increase your chances exponentially is to always hitchhike with a female when one is readily available. You can even borrow one to hitchhike for you while you hide somewhere out of sight, then let them go on their way after your ride has stopped. This kind of decoy cheating will sometimes backfire when your ride sees you step out of the woods and the girl step back into the woods, but sometimes you have to take risks.

When people see a female on the side of the road hitchhiking, they usually associate it with "damsel in distress" as opposed to "she looks like she might cut my head off and put it in her backpack." As a result of this thinking, the lone female hitchhiker almost always gets a ride right away. This also goes for the male hitchhiker that teams up with the female hitchhiker. Your potential ride will think to themselves, "Oh, what a lovely couple, they seem harmless, I'll pick them up!" or… they will think, "If that girl is hitchhiking with that guy, then he must not be a murderer because she is obviously still alive and therefore safe to pick up." I'm telling you, this is what lurks in people's minds.

Another strategy is to use the weather to your advantage. If it's raining, windy, freezing cold or any combination of the three of those things, then you're in luck. As the cars go by, try to look as miserable as possible, but also manage a hopeful look/smile as they approach. This will tug on the heart strings of your potential ride. No one wants to feel like they're responsible for another person's suffering... hopefully.

The next strategy is hitchhiking with a dog. People instinctively associate someone who owns a pet with being stable. Why is this? It's because unstable people don't usually own pets. They don't own them because their pet has died or they don't want a pet in the first place because they're, well... unstable. Your potential ride will see you and your lovely animal, then think to themselves, "that guy is definitely stable enough NOT to be an axe wielding murderer... I think I'll pick him up."

Last but not least is what I call "active hitchhiking." There is a saying that goes like this, "No matter what you do, never do nothing." This can be true for hitchhiking. Sometimes the distance you're trying to hitchhike isn't far at all; maybe it's less than two miles. This is a very walkable distance. In fact, it's so walkable that you might be able to walk it faster than you can signal down a ride. When you find yourself in this situation, you should start walking and hitching at the same time. Hold that thumb out loud and proud as you saunter down the road towards town. If you're lucky or helpless enough looking, then someone will pull over and get you into town that much quicker.

The strategy of active hitchhiking can also backfire. In some situations, you may have a longer walkable distance. We will say between three to five miles or more in some cases. You start walking under the assumption that someone will feel bad for you and pull over. No one does and eventually the side of the road may get so narrow or winding that there's simply no way for your potential ride to safely pull over even if they wanted to. In cases, such as this, you have officially screwed yourself and your chances to get a ride have just gone to zero. Your options are to grit it out and walk the rest of the way into town, or walk back to the trailhead and continue stationary hitchhiking.

Here are a few other quick nuggets. You should never hitchhike in a group of more than three or four people at the most. Any more people than that and most folks won't have room in their vehicle or even want to deal with that many individuals. Also, you can just forget about hitchhiking at night. It almost never works unless you're a female or your potential ride is an overly trusting saint.

That is the fine art to hitch hiking along the Appalachian Trail and can probably be applied to almost anywhere else. Of course, there are exceptions to every rule, but for the most part, those guidelines will hold true in almost any situation. I can proudly and not so proudly say that every situation I've described above has happened to me during my adventure at one point or another.

Towns

The unique towns that reside along the Appalachian Trail are as much a part of the thru-hiking experience as the mountains and forests. While I wish it wasn't the case, it's nearly impossible to visit them all in a single thru-hike attempt without going broke or running out of time. Some towns you'll pass by without the need to go in for resupply, while others will be passed up or missed due to the fact that you chose a different town located near the same road crossing for whatever reason. From the southern half of the trail to the northern half of the trail, every single town is unique in its own way. Some will be nothing more than a bump in the road, with populations of only several hundred people and the only businesses being a gas station or small convenience store. There will also be towns that you couldn't miss even if you wanted to. This is due to the fact that the trail winds straight through them.

When exploring, or staying in towns, it's important to remember one cardinal rule; be respectful. Be polite, respectful, and gracious to any and all townsfolk you meet out there. Think of yourself as an ambassador of the trail. Your actions, as well as your demeanor will reflect on all thru-hikers, as well as influence local opinion and treatment of future thru-hikers.

Gear Replacements

While you're out there, gear is going to break, wear down, or be found inferior or less practical than other choices available to you. The one piece of gear you are sure to replace at least once, if not two or three times, are your shoes. While some people do manage to use their original footwear the entire way, it's usually because they were wearing some god-awful heavy boots. Others may wear out their packs (I did), lose stuff, or opt for lighter or warmer versions of sleeping bags, sleeping pads, shelters, or clothing. Some opt for different cookware, stoves, water filters, or any other miscellaneous items. The question is, when you need something out there, where can you get it? Many of the towns you pass through will have outfitters that carry absolutely anything you could possibly need or want for a thru-hike. The very first outfitter you come to is only thirty miles into the trail (if you start in Georgia), and lucky for you, the trail passes directly through it, literally. It's called "Mountain Crossings," and besides being an outfitter, you can resupply, sleep, and seek out invaluable advice while you're there. Thirty miles is enough time to realize that you might have made some bad gear selections, but it may take longer to figure other things out. A couple freezing nights, or a few days of torrential downpour can reveal some serious flaws/weaknesses in your gear selection, but you might be a good distance from the nearest outfitter where you can rectify any mistakes. In reality, I wouldn't worry too much about it. Outfitters are fairly common, and they're also listed in many of the guidebooks.

Resupply

If it wasn't for the need to resupply, you'd never have to go into an Appalachian town. On the trail, you'll resupply on average every three to five days. You'll buy foods at gas stations, convenience stores, hostels, grocery stores, Wal-Mart, and a myriad of other stores you may or may not have heard of. Long story short, you'll resupply where it's most convenient, or where prices and selections will be best. Before I began the trail, resupply was something I worried about quite a bit. I was plagued with thoughts of "What if I don't reach town in time?" "What if I can't get into town?" "How will I get around town once I get there?" and "How do I get back to the trail?" Well, I'm here to once again put your mind at ease. While these sorts of questions seem legitimate prior to the trail, you'll find that all these potential problems seem to work themselves out, solutions falling into place on their own. You'll learn to love the challenges and logistics of hitchhiking as well as navigating new towns and roads. It seems scary and overwhelming at first, but the mini adventures which take place during your efforts to obtain a resupply are a major facet of excitement while hiking the trail. With caution and good judgment, you're not going to starve, you're not going to get lost forever, and you're not going to get stranded for some crazy, indeterminable amount of time. Sure, there will be hiccups and obstacles of varying degrees, but you're going to overcome them. You're going to learn to look forward to, even invite the challenges of getting around strange new lands with nothing but your wits and your own two feet.

Mail Drops

In terms of re-supply, or simply having mail or care packages delivered; you can have all of the above sent to you in just about every town along the trail. Most people will have packages sent directly to the post offices within the towns, but you can have mail sent to just about any establishment that caters to hikers, or is familiar with hikers. Besides post offices, almost all hostels, many hotels, some outfitters, and certain other establishments will hold packages for up to two weeks or more for thru-hikers. Of course, there is a protocol to follow in order to ensure the package is held and given over to the right person. You have to address it differently depending on whether you're sending it to a post office or other location. I will provide the layout below, but firstly you must address the package to the person's real name, not their trail name; this is because they will be asked to provide identification upon retrieving the parcel, especially at a post office.

When sending anything to a post office, use the following format:

John Doe

C/O General Delivery

"Address of post office"

Trail Town, GA, 12345

Please hold for thru-hiker

ETA: July 4, 20xx

After you have the correct information in the address column, make sure to write "hold for thru-hiker" once or twice on the package or envelope, as well as an ETA (estimated time of arrival) date next to those instructions. If you are able to fit this extra information under the address column, then I wouldn't worry about writing it on the sides, but you can if it makes you feel better.

When sending mail to a hostel or anywhere else that isn't a post office; address in this format...

John Doe

C/O "name of business"

"Address of business"

Trail town, GA 12345

Please hold for thru-hiker

ETA: July 4, 20xx

Mail drops are an excellent system, as the post offices around the Appalachian Trail are very familiar with the procedure and are happy to help. In fact, many people re-supply only by mail, choosing not to use any stores for the bulk of their resupply. If the postage costs are coming out of your pocket, then this can be less economical. However, if a support team back home is footing the bill, then it can work in your favor. In an effort to make your life easier, I'm going to provide the names of several crucial towns you will stop in that have very poor, or very expensive resupplies; I'll also include their approximate mileage into the trail. Many people will send mail drops to themselves in these towns to keep from paying an arm and a leg at expensive stores that provide limited options. You can have someone back home mail you the resupply, or simply mail it to yourself from the previous town before you hike out.

Nantahala Outdoor Center, NC (The NOC)/Mile: 137

Fontana Village, NC (Fontana Dam)/Mile: 164

Bland, VA/Mile: 587

Harper's Ferry, WV/Mile: 1,020

Caratunk, ME/Mile: 2,043

Monson, ME/Mile: 2,071

In an effort to keep this book as accurate and timeless as possible, I am not going to provide the addresses to any business or post offices in these towns. Businesses move or shut down, as do post offices; you can very easily find any current addresses with a quick online search.

Bounce Boxes

Although I never used one, many people utilize bounce boxes when hiking the trail. A bounce box is simply a cardboard box, or any container for that matter that you continuously mail ahead to yourself in future towns that you have yet to reach. The box usually contains extra gear, extra supplies, extra toiletries, or extra food that you may or may not have needed or used through certain sections. It's also smart to fill them with packaging tape, labels or permanent markers; this way you have everything you need to repackage and send it ahead should you open it. As long as you do not open the box, you can continue to mail it ahead to further towns for no extra charge. It's recommended that you use "Priority Mail," as its faster than parcel post, but can also be forwarded at no extra charge. Once you open it, you will have to pay shipping costs to get it moving again; if you reach the town where your bounce box resides and decide that you don't need anything inside it, you can call the post office and have it sent ahead to the next post office of your choosing. Sometimes you can simply forward it over the phone, but sometimes the post offices will require you to personally come in and send it ahead. If you send it anywhere other than a post office, you will be paying new shipping costs, regardless of whether you open it or not.

Hiker Boxes

A "hiker box" is something that exists along the entire trail. You can find them in every single town, and usually quite a few of them. They're nothing more than a container, room, or area filled with items that have been discarded by other hikers. You can find food, gear, fuel, and tons of other miscellaneous items within these little treasure boxes;

you never know what you'll get. Almost every single establishment that houses, caters to, or shelters hikers will have a hiker box somewhere on the premises. These establishments are usually hostels, certain hotels, outfitters, and sometimes private residences that frequently take in hikers. However, you can find them in less likely places. If you get to a hiker box at the right time, you can often find incredible stuff in regards to gear and food. It's a shining example of "one man's trash is another man's gold." Early on in the trail, when the majority of people are quitting is when hiker boxes are at their best. Some people will be so fed up; they throw away entire backpacks or gear worth hundreds or even thousands of dollars. All of it is first come, first serve, however there is certain etiquette to using hiker boxes. Some hikers who are on an extreme budget, or even the ones who have totally run out of money will sometimes try to resupply their foods solely from hiker boxes, taking anything and everything edible from them. Some people take no issue with this, but others take great issue with it. As a courtesy, one person should never clean out an entire hiker box of all its food. Every hiker box is different, and if there is hardly anything in it to begin with, then it's not a big deal. Simply don't raid a hiker box full of abundance, leaving it decimated for the people behind you.

Hostels

They're not Hotels, but they're the next best thing, or better. A great majority of the towns along the Appalachian Trail will have hostels that cater specifically to hikers. Some will come across as serious business operations, determined to make a dollar off your weary and hungry traveler. Others will come across as hang outs, operated by people who truly just enjoy the endless stream of company and colorful characters that hiking season provides. Hostels can be as cheap as $5 a night, to sometimes more than $30 a night, while others are set up as "free," operating solely on a donation basis. Many of the hostels will have shuttle services that take you to and from grocery stores, post offices, or wherever you need to go. Of course, some of these services will cost extra, but sometimes they are included in the price of your stay. Many hostels will also have a "work for stay" option, where you can choose to do chores around the facility in exchange for a place to sleep, without any type of monetary exchange.

Hostels are another major cornerstone of the Appalachian Trail culture and spirit. They are havens and hubs for hikers passing through towns, as well as amazing locations to meet new people, kick back, relax, and enjoy the smaller pleasures of life, as well as some of the ones we take for granted.

Shelters

There are quite literally hundreds of shelters set up along the AT, and every single one of them is unique. They can be anywhere from several to ten miles apart, or even fifteen to twenty miles apart in some sections of the trail, but the overall average is eight miles. The shelters are usually nothing more than a three-sided wooden lean-to that is completely open to the elements on one side.

Your typical shelter can accommodate anywhere from five to thirty people, and forty to one thousand mice. The average is usually five to ten people and one hundred mice, but all along the trail fantastically elaborate and beautiful shelters of varying sizes can be found. It's never a bad thing to plan your daily miles around the shelters that lie ahead of you, because they're normally placed in ideal locations that are almost always next to a reliable water source.

Your average shelter will have a fire ring/pit, flat areas to tent nearby, sometimes a picnic table, and sometimes bear cables to hang your food. Most times the inside will be a simple raised platform for sleeping, but some have what might be considered a "porch" area you can stand or sit around, that's also protected from the rain.

Shelters are a huge part of the AT, and funny enough there are a lot of people that look down on the AT because of the abundance of shelters. I'll admit, when I first learned of all the shelters during my research prior to my thru-hike, it kind of turned me off. I thought they would take away from the wilderness experience, as well as some of the challenges of wilderness camping. In truth, they do help to ease some of the challenges of wilderness camping, especially during inclement weather, but the shelters are incredible. If anything, they add to the experience of hiking the Appalachian Trail, and feel as much a part of the forest as the trees surrounding them. There is nothing better than being at the end of a long day of hiking when you smell a shelter fire you know is somewhere nearby. You know warmth and safety is close, as well as the kinship of your fellow man, possibly a familiar face, or new friends waiting to be made.

Trail Registers/Shelter Logs

All the shelters along the Appalachian Trail have what is known as "Shelter Logs" or "Trail Registers" inside them. They are usually nothing more than a simple spiral ringed notebook and a pen that's been stuffed inside a Ziploc Bag to protect it from moisture. The purpose of these log books is to keep track of where people were on certain dates, but also to pass messages or thoughts to friends and strangers that may be behind you on the trail. Whenever a person goes missing on the trail, it's the shelter logs that are checked first in order to better understand their last position on specific dates. It's completely up to you whether you sign them or not. Some people do it religiously, while others do it semi-frequently or not at all.

You don't even have to sign your name and date; you can write whatever you want in a shelter log. You can talk about your day, write a poem, draw a picture, leave an inspirational quote, tell a story, or simply pass on information or advice to whoever is behind you that might read it. Advice and information like, "This shelter leaks, don't sleep here," or "There is a large black snake living under this shelter," or "The mice at this shelter are worse than other shelters," or "Hiker so and so is a snore bastard, avoid him at all costs." You could find almost anything in a shelter log. I even found a Marijuana joint that was taped to the inside of a shelter log that had "Cheers" written underneath it. That's the sort of crazy random things you could find in one of these journals... not just signatures.

I've seen people obnoxiously take up entire pages to themselves writing nonsense messages or even just writing their name really big like a kindergarten child. You can be sure to find a little bit of everything in a shelter log, but most importantly you will get a better idea of who's ahead of you. Not only that, but it can also give you something to talk about with a hiker you're meeting for the first time. For instance, much further along in my journey while meeting a fellow hiker for the first time, I recognized their name from a journal entry I'd read many weeks before. After learning their name and remembering their log entry, the conversation went something like this. Me: "Oh I read you were attacked by a donkey while crossing that field outside Daleville; how have you been since then?" Them: "Oh yeah, I had to fend it off with my trekking poles, but I've been good! Just climbing mountains and shit every day, you know how it is."

In the beginning, I signed almost none of the shelter logs, but as time went on they became a bit of a game as well as an outlet to relieve boredom. I would write the lyrics of songs that were stuck in my head, or write excerpts of a fictional story I'd made up while walking along. I always left the story in a state of suspense and "to be continued" at the next shelter log. It kept things interesting, as well as entertaining while out there in the wilderness. We had few diversions and did what we could to bring the entertainment to us.

Towards the end of the journey, I signed or read almost none of the shelter logs. The novelty had worn off and there were so few people left on the trail that there was hardly anything worth reading in them anymore. Everyone had run out of things to say besides simply signing their name and dating it. "So-and-so was here on such and such date"- period. Unless you were curious about who was in front of you, there was almost no reason to even look at them anymore.

Trail Magic/Trail Angels

You may or may not be familiar with the terms "Trail Magic," or "Trail Angel," so allow me to familiarize and explain. Trail Magic is any form of unexpected kindness that may appear as: a good deed, food, a ride, supplies, a place to stay, etc. Trail Angles are anyone and everyone who provide these unexpected good deeds and acts of kindness. Trail Magic, as well as Trail Angels, will be prevalent throughout the entire trail, but is decidedly more common below the Mason Dixon Line. The most frequent type of trail magic is normally food; food that's been left at road crossings or trail heads, as well as picnics or feasts laid out at churches, private residences, or the middle of the woods with the Trail Angels themselves in attendance. After food, the next most common form of trail magic are favors and general acts of kindness in the form of rides into or around town, without requesting them; someone paying for your meal or laundry; someone opening their home to you; anything you can think of that makes your life easier or more pleasant that's provided by someone else. It feels good to receive Trail Magic, but I must admit, it feels much better providing it.

Food Storage at Night

When do the creepiest of creepy crawlies come out? Nighttime of course. What do they want? Besides you (kidding), they want your food. So, what are you supposed to do with your food every night while hiking the trail? Convention and common sense tell us we should at the very least put it somewhere out of reach of all animals, but where? On the AT, you have a lot of options for what you can do, as well as recommendations. Whichever way you choose to store your food at night will be a matter of personal preference based on what makes you comfortable, or based on prior experiences you've had with storing your food in the past (your methods may change as your time on the trail progresses). Some people will hang their food out of reach of animals religiously every night; others will sleep with their food, not worried about any potential consequences. Unless you're in a national or state park/forest that has specific rules governing how you should store your food (hanging, bear box, bear canister, etc.), then it's pretty much your choice what you do the rest of the time. Please note: Carrying a bear canister is not a requirement while hiking the AT, although some people will choose to do so. There is one section that is only several miles long that resides within the first 30 miles when going north from Springer Mountain that requires bear canisters to camp in; almost no one camps in this tiny section, instead choosing to camp on the boundary (it will be marked) of either side. Don't sweat it.

While on the trail, you will have at least one of several options for storing your food at night, no matter where you are. You can hang your food from a tree limb, off the ground and out of reach of bears and other creatures; you can hang it from bear cables or bear hooks at a shelter or campsite, provided they have them (not all do); you can store it in a bear box if one is available (usually in national or state parks/forests, and usually at designated campsites or shelters). You can also choose to store them inside the shelters themselves. Almost every shelter on the AT will have multiple spots within the shelter to hang food bags or gear; usually in the form of wooden pegs, hooks, or nails. Some will also have what is known as a "mouse hanger." Mouse hangers are thin strings or cables that hang from the ceiling or frame of the shelter, draping down just far enough to reach up and grab. These strings or cables will have a short stick or straight, sturdy object tied at the bottom; these work as marlin spikes to hang the loop of your pack or food bag over. About halfway up the line will usually be a can, or lid, or some form of disk the line runs straight through. Whatever the object halfway up the line is, its purpose is to create an impassable obstacle for mice if they were to climb down the line in an attempt to get to your pack or food bag. Besides keeping food safe, the mouse hangers and pegs within shelters help store any loose or wet gear off the floor of the shelter, making more room for any potential shelter dwellers. Your final option for food storage is to carry a bear canister, but these are rather cumbersome and heavy; pretty much no one carries them on the Appalachian Trail.

So, those are your options for food storage at night, but of course you can always opt to not store your food anyplace special and simply sleep with it. A great number of people sleep with their food every night and never had/have anything happen, myself included. So far, I've logged well over 300 nights of sleeping with my food, and only twice have I had an issue. One time I had a mouse chew its way into my hammock and come after my food; another time I had a raccoon reach in and try to pull my food bag out; those are the only incidents, so far. I hang food if I sleep in a shelter, but other than that, I've always slept with it in my hammock. I will not do this in grizzly country!

Having said all of this, sometimes no matter what you do, the animals will still get to your food. I've been present to see squirrels get into food that's been hung off the ground; mice chew into tents and get into food bags; and bears make off with bear canisters, never to be seen again. I've also heard first hand, as well as second hand accounts of bears pawing at hammocks or tents that have food in them; a bear biting someone through a tent while trying to get to their food within; bears stalking shelters or campsites full of people with food; bears climbing and breaking off branches that have food hung from them; porcupines chewing on backpacks for the sweaty salt soaked materials; a skunk biting a hiker on the toe while looking for food within the tarp he was sleeping under; and every kind of mouse chewing into your gear story you can imagine. Sometimes you just can't win; the choice is yours, whatever you decide. I only ask that you keep one thing in mind... if you decide to sleep with your food in areas with high concentrations of bears and something does happen, that bear will most likely be put down. So please do not put the bears in jeopardy if you decide to camp in an area that's been having a major issue with one.

Privies

The majority of shelters will have a "privy" (outhouse) somewhere within the vicinity. The reason for the privies is to consolidate human waste. If everyone went to the bathroom in any convenient spot within the vicinity of a shelter, then things would get pretty crappy and unhealthy out there. The privies certainly help to keep the waste centralized, but are not always the better alternative to simply digging a hole. This is due to the critters that tend to call these small wooden outhouses "home." The standard privy will be filled with spiders, spider webs, flies, and other insects as well as mice, rats, chipmunks, woodchucks and sometimes the snakes that come to feed on them; not to mention the smell is wooonderrfuulllll. Yes, the Appalachian Trail privy is a miniature ecosystem in itself, and it takes a special person to get used to one. Just imagine a Brown Recluse Spider sitting just under the lip of the makeshift seat you're sitting on as you do your business. I promise this thought will be stuck with you for the next several dozen times you sit on a toilet, especially an Appalachian Trail privy...

Defecating

Are you accustomed to pooping in the woods? Popping a squat or holding onto a tree, then depositing your waste into a little hole that you dug? It may not seem like that big of a deal to some people, but to others, the thought of making number two anywhere but a toilet is horrifying. While there are privies at nearly every shelter (excluding all shelters in Tennessee) on the Appalachian Trail, as mentioned earlier; they are not always the best option, or available when the need arises.

Defecating out on the trail will become something that you will become accustomed to - that is if you're not already comfortable with it. When the need arises, you'll simply stray off the trail (wherever you are) in search of a decent spot to make a deposit. What constitutes a good spot? A good spot is somewhere that's not immediately in view of the trail, or somewhere likely to receive little to no foot traffic. After you've established that no one might accidentally be subjected to watching you take care of business, or stepping on or near it later, then you can start finding the perfect spot. Since most of us are accustomed to sitting down when we do our business, I like to search for a log, stump, or rock that might provide a semi comfortable base to sit on while the deed is done. If no comfortable, seat-worthy object or surface is readily available, then I look for something to brace myself against, whether it be holding onto a small tree or rock, or bracing my back against a larger tree or rock. If no brace-worthy objects are readily available, then you simply have to squat. Once you've decided if you're sitting, bracing, or squatting, it is then up to you to dig what is called a "cat hole," or a small hole deep enough to deposit your waste in and cover up without it protruding or being a hazard if that spot were to be stepped on by someone else. Be sure to completely bury any toilet paper as well. Many people will insist that you pack out any used toilet paper, and while this is being very conscious of the environment, you won't find many thru-hikers carrying around used toilet paper to deposit in the next town. How deep is deep enough? The rule of thumb is no less than six inches.

    Some nuggets of advice (no pun intended) when taking care of business is to remove one of your legs completely out of your bottoms and underwear (if you're wearing any). This will help to ensure that you don't accidently take a dump in your pants while they're around your ankles (not everyone can achieve a perfect squat.) Ladies, there are many feminine products out there that assist women with peeing outside. I have no business going into any detail about them, but they are easily researched and found. I personally like to take my pants and underwear completely off when I'm going number 2. It allows me the most freedom and range of motion to do business, but your preference is your own.

Leave No Trace (LNT)

Leave No Trace is a phrase you will hear many times throughout your hike. There are some finer points to this practice, but it can be summed up with an old saying; "Leave only footprints, take only pictures." LNT is the practice of having as little an impact on the environment as possible. There are seven main principles to LNT that I will touch on briefly.

Plan ahead and prepare: This refers to knowing any rules and regulations of the places you plan to visit or hike through in advance. If you're aware of the rules and regulations, you don't have to worry about breaking them by accident, or having a negative impact on something you weren't even aware of.

Travel and camp on durable surfaces: This refers to walking on the established paths, and camping in designated camp spots. If you stray off the trail, or make camp in a place that hasn't been previously established, your chances for trampling or damaging sensitive flora/fauna are increased.

Dispose of waste properly: If you packed it in, then you pack it out. Any trash that you generate needs to be kept on your person until you reach a designated waste disposal area. This also encompasses burying your waste properly, and not leaving it on the surface of the ground to be seen, stepped on, or smelled. It also covers the use of chemicals; if you plan to wash dishes or yourself with any kind of chemicals, make sure you do it at least two hundred feet away from any source of water.

Leave what you find: Don't touch/take historic structures or artifacts. Don't take any rocks, plants, or other natural objects that you may find. Don't build any unnatural structures, dig any trenches, or introduce any non-native species.

Minimize campfire impacts: Only make campfires where they're permitted, and keep them small. Don't cut down live vegetation for fuel, only use dead branches and logs for fuel. Put out your campfires completely and make sure everything within them has been burned to ash.

Respect wildlife: Observe wildlife from a safe distance, without trying to approach or follow them. Do not feed the wildlife or leave your food where wildlife can get to it. Also, control your pets from harassing or attacking the wildlife, or leave them at home.

Be considerate of other visitors: Respect the other people that you meet and protect the quality of their experience. Treat everyone you encounter with respect, and always give the larger group or the individual going uphill the right of way. Don't make excessive noise, and be considerate to other people hiking or camping around you.

Campfires

Campfires - beacons of the night that bring people together in a sphere of warmth, comfort, and camaraderie. Undoubtedly, many of the most social, surreal, and genuine interactions on the Appalachian Trail will take place around campfires. Besides certain state and national parks, as well as some sections of the trail that may be under a "burn ban," you can make a fire on the trail pretty much anywhere, anytime. Nearly every single shelter will have a designated fire ring, some bigger and more elaborate than others, but a fire ring none the less. Fire rings are not only specific to shelter areas, and can be found throughout the trail in obvious, as well as not so obvious places. Some fire rings have lasted throughout the decades and can be found all over the trail in out of the way places; you simply have to find them. Some will be just off to the side of the trail, some will be in epic locations, while others will be somewhat hidden, discovered by chance as you investigate different areas, or stray off trail for whatever reason. Always be wary of where you make your fires, how big you let them get, and how strong they are when the last person turns in for the night. It's usually best to put them out before bed, but the soft crackling and dull glow of a dying fire makes for a sweet lullaby against the back drop of nocturnal noises.

Making fires in wet conditions*:* This can sometimes be hit or miss, as well as time consuming depending on how long it has been wet in the location you're trying to make a fire. Collect the dead sticks or branches you need to get your fire started, then with a sharp knife, shave off the top layer of wet bark until you've reached the driest part.

For kindling, use very small twigs or dead/dried out vegetation. These are small enough that you can dry them yourself, or they can be lit up fairly easily even when damp due to their small size. Once you get the fire going, place all other branches/logs/sticks next to the fire in an attempt to dry them out as much as possible before adding them to the blaze.

Trash Disposal/Burning

During longer stretches between towns, you can accumulate a surprising amount of trash depending on the sorts of food you've packed out. What do you do with all of it? You carry it to the next town and throw it away in the proper receptacle, that's what. Something you'll see on the trail all too commonly is people burning their trash; this is considered a bad LNT practice. While the trash is probably going to end up getting buried or burned at a landfill anyway, burning plastics or foils in a camp fire can release chemicals into the ground, air, or be ingested by animals at a later time. If you feel like you absolutely must burn something other than dead branches, make sure it's purely of the paper or cardboard variety. When I find myself with purely paper or cardboard trash, I sometimes like to use it as kindling to get a fire started if nothing else is immediately available, or conditions are a little damp.

People

You will meet plenty of people on the trail. Some of them you'll like, while some you won't stand to be around; some of them might even scare the hell out of you. A few people find temporary love or even life partners while they're out there. Basically, you really don't know who you're going to meet. The Appalachian Trail attracts some interesting characters to it every year, while other characters are fixtures. Many are fun to talk to and wonder about, while others may even become your best friend. I've met ordained priests of Satan, millionaires, self-proclaimed geniuses, entrepreneurs, gurus, trail legends, authors, homeless people, business owners, adventurers, people who'd taken oaths of silence, drug dealers, foreigners, past criminals, current criminals on the lam, hunters, and every type of person in between. You can't be afraid to encounter these types of people, because they are the ones who enrich the experience. There will be stretches of utter solitude, but for the most part, you will constantly be running into other hikers and citizens on the trail, as well as within towns.

Self Defense

You're walking across the country by way of the forests and mountains, a stranger in strange lands; how is one supposed to protect oneself? This is something that crosses the minds of almost everyone prior to embarking on their journey. It also crosses the minds of those you come in contact with who aren't on the journey. It's one of the most commonly asked questions by friends and family, as well as strangers you meet while thru-hiking; "What do you carry for protection?" First of all, ask yourself this...what do I need protection from? Immediately you might think, "dangerous animals and crazy people, duh!" This is a reasonable answer, but largely does not apply to the AT. The wildlife you encounter will be 99.99% peaceful, requiring no defensive actions on your part. As far as the people go, there are plenty of crazy individuals you'll encounter out there, but 99.99% of them will also be peacefully harmless. Even in the off chance you were to be involved in some kind of altercation out there, it most likely wouldn't require the need for a weapon (I did see one drunken fist fight).

I understand that weapons, especially guns, are a very sensitive topic to many people. Some lobby passionately for them, while others lobby passionately against them. I personally have no problem with guns, nor the people who love or despise them. As long as they are used responsibly, I have no qualms. I'll go ahead and say it... you do not need a gun to hike the Appalachian Trail, and almost every single thru-hiker who has completed it will tell you the exact same thing. The trail itself, as well as the towns around it are incredibly safe, believe it or not. You also don't need a machete or giant combat knife for protection either (serious waste of weight). To be honest, you don't need much more than your wits and good judgment.

When I did my thru-hike, the closest thing I carried to a weapon was a three-inch knife, and my 6-ft. walking stick. I only used the stick for walking, and the knife for cutting certain foods, or performing simple tasks around camp. I never once found myself in a situation where I felt I needed protection of the deadly weapon variety.

Now for a little bit of reality... While the chances of something happening that require you to need protection are basically slim to none, things have happened to people out there. Things like being robbed, jumped, attacked, held at gun point, murdered, or people being held against their will; these things have happened to thru-hikers over the decades, and I'm sure most, if not all of them wished they had some extra form of self-defense after the fact. I've met people who have been robbed or jumped, but I've only heard the stories of documented events where people were shot, held at gun point, or viciously attacked without provocation. These sorts of things are few and far between, but they can happen anywhere, at any time; not only while hiking the trail. It's the feeling of vulnerability from being someplace new, with few resources readily available (as well as the absence of our familiar safety net back home), that cause us to feel like we need extra protection when on an adventure of this magnitude.

All that being said, I have met people who carried a small firearm in their packs, or a large knife the entire way through. Most notably, I met a young woman who carried a gun in her pack because her father insisted on it; she began the trail hiking by herself. If you are a woman, or individual who has been plagued by a terrible experience, or terrible thoughts, and feel you absolutely need to carry some form of protection for your own peace of mind; then who am I to tell you not to? If you plan to do it, then do so discreetly and responsibly, and don't tell others what you have. Every time you cross into a new state, there are new laws which govern that land. Many of the states in New England have very strict gun and knife laws, and while the chances of your pack being searched are virtually zero, you never know when you might end up in a freak situation where it happens.

Hiking Alone

Some people are distraught at the thought of being alone in any situation or environment; some are utterly terrified at the thought of being alone in the wilderness. There are people every year who abandoned their plans to thru-hike due to their hiking partner bailing out on them; they were too afraid to go it alone. The fact of the matter is... the majority of people who thru-hike the Appalachian Trail begin it alone - women and men alike.

In the not so distant past, beginning the Appalachian Trail alone really meant you were alone. These days, with the trail popularity growing exponentially, you'll almost never be truly alone, unless you begin the trail at an extremely unpopular time - like say the first of the New Year. In terms of being afraid of hiking alone, please don't be; there will be more than enough people on the trail to make you feel comfortable, and almost everyone makes friends of the lifelong variety while they're out there. In regards to hiking alone by choice, this is also easily achieved. It won't take you long after getting on the trail to figure out how to be by yourself and avoid any potential crowds. As a rule, shelters will always have the most people around them, so if your goal is to avoid human beings, then make it your business to avoid camping or hanging around shelters and/or large designated camp spots. Camp in smaller, obscure sites, or if possible, choose your own stealth spot; this is easier for hammock-hikers since they don't require flat ground, or even to be on the ground. As always, it's best not to go stomping off the trail, or clearing out areas so you can set up your tent; simply find a small, out of the way area that's already been established; there are plenty of them.

The longest I ever went without seeing another person on the trail was three days, and this was due to the fact that a festival was going on; the majority of people in the area were partaking in festivities instead of hiking. Despite any special circumstance, by and by, you will be as alone as you choose to be while hiking the trail.

Hiking at Night

Are you afraid of the dark? Does the thought of hiking through the woods at night by yourself or even with the added security of other people send shivers down your spine? If the answer is yes, then you're like probably 99% of the rest of the earth's population... but not former thru-hikers. When spending months and months hiking around the clock, it's only logical that some of those times will fall during periods of darkness. Do not be afraid.

Before I began the trail, night hiking never crossed my mind; it wasn't even a possibility to me. I assumed I would only be hiking during the day, then be safely within my shelter by the time darkness set in. Boy was I wrong! I night-hiked my little buns off; sometimes because I wanted to, and sometimes because I had to, or felt I needed to. Oftentimes I was alone with my dog, but many times I was among friends or other hikers. While the thought of night-hiking might seem like an improbability for you now, I promise you will eventually become so comfortable with the forest at all hours that it will become second nature - or even a preference to hiking during the day.

I spent many a night trudging through darkness, and knew several people personally who only hiked at night. Sometimes I did it to beat the heat of the day, while other times I did it because I'd made up my mind to reach a certain distance or destination, then simply ran out of daylight before getting there. Whatever reason finds you hiking at night, you can be sure of several things... you will for the most part be the only one on the trail, wherever you are (plus whoever you're with-if applicable); it will be much quieter than during the day, and you will gain a new found supreme confidence in yourself, as well as your abilities. There is an incredible surreal feeling which comes from night hiking, especially when you're new to it. I urge you to be open to the idea and not be afraid when the opportunity presents itself.

Sexual Harassment on Trail

    I suppose this subject would be of greater interest to women, especially women who are thinking of going out there alone. As we all know, sexual harassment comes in many forms; the physical, the verbal, and in some cases...the psychological. Much like at the bar, at work, or anywhere people might gather, sexual harassment does exist on the trail, and mostly against women. It's not a major problem of the trail that should have you up at night worrying, but it does happen. As it goes, more men than women partake in thru-hikes; more women are getting into it every year, but for now the ratio is tipped much further to the men's side.

    The sexual harassment that exists on the trail is mostly in the form of verbal innuendo, or unwanted sexual advances or passes. These are also the types you will encounter most commonly back in modern society, so no surprises there. What makes it more unpleasant on the trail is the feeling of isolation and vulnerability that comes from being in the woods. The type of sexual harassment women on the trail might encounter that is decidedly less common off trail is being pursued or followed. I'm not talking about someone chasing you down the trail wielding a knife trying to "get you." I'm talking about men following women on the trail; hiking the same pace as them so they can talk to them throughout the day; taking breaks at the same spot as them; trying to camp in the same areas as them every night. This is the most common form of truly unwanted sexual harassment on the trail. Many times, it's simply a hopeful guy trying to spend more time around a girl he finds attractive, but doesn't get the hint. Other times it's a guy who doesn't care if his attention is unwanted, and continues to follow and pursue even though it's been made clear the woman is not interested. This is where it can get scary for women. I've personally seen this type of "pursuit" several times on the trail, and it genuinely freaks the women out. Although frequently the pursuer has no bad intentions, and is simply a creepy guy who may or may not know how creepy they are being; it makes it no less wrong. If you find yourself in this situation, you have options... Firstly, you may confront the individual and outright tell them how you feel; most times this will work, as the person is simply terrible at reading signals and needs everything spelled out for them.

However, if you think confronting them might exacerbate the situation, then you still have more options. Secondly, you can join up with a group or fellow hiker, skip ahead further on the trail, or get off trail for a couple days and let the individual get far enough ahead that you won't see them again. Lastly, if you feel threatened, and you feel the individual has crossed the line or may be dangerous, get in touch with authorities as soon as possible. I've seen and talked to women who have utilized these options to great effect.

Without going on forever, I'll close out this subject by saying this: sexual harassment is real, and it can exist on the trail in all its forms. If you find yourself in an uncomfortable situation, utilize the network of other people out there. While on the trail, other thru-hikers are a thru-hiker's best friend - we take care of our own. We confide in each other and help one another out whenever and however we can. Don't forget that.

Drugs and Alcohol

Yes, there are drugs on the trail. You might even say that drugs are a sub-culture of the Appalachian Trail. Mostly your hippie drugs like marijuana, mushrooms, and acid; but you can encounter more. They're easy to avoid or find, depending on what your goals are, but they do exist in all their forms. What you may or may not find surprising out on the trail is the open use of marijuana. It's passed around, even given out freely, and on any given day, you can find someone smoking it or offering some to you. It's nothing to be worried about or afraid of; it's simply another aspect of the "living in the wilderness/hiking culture" that you'll find out there. As I said, all of it is easily avoided or ignored if you wish to do so.

Alcohol is more common within towns. Since alcohol is a liquid, and liquids are generally heavy, most people do not carry it unless it's hard liquor in medium to small containers. It's tough to get a buzz when you're constantly sweating, so most forms of alcohol are reserved for town visits and around campfires at the end of the day.

Abandoning Social Norms

You will undergo quite a few personal transformations while on the trail; some of them physical, others psychological or spiritual. The transformation I want to focus on briefly pertains to the mental and physical in regards to societal norms. What is a "social norm?" In short, they're universally accepted rules, values, and behaviors within a society that are expected to be followed without question or disruption. Some examples of social norms are, but not limited to; shaking hands when you meet someone; not talking about bodily functions while in polite company; looking presentable when you go out in public; not talking with food in your mouth; not picking your nose, farting, or burping in public; showering regularly. While some of those examples are things you might never abandon (being polite to everyone at all times is never a bad thing), there are plenty of norms we end up disregarding after being on the trail for an extended period of time.

It first begins with bodily odors; you're out there sweating in the same clothes for days on end without a shower. At first you may feel self-conscious and even offensive to yourself and others by the way you smell. However, after a short time you grow immune to your own smell and soon stop caring about the smells of others. You're all on this journey together, meeting the same obstacles day in and day out. The smells and the filthiness become an accepted natural by-product of the adventure itself. After you make this unconscious connection, you begin to realize these smells are who we are when we're at our best, our happiest. This is the first domino to fall in a long line of socially acceptable dominos. Next, we stop caring about our appearances; women stop shaving their legs and armpits; guys don't shave their beards or heads; both stop caring about clothing appearances. On any given day during the warmer months on the Appalachian Trail, you can see individuals hiking in their undergarments, or wacky, mismatched outfits they've picked up at thrift stores in small towns; sometimes you'll even see men hiking in dresses. Aside from the fragrances and visual spectacles, people will cut loose from the stigmas regarding suppression of bodily functions, literally. You become so used to farting, belching, and using the bathroom whenever the need arises; you won't think twice when doing it, talking about it, or excusing yourself to do it within speaking distance of those around you. Men and women fart and belch with reckless abandon while in the presence of one another; free of judgment, embarrassment, chastisement, or alienation from others. It's absolutely wonderful.

Extended life in the woods teaches you something about being human and embracing all our natural little idiosyncrasies. Submerging yourself in nature breeds back a lot of natural behavior we've shunned or been taught to look down upon, and guess what? You'll love it. All of these inane things we concern ourselves with on a daily, almost moment by moment basis while living in "modern society" are finally revealed for what they are - ridiculous.

As you realize these changes taking affect within and around you, it opens up the doors to even more change, more questions. It all begins with the little things, but once you're conscious of those little things, the real-life changers begin to manifest…

<u>Personal Growth</u>

What is personal growth? In its most basic definition, personal growth is an improvement of awareness, self- awareness, identity, talents, potential, quality of life, and self- knowledge; it contributes to the realization of dreams and aspirations, as well as the enhancement of all aspects of being human. Absolutely everyone undergoes some form of personal growth during a long-distance hike; even the ones who don't make it the whole way (even when that was the original plan). To what degree and in what areas you grow in will always vary from person to person, but I guarantee you will grow in one way or another.

We left off the previous subject of "abandoning social norms" with the manifestations of life altering changes and realizations. People choose to do a thru-hike for many different reasons; thrill of adventure, physical challenge, weight loss, time away to think, get in touch with nature, test themselves, etc. Sometimes these reasons are brought on due to major life events; loss of a loved one, divorce, losing a job, or maybe plain boredom with the way they've been doing things. Regardless of why or what drives you to go out there in the first place, almost every single person goes out there expecting one thing at the very least; to be changed in some way, hopefully for better.

Once notice has been taken of the small changes regarding social norms, it opens up our consciousness to new changes. We realize how easily we changed the way we did certain things for the better part of most of our lives, subsequently beginning to notice and question other things, bigger things. Things like "happiness," and how we define it personally to ourselves. We learn what true freedom is, as well as the value of our time; the most precious resource we possess. Other's expectations suddenly become worthless as we begin to question what's expected of us from society, as well as the order of events our lives are expected to follow; study hard, college, career, marriage, children, nice car, nice home, picket fence, bills, debt, etc. You learn to put value in things you consider personally valuable, not what society deems valuable.

All of the above is only a single example of a small facet of personal growth you could undergo. I mainly used examples from some of my own personal growth experiences during my time spent long distance hiking. In reality, your guess is as good as mine as to what sort of personal growth you will undergo, as well as to what degree. I will say this however, while you certainly undergo noticeable changes while making multiple revelations about yourself, as well as the world we live in and those who inhabit it - while on the trail, a great deal of personal growth will take place after you've finished your hike and come home. This is what I call retrospective personal growth. You've gone home and are now attempting to (perhaps grudgingly) assimilate back into civilized society. While this assimilation process is taking place, you have a lot of time to look back on your journey, as well as take a closer look at the society you've just rejoined. You begin to reassemble all the puzzle pieces that were scattered during your journey. However, they don't all fit together the same as they did before you left. It's during this down time of looking back on it all while trying to make sense of it-that your final, sometimes most profound burst of personal growth takes place. Mine did.

Relationships-On the Trail and Off

A question I see pop up pretty often pertains to "romance" on the trail; people are curious what the romantic scene is like. Some would just as soon assume its non-existent, not sparing a second thought on the subject. Others are very intrigued by the notion of a romantic encounter while in the throes of an epic adventure; and why shouldn't they be? It's the stuff of Hollywood movies. Without going into a heavy amount of detail, the short answer to the inquiry of trail romance is...yes, it does happen, and more often than you'd think. We are human beings, and where there is a will, there's a way; sweaty, dirty bodies and all. Having gotten that out, it's more common to see romantic relationships form between hikers, rather than one night stands. Don't get me wrong, the one night stands exist out there, just like anywhere else, but they're less common than your wholesome relationship. This journey unites people like you wouldn't believe. It provides a major commonality between you and everyone else you meet. This common ground that is defined by the adventure you're on, can be an incredible catalyst for short or long term relationships. Some people will meet on the trail, get into a relationship, then go their separate ways at the conclusion of the hike. This may be something which was discussed and agreed upon ahead of time; but mostly it's simply because the greatest thing the individuals ever had in common was the adventure itself and the struggle to complete it. Adversity and struggle brings people together in a way unlike any other; however, once that adversity or struggle is over, so is the relationship, by design. Sorry for the negative aspect of this, but it's a reality of life, as well as the trail. Here's a bit of good news though...I know many people, and have met many people who found the love of their life while thru-hiking. I know some who are married with children now, and I know others who are still in relationships years after meeting on the trail. So, there's your answer on that one; anything can happen.

I know I touched on relationships back home a little earlier in the book, but I didn't inject any personal experience or really give any advice based on what I saw and did on the trail. I'll give you the real-world stuff first; some relationships last the length of the trail, and some don't. I saw people who ended relationships back home while on the trail, and even a couple of divorces initiated from the trail side, as well as the home front. I also saw plenty of people who happily maintained their relationship back home for their entire hike; I'm one of them. Now, some people end up growing and changing so much while they're out there, they realize what they have back home simply isn't in line with the person they have become/becoming, or the new direction they want for their life; it happens.

As far as any good advice I can give you based on my own experiences, as well as what I saw from others who successfully thru-hiked with significant others back home; I do have some. Make your significant other as much a part of the journey as you possibly can; make them feel useful, and not like they're sitting on the sidelines. If it's possible, have them come out and hike a section, or visit you in town for a weekend. You can always go back home if you want, but from what I've seen, it's usually better for them to come to you; it makes them part of the adventure, and feels more like a vacation on their end. What also works when trying to include them on the adventure without physically having them come to you, or vis-versa, is to make them feel like they're helping you while you're out there. Encourage or let them send you care packages, gear replacements, mail drops, or whatever. When they send you things on the trail, it's like them sending a piece of themselves; and the more appreciative you are, the more they feel like they're right there with you, in spirit, helping you along. For example: My girlfriend sent me a care package full of pay day candy bars and bacon jerky; these are things I love. After I received the package, I called her and let her know how much they meant to me. I told her I'd been having a terribly rough day, missing home, but the sight of the bacon jerky and the little love note with it had turned my mood around (for the record, food can make a bad day into a great day, believe me). Something as simple as letting them know they improved your day or made life easier for you in whatever way, can make all the difference. Intermittent phone calls don't hurt either; especially if you call them from beautiful locations on the trail and describe to them what you're witnessing; it can make them feel like they're with you, but also lets them know you're thinking of them during beautiful and special moments.

That's the best I can offer for relationships based on my own personal experience, as well as the experiences of others whom I've met or am friends with. As with anything in life, sometimes it's meant to be, and sometimes it's not; don't be afraid of change, it's how we grow.

Challenges Back Home

Believe it or not, quite a few people end up quitting or going home through no direct intervention or challenge of the trail. I've seen many people quit, due to pressures from family, spouses, loved ones, significant others, or problems back home having to do with personal business, work, relationships, or family dynamics. While some of these are unavoidable, unforeseeable, and can't be ignored; some measures can be taken to help lessen the likelihood of any of these occurrences rearing their ugly head. Those measures for the most part require that you have all of your affairs meticulously in order before you leave in the first place. Things like money, work, and prior commitments/responsibilities can be and should be completely ironed out before you leave. If they're not, then you're taking a gamble. Pressures from loved ones, family, friends, spouses, etc., are a little less predictable. While any situation involving the aforementioned subjects will be unique, it's up to you to decide what's most important to you when making the decision to possibly leave the trail permanently at the request of others...

Terrain/Obstacles

The Appalachian Trail is chock full of different types of terrain and obstacles that tend to vary based on which section/region of the trail/states you are in. While the majority of obstacles will consist of nothing more than seemingly endless ascents and descents of varying steepness and height, there are plenty of other terrain types and obstacles to be found. You're going to be hiking over rocks, through boulder fields, washed out root beds, logs, fallen trees, grassy fields, rural roads, walls of smooth rock, mountains of jumbled boulders, interstate overpasses/underpasses, across, over, around, and through streams, creeks, rivers, ponds, and lakes. You'll climb hand over hand up short climbs and good portions of certain mountains. You'll slog through puddles, swaths of moss, bogs, seemingly endless fields of mud, tall grass, overgrown vegetation, pastures full of livestock, spider webs, bug hoards, herds of ponies, and people's back yards. Sometimes you'll encounter snow and ice depending on what time of year it is, or during freak, out of season weather. You'll hike in rain so heavy and furious that you can't see ten feet in front of you as the trail becomes indiscernible from a fast-flowing stream. In the south, you'll encounter never ending switch backs, while further north the trail will shoot straight up the mountain side for thousands of feet. You can be sure that you're going to hike over just about every kind of terrain you can imagine, besides desert or frozen tundra.

Saving your shoes on the rocks: By wrapping duct tape around your shoes throughout the rockier sections of the trail, you can prolong their life and save them from extra damage. This also works when your shoes are on their last leg and you need to give them a little extra support until you reach a location where you can get another pair. The downside is that on hot summer days, this can keep your shoes from venting properly, subsequently baking your feet. Duct tape works, but unless you're going to get very creative, or keep re-applying it, it's only a temporary fix.

Weather Conditions/Temperatures

Some of your worst days and lowest moments on the trail are going to come during inclement weather. If you spend any prolonged amount of time in the woods, you're going to run into some bad weather conditions. Not only does the AT have a wide range of different weather conditions, but it's also home to the most unpredictable and extreme weather conditions found anywhere else in the United States; that location is the White Mountains of New Hampshire. Now, granted there is plenty of extreme weather in the winter, we are going to focus on weather throughout the entire trail during the most common thru-hiking times. Those times are early spring to early fall. Within the span of that time frame, you can expect to potentially encounter torrential rain and thunderstorms, possibly even hurricanes in the summer and early fall. You can expect to potentially encounter hailstorms, ice overs, snow flurries, or light snow storms; severe winds, lightning storms, cold snaps, cold fronts, and heat waves. You'll get caught in these conditions while hiking, sleeping, or within towns. The important thing when confronted with severe weather conditions is to make smart decisions. Smart decisions can include: Knowing when to call it quits; setting up your shelter before the conditions are so bad that it's nearly impossible; not hiking with too many layers on so that your innermost layers become drenched with sweat, or get soaked anyway during heavy rainfall; camping in low or high altitude locations during certain weather conditions or temperatures.

When it comes to being mindful/aware of temperatures, there are a few facts you should know that will make your life easier. In regards to altitude, for every 1,000 feet you ascend, the temperature drops three degrees. This is true for descending, except the temperature will rise three degrees. Knowing this can be very helpful when you're trying to choose a camp spot that will beat the heat, or beat the cold. Keep in mind, if you're going to camp at high altitudes during the summer, you always run the risk of being caught in a storm on a mountain top. Also, while it may only drop three degrees for every thousand feet that you ascend, you must also take into account that there are higher winds at higher altitudes, and sometimes less foliage and trees to block them - thus, resulting in a much higher wind chill factor. Colder temperatures can also be found close to water. So, when camping directly next to a water source, or within the vicinity of a large water source, you can expect cooler temperatures than you would encounter if you were to camp slightly further away. These sorts of tips don't usually make that big of a difference on a day by day basis, but during unique or severe weather conditions when every degree lost or gained counts, they can be very helpful. Also, the coldest part of any night will fall between the hours of 2 am and 5 am.

The White Mountains of New Hampshire

There was much more to the White Mountains than their steep climbs and inhospitable terrain. This entire range was billed as having the most extreme, as well as unpredictable weather in all the United States. Exposed rocky ridgelines, freezing temperatures, and hurricane force winds were unpredictable and commonplace all year round in the

White Mountains. The strongest gust of wind ever recorded in history for over sixty years was measured on top of Mount Washington in the Whites, at 231 miles per hour. This record was beaten only by a typhoon in Australia in 1996, with the measurement of a 253 mile per hour wind gust. More than a hundred people have died from falls, exposure, and other accidents over the past decades in these mountains.

Being a very popular national forest, the White Mountains also come with some very specific rules. The main rule is "NO stealth camping." Just like the Smokies and Shenandoah, this means you aren't allowed to camp in undesignated camping spots. The only difference in the Whites is that all the designated camping spots cost money, even the shelters.

The other option is the "Huts." These are lavish lodges that house anywhere from forty to ninety people depending on their size. The huts have crews (Croos) of three to five caretakers that live in them for months at a time while cooking for the guests and taking care of them during their stay at the hut. Every hut is placed in a remote yet ideal location that is only accessible on foot or by helicopter; all the supplies at these lavish cabins are either packed in on foot by the caretakers or air dropped. Staying at huts is referred to as "rich man camping" amongst thru-hikers. At around $140 per night, you can enjoy your nice bunk, baked goods, hot drinks and hot meals provided by the caretakers while you spend the day hiking the surrounding trails and admiring the beauty of the region.

After eighteen hundred miles of camping wherever you want, the vast majority of thru-hikers opt not to pay money to camp in the wilderness, or the exorbitant prices to stay in something that has fewer amenities than a hostel costing $10 per night. So, you have three options to choose from.

Option one is to follow all the rules and pay the prices of whatever sanctioned area you decide to lay your head. This is the more expensive, honorable, but ultimately least chosen option by thru-hikers. Most North bounders are all but broke by the time they reach New Hampshire anyway.

Option two is to avoid the sanctioned areas and stealth camp off the trail wherever you can find a good spot. This is the most chosen option by thru-hikers, and even though the "No Stealth Camping" rule is in place, it's very difficult to enforce. The terrain is harsh and the temperatures cold, so there isn't a squadron of National Forest Police running around the mountains every night, searching high and low for people camping in undesignated areas. The trail itself is challenging enough, so no one is going to stray very far from it, least of all the officials. I never heard of a single person getting busted for stealth camping before, during, or after the Whites. If you choose to stealth camp, or get caught in a situation that forces you to stealth camp, then please do so while having as little an impact on the surrounding environment as possible; no fires, no trampling vegetation, no litter (fires are not allowed in the Whites anyways).

Option three is "work for stay" at a hut. Work for stay refers to doing chores for the caretakers (i.e., washing dishes, sweeping, cleaning bathrooms, etc.) in return for a warm and dry place to stay, as well as receive some food. They don't give you a bunk or a bed, but instead let you sleep on the floor in the dining room. This is perfectly fine because that's basically what you've been doing for all those months anyway. The food they give you in exchange for the work is left over from whatever the "hut guests" didn't finish. Leftover "hut food" beats the hell out of backpack food any day of the year, so no one complains.

The only downside is that work for stay is not always available and you can't predict when it is. Hikers can sometimes be vulnerable to a caretaker's philosophy of not wanting to give any unused floor space or uneaten food away for free (even at the expense of a hiker's safety). This means you could potentially find yourself on the bitter end of an exchange that finds you stuck more than four to five thousand feet up a mountain at night, during inclement weather. Your best bet is to never rely on the huts for shelter unless you absolutely have to. One trick/charitable offering that can sometimes ensure your free stay at a hut is to bring liquor. The hut crews are normally college aged young people with one thing on their mind; having a good time (and believe me, they do). If you don't mind the extra weight, pack out a small to medium plastic bottle of liquor to offer the crew at the hut of your choice. I spoke to a group of three hikers who used this approach and were able to stay at five different huts; they were never turned away from any of them. My liquor-less-self, on the other hand, was turned away from three huts and only scored work for stay at two of them.

Those are the options in the Whites; options made even more critical by the topographical layout of the Whites themselves. There are hardly any roads and barely any towns throughout the 100-mile stretch of the White Mountain range. Resupply options were usually very slim, and depending on how fast you make your way over the harsh terrain, you might find yourself resupplying with the over-priced snacks and baked goods from the Huts.

Many areas through this section were so high in altitude, they were above the tree line. This meant there were no trees or vegetation to shelter you from the high winds and extreme weather; all you had was bare, exposed rock. The exposed ridges that reside above tree line can go on for many miles before dipping back below tree level. In the event of an emergency weather situation, you could find yourself stuck on one of those ridgelines in life threatening conditions with only several options. Those options include: Grit it out, hide amongst the rocks, run down the mountainside to the tree line (not usually a viable option), or seek shelter in a Hut that's strategically placed on some of the above tree line sections.

When you've never been to this region before and have relatively no idea what to expect, things can get tricky. Even when you know where everything is, it's almost impossible to know how long it'll to take you to traverse certain distances. This makes it very hard to plan your miles, stopping points, and safety areas along the way. No matter how fit you are, or how fit you think you are, the Whites are unlike anything you've encountered previously to the south. Of course, there are exceptions to every rule, but most will find their hiking progress slows dramatically upon reaching the Whites. You may end up not being able to reach certain distances that you would normally have no problem reaching. This could unexpectedly leave you in dangerous locations or situations at the wrong time. A good rule to follow and remember in the White Mountains is for every mile you hike there, it will feel like two miles. A ten-mile day will take the effort, and in many cases, the time of a twenty-mile day anywhere else. I learned this the hard way more than once during my stint in the White Mountains.

Hiking in Rain

It never ceases to amaze me how often this question arises… "What do you do when it rains?" While thru-hikers view this question as a no brainer, your average person most likely already knows the answer, but simply wants to hear you say it… "You hike through it, or you set up your shelter to get out of it." Most people stay inside when it rains, cancel their plans, read a good book, or watch television; the thru-hiker's options are slightly less comfortable. When rain begins to fall during your thru-hike, you have decidedly less options than say…someone playing in their backyard or out for a picnic. You don't get to simply come in out of the rain. No, you're in it for the long haul. When the rain drops are falling on your head, you have several options. First, you can hike through them depending on severity, temperature, and other conditions that will influence your personal threshold and preference. Secondly, you can simply erect your personal shelter in the next safe/viable spot, or make it to the nearest Appalachian Shelter available. I'll go into greater detail on hiking in the rain with various pieces of gear later on in the "Gear" section of this book.

Injuries

I don't think I ever met a fellow thru-hiker who didn't suffer some form of injury (or injuries) on their thru-hike. If you're walking thousands of miles over tough and sometimes treacherous terrain, the odds are not in your favor to come out unscathed. Cuts, scrapes, punctures, bites, breaks, fractures, tears, strains, pulls, rolls, overuse injuries, splints, lacerations, bruises, rashes, stubs, jams, bangs, bumps, you name it – some form of injury is inevitable. You're going to encounter at the very least one of those, several of them, or most of them over the course of your long stay in the woods. You'll trip, fall, stumble, slide, brush up against sharp objects, get attacked by bugs, touch things you shouldn't touch, and probably lose your balance more times than you can possibly count. How bad the outcome could be for every single one of those occurrences is a mystery. What isn't a mystery however, is that it's going to happen to you in one form or another. You might as well come to terms with it now, then keep an extra dose of vigilance and awareness if you're accident/injury prone (like me). Living on the trail will harden you, but it will harden you through experience.

Nevertheless, many of those experiences will be painful and/or somewhat miserable.

Foot Pain, Shin Splints, Plantar Fasciitis, and Other Ailments

Regardless of whether you have the perfect shoe or not, you're still likely to experience some form of foot pain. While chronic foot pain, shin splints, and other injuries can be linked directly to improper footwear, we're going to go over some treatment of these injuries, as well as some other ailments that might arise from issues not directly related to improper footwear.

Aside from improper footwear, shin splints can be caused by anatomical abnormalities such as flat feet, muscle weakness in the thighs and gluteus, inflexibility, improper training techniques, and repeated impact due to walking or running on slanted, downhill, or uneven surfaces. As you might have guessed, the Appalachian Trail provides the perfect environment to get shin splints, especially if you are prone to getting them due to any of the factors mentioned above.

So how do we help prevent and treat them? To prevent them from happening in the first place, try not to overdue your miles right off the bat when you first get out there; gradually work up to them. Strengthen your calves, shins, and ankles prior to beginning your hike. You can easily research exercises to implement at home or in the gym for these areas. Stretch your calves and ankles at the end of physical activity, especially at the end of a long day of hiking. Shortening your stride while taking smaller, more frequent steps, can also help to decrease your chances of getting them. If you're especially prone to getting shin splints, then you may want to think about getting some shin compression sleeves to wear, or wrap your shins with an ACE bandage; this technique can help treat as well as prevent shin splints.

Realistically, the best thing you can do to treat shin splints is rest and stop hiking until they've healed, usually a week or more. Unfortunately, this is not an option many thru- hikers like to utilize, as not everyone wants to take this much time off the trail in a town or back home. I've seen people quit, due to shin splints. They went home and came back once they were better, or stayed in a town until they healed. I've also seen people simply hike through the pain until they were better, or in so much pain they had to make a decision about the future of their hike. If you decide not to take the "rest" route, there are steps to treating them on the trail besides compression sleeves and ACE bandages. Every time you break, and even when you sleep, try to elevate your legs by putting your backpack underneath them, or propping them up with whatever is available. This can take a bit of ingenuity in your tent, but I have faith in you. It also doesn't hurt to take an anti-inflammatory such as Ibuprofen to help with the pain, as well as any swelling. Lastly, when you stop for the day or even long breaks, try to soak your shins in a cold- water source for as long as you can. I wish I had some personal experience to share with you regarding shin splints on the trail, but I've only had them once as a teenager when I first got into running.

Plantar Fasciitis is another deal breaker for people's thru-hikes; especially the middle aged and older crowd. It's the most common cause of heel pain, and results when the ligament that attaches your heel bone to your toes becomes weak, swollen, or irritated due to strain. These strains occur due to walking or standing for long periods of time, having a high arch or flat feet, wearing shoes that don't fit well or are worn out, excessive pronation (feet rolling inward), and being overweight. If you continue to walk on feet or a foot that has the beginning symptoms of Plantar Fasciitis, it can lead to tiny tears in the ligament and a whole lot more pain.

I've seen a lot of people get Plantar Fasciitis on trail, and most of the time it's one of those things that don't get better quickly; or once you get it, you're more prone to getting it again. The best way to prevent "PF" is wearing shoes with good arch support and heel cushioning; also do exercises to stretch the Achilles Tendon at the back of the heel, especially in the morning before hiking, but also the evening, and throughout the day if you can.

As with almost everything, the best treatment is prevention; but if you find yourself with the onset of Plantar Fasciitis while on trail, you can try to actively treat it. The best way will be to cut back on your physical activity, which means shorter days and smaller miles. Much like shin splints, try soaking your heel in cold water at the end of the day and throughout the day if you can. Also, do toe stretches and calf stretches first thing in the morning. Everything mentioned can help, but as with all things pertaining to a thru-hike, a lot will simply ride on how much you can take; take the lick'n and keep on kick'n.

You may or may not have thought of this, but losing toenails is fairly common amongst thru-hikers; although it doesn't have to be. I must admit, I've lost a toenail or two on each of my thru-hikes; mostly due to hiking, but on one occasion due to traipsing about in a rocky, fast flowing river while barefoot. The best way to prevent losing toenails is to firstly keep them trim at all times; don't let them get too long. Don't wear shoes that are too small or tight fitting; however, you can get away with wearing a shoe that's half a size too big (this can help with foot swelling, as well as blisters). Try to keep your feet as dry as possible. When your feet are wet or soggy for long periods of time, due to sweat or rainy/muddy conditions, your skin and nails can become extremely soft, allowing the toenail to simply slough off. You can fight this by airing your feet out during breaks, and also wearing a sock liner to help wick moisture away from your feet. If you've never lost a toenail before, I promise it's not as bad as it seems or sounds. Oftentimes, you won't even notice until you look down and realize it's missing.

Blisters

They're the bane of our feet! No matter how prone or un-prone you are to blisters, you better expect to get one or two at the very least while you're out there. They are nearly impossible to avoid when walking thousands of miles over uneven ground, but there are measures you can take to prevent them and certain instances when you become more vulnerable. You become most susceptible to blisters when you're wearing incorrect footwear. Not so much incorrect in the sense that your shoes weren't made for hiking, but more in the sense that your hiking shoes simply aren't made for your specific foot. Even when you find the right shoes, breaking them in can sometimes be met with the odd blister or two before the shoe material submits to your might. Even if your feet have been toughened by hundreds or even thousands of miles, switching to a new pair of the same shoe you've been wearing (after the original pair has worn out) can sometimes be met with some hot spots and/or blisters before you quickly break them in.

Despite the pain and annoyance that blisters cause, they do have a positive side. After the blister has run its course (sometime two or three times), it transforms into a callus, or thick pad of hardened skin that's designed to further protect and insulate a specific area from friction. So "friction" - the very thing that creates blisters, and subsequently calluses, are what the calluses are designed to protect you from. They basically defend you from their creator. Calluses are your friend, but it will take a good bit of pain and "sucking it up" to get them built up to where you want them. You'll develop them on the bottom and sides of your heels, the front pads of your feet, the outsides of your feet, and the bottom of your toes.

If you really want to prevent blisters, the first stage of the fight starts with your shoes. Make sure you're wearing proper footwear that's designed for your specific foot shape. Secondly, make sure your socks are not too tight, or too loose. Thirdly, try to keep your feet as dry as possible; soggy, moist skin is more susceptible to friction than dry skin. You can keep your feet dry with certain foot powders and lubricants.

Chafing

Probably as common, if not more common than blisters, is chafing. Some of my absolute worst days hiking have been due to extreme chafing. Anywhere your skin can potentially rub together is a place you can chafe. The most common areas that chafe while hiking are your inner thighs, your butt, your armpits, men's testicles, and men's "gooches" (area between anus and testicles). It feels really awkward addressing this particular detail, but get used to the idea, because people will chafe in all these areas, and you'll all complain and talk about it together.

I'll be honest with you, chafing haunts my nightmares, and I'm sure it's the same for many other people. If you know you have the potential to chafe, but don't do anything to help prevent it while hiking; you could be in for some of the most miserable days of your life.

So, what are some of the greatest causes of chaffing in regards to hiking? Clothing that is too tight or too loose; excess moisture from sweat or water; fabrics that don't wick moisture away; sand or gritty dirt getting on your skin in areas where any kind of friction is present; and salt residue on the skin from sweat. What are the best ways to prevent it? First, you need to stay hydrated. Then, you need to form a gentle barrier between the areas that rub together using either clothing or some type of substance you apply.

Most people wear some form of compression underwear in an effort to prevent chafing while they hike. Compression underwear will prevent thigh chafing almost 100%, but when it comes to butt, testicle, and gooch chafing, it can sometimes make them worse. This is where having the proper fitting underwear comes in. If your compression underwear is too tight, then it's going to squeeze your buttocks and other areas closer together, thus creating more friction, as well as the potential to chafe. If you know the areas you're most prone to chafing, then you can either wear the proper compression underwear, or forgo the underwear all together and simply wear running shorts with their loosely built in underwear. I personally switched between wearing just my running shorts, and my running shorts with compression underwear beneath them; most of the time I don't chafe, so I prefer to wear less clothing. However, in the off-chance I feel a thigh chafe coming on, I immediately put my compression underwear on to eliminate skin to skin contact between my thighs.

When it comes to applying substances to your skin, the thru-hiker favorites are body glide, baby power, body powder, and Vaseline (of course, there are other products out there you might prefer or want to try). When you apply these substances, apply them to all or any areas that you know are prone to chafing (yes, get in there good and proper). I used to use body glide and Vaseline religiously, but eventually found that Gold Bond Body Powder was more than enough to keep me from chafing in my problem areas.

If you end up chafing badly, I do have some good news - most of the time your chafing injuries will heal overnight, leaving you fresh in the morning. This isn't always true, but I've found it to be accurate for most people, including myself. In order to speed up the process at night, try and air yourself out as much as possible. Laying spread eagle on top of your sleeping bag within your shelter helps greatly. Also, if you have them, apply baby or body powder to those areas before you go to sleep. Lastly, if you have it, you can take a wet wipe or alcohol pad and wipe the chaffed areas clean; this burns like the dickens, but will help speed up the dry-out process and help get rid of any excess salt crystals.

Dealing with chafing is something you'll get better at handling as time goes on. If you're not used to prolonged physical activity, or even chafing itself, then sometimes going off what you read on paper won't always immediately work for you personally. Don't get discouraged, experience is the greatest teacher, and necessity is the mother of invention. I promise you'll figure out what works for you eventually - hang tough until you do.

Diseases/Viruses

As if you don't have enough things to worry and think about while you're out climbing mountains all day, there are some diseases/viruses that are all too commonly contracted while on the trail. The most common ailments contracted or encountered on the Appalachian Trail are Lyme disease, Giardia, and Norovirus. There are plenty of other little ailments and coughs you can get, but those three are the most serious, most unpleasant, and most feared contagion you could potentially contract. I'll examine each one - how it's contracted, symptoms, prevention, and treatment.

Lyme disease: Lyme disease is only passed on to humans by ticks. Deer ticks are the most common carriers (out of any other tick species), and can be better identified by their smaller size in comparison to other ticks. Lyme disease is first characterized by a bullseye like rash (although you don't always get one), then headache, fever, chills, and further on by possible arthritis, neurological, and cardiac disorders. Lyme disease is a very real, very common, and very dangerous threat on the trail. Dozens upon dozens of hikers do contract Lyme disease every year. It's treatable with oral antibiotics if caught early, but can cause permanent ailments if left untreated. For some of the neurological and cardiac disorders, intravenous treatment is required.

The best way to avoid Lyme disease is to avoid letting ticks attach to you, or allowing them to stay attached for prolonged periods. If you hike through thick vegetation, or brush against thick vegetation, or tall grass, immediately check the tops of your shoes, socks, legs, clothes, or any body parts that came in contact with the vegetation containing ticks. You'll almost never feel them, instead having to physically see them with your own eyes. Whenever you stop for a break with other hikers, ask them to check your back, or other hard to see/reach areas; the buddy system helps. You can also treat your clothing and gear with a chemical called "Permethrin." Wash your clothes or other gear in this chemical and they will stay treated for weeks, killing any ticks and some other insects on contact.

Giardia: Giardia, or Giardiasis, is a diarrheal disease brought on by an infection caused by microscopic parasites in the intestine. It can affect almost any mammal and is common throughout the entire United States. The parasite is passed on through fecal matter. It can be contracted through direct contact with fecal matter, but is more commonly ingested through the drinking of water that has come in contact with infected fecal matter. The symptoms are diarrhea, bloating, gas or flatulence, greasy stool that can float, stomach or abdominal cramps, upset stomach or nausea, and dehydration. In some cases, there can be no symptoms, or the symptoms can be delayed for many weeks or months.

The best way to prevent Giardia is to be smart about where you get your water, but also make sure you always filter or treat it. On average, your best chances of contracting Giardia are going to be at low altitude water sources, especially sources that run through or near farm land/residential areas. It's easily treated within a week following a dose of powerful antibiotics.

Noroviruses: The Noroviruses are one of the most common contractions on the Appalachian Trail and can infect entire groups of hikers, if not careful. They are a group of viruses that cause inflammation of the stomach and large intestine lining, and are also the leading cause of gastroenteritis in the United States.

It's characterized by nausea, vomiting, watery diarrhea, and stomach cramps. Other symptoms include low grade fever, chills, headache, muscle aches, and fatigue. You can feel perfectly healthy one moment, but have all the symptoms hit you suddenly over the course of one or two days. People contract Noroviruses when they eat food or drink liquids that have been contaminated. You can also catch the virus if you touch an object or surface that has been infected and then touch your mouth, nose, or eyes. Noroviruses, just like all viruses, do not respond to antibiotics. Most healthy people that contract the virus get over it after several days with no long- lasting effects.

The best way to avoid catching Noroviruses on the trail is to avoid congested areas where people stay in close quarters. This mostly includes hostels and shelters, but technically you can pick it up anywhere. Don't let Norovirus scare you from staying in shelters or hostels, but listen to the hiker grapevine and be on alert for recent outbreaks at certain locations.

Universal Hygiene/Hand Sanitation/ Other Practices

This short section will cover certain protocols in regards to hygiene activities we all perform on a daily basis; especially while in camp. Before leaving camp or a shelter, almost everyone goes through their morning routine of brushing their teeth, going to the bathroom, etc. Some people wonder, where do I spit after I brush my teeth? Or, where do I go if I only need to pee and I'm in a campsite with other people, or at a shelter?

In regards to brushing your teeth, as a courtesy to other people, don't spit in the water source unless you are a good distance downstream. Additionally, don't spit in the immediate vicinity of where people are going to be walking, or where people are going to readily see whatever it is you spit on the ground. Spitting your used toothpaste isn't usually something that people get grossed out about, but it's simply a courtesy to do it somewhere out of the way. After all, these are your germs we're talking about.

A fun fact about Appalachian Trail Privies: You're only supposed to poop in them. If you only have to pee while at a shelter, you are encouraged to do so somewhere other than the privy. Urine can inhibit the breakdown of other waste within the privies, thus slowing down the natural process. So, please do your part to keep everything working smoothly. When at a campsite, or around a shelter, simply walk to an area that's out of sight, as well as out of range of standard foot traffic (chances are your peeing somewhere that hundreds of other people have peed).

When around campsites or on the trail, when the call of nature arises, the most courteous and safe thing you can do is to perform business away from any water sources. Even when you're maintaining the proper distance from water sources while taking care of business, always try to do it down stream of wherever the obvious water collection point is. This is a great courtesy to all human beings coming behind you.

Cleanliness is next to godliness, so make sure you keep your hands clean. Use hand sanitizer, or wet wipes if you plan on carrying them. Sanitize your hands before you eat, as well as after major bathroom breaks (you know what I mean). In an effort to not spread germs, thru-hikers almost never shake hands; we fist bump. This minimizes skin to skin contact in an effort to keep us germ free and healthy. I practice this method while in towns with strangers as well, but always lead or follow up their sometimes puzzled looks with, "Forgive me, my hands are dirty." Trust me, they understand.

Feminine Hygiene

I really don't have any business telling women how to take care of their feminine hygiene while on the trail, but I feel like this book wouldn't be complete if I didn't at least touch a little bit on this subject. The following is a mixture of heavy research, as well as other information I've picked up over time while being around A LOT of other thru-hikers.

The two biggest problems females need to avoid when it comes to hygiene during any kind of extended wilderness backpacking are vaginal infection and urinary tract infection (UTI). Preventing the UTI's is the most important due to the seriousness of the infection spreading into the bladder and kidneys if not treated quickly. You can help stop a UTI in its early stages by staying very hydrated and flushing it out of your system.

*Keep everything (downstairs) dry.

-Wear comfortable underwear.

-Cotton is the most comfortable underwear, but may take a long time to dry under your clothing.

-Synthetic underwear is good, but tends to smell very quickly

-Wool is odor resistant and easy to clean, making for a smart underwear choice.

*Keep up with your hygiene

-The vagina is a sensitive self-regulating environment full of good bacteria and bad bacteria. It's just as critical to maintain the good bacteria as it is to avoid the bad.

-If you use an alcohol pad to clean yourself, it will kill both good and bad bacteria alike; it would be better to use a gentle soap, washing around but not inside the vagina; the ideal would be daily, but doesn't have to be. If you've had an exceptionally dirty, sweaty, or humid day - clean it.

-Wash your underwear as often as you can.

-If unable to wash the underwear often, use a panty liner and swap it out every day.

*Wipe Well

-Carry a pee rag in the form of a soft micro fiber towel, or cotton bandana; however, over time, a cotton bandana remains immediately more absorbent than a microfiber towel.

-After pooping, always wipe front to back; fecal matter getting into the vagina due to bad wiping is one of the leading causes of infection.

Stay Hydrated and go to the Bathroom

-If you are dehydrated, or hold urine in when you need to go to the bathroom (not wanting to get out of your shelter at night to pee because it's cold), you increase your chances for UTI by not adequately flushing your system.

Manage your Period

- You can use a traditional Maxi Pad or Tampon.

-You can use a "Diva Cup," which is reusable and eco- friendly, can be worn for 12 hours, and eliminates the need to pack out any waste in the form of used tampons or pads. The diva cup is a bell shaped menstrual cup that is inserted into your vagina to catch menstrual flow. It's becoming very popular, but the insertion can be uncomfortable to get used to.

Laundry

Thru-hikers are so dirty all the time out there; a fresh set of clothes can feel like the closest thing to heaven. What about doing laundry in town or even out on the trail? Yes. Besides food, laundry and showers will be the greatest things you look forward to when getting into towns. Doing laundry in a town is fairly straight forward, but you'll usually have one or all of these following options: You can walk to a laundromat if the town has one; use the machines at a hostel or hotel (provided they have them); or sometimes people will take you in and let you do laundry at their private homes. It's really not difficult to find somewhere to do your laundry once you get into town, so don't sweat it.

Washing your clothes while on the trail is a totally different challenge. Some people attempt this, while others don't even worry about it. I don't think I ever met a single person who actually tried to wash their clothes with soap or chemicals while on the trail; mainly because no one wants to carry anything extra. If you do decide to wash your clothes with soap and chemicals on the trail, then research the correct environmentally safe products, and when you do it, make sure it's downstream from any potential drinking areas.

The most common way people attempt to wash their clothes on the trail is simply dunking them and squeezing them out in water without using soaps or detergents; I actually did this quite often. There are some advantages and disadvantages to this method. If you're dunking your clothes in a stream, creek, or lake without any type of cleansing chemicals, your clothes aren't going to get clean. They will get "cleaner," but nowhere near as clean and soft without cleansing products. You won't eliminate any odors by doing this either; maybe change the odor of your clothing, or dilute it, but you won't get rid of it. The greatest advantage to wringing your clothes out in a stream of fresh water is removing some of the caked-on dirt and sweat; the crustiness. If your clothing or socks are in bad need of a wash, but you're still days from town, dunking them in fast flowing water certainly helps. As I said, you won't fix the problem, but you will improve it... This is also where having a bit of cordage (or line) comes in handy for hanging them up to dry.

Bathing on Trail

When you're covered in mud, dirt, sweaty grime, maybe some dried blood, and town is still two days away; what do you do? Deal with it, or find a way to wash yourself while on the trail. As far as swimming holes go, they do exist throughout the entire trail, but mostly in the form of rivers, waterfall basins, creeks, and streams, up until about New Hampshire (when going north). There are some fantastic lakes and ponds worth taking a dip in before New Hampshire, but the majority of good swimming mountain lakes and ponds will be in New Hampshire and Maine. When it comes to bathing yourself on trail, just about any running water will do. I can't even explain how refreshing it is to lower yourself into the shallow pool of a mountain stream at the end of the day; washing away all the dirt and grime before settling next to a campfire or crawling into your sleeping bag. The majority of on-trail showers you take will come in the form of rain showers, but you can bathe yourself in creeks and streams just about every night if you so wish. I knew an elderly thru-hiker gentleman from Taiwan who took a bath in a stream or creek every single evening, and sometimes every morning without fail. Most people will bathe in their underwear as a courtesy to anyone nearby, and always downstream of wherever the main water collection point is. You can use "camp soap" if you really want to, but my recommendation would be to leave the soap at home. An ice-cold wash at the end of the day to remove all the surface dirt and grime is more than enough. To conclude this subject, I'll include a personal fun fact: Not counting walking in rain, 18 days was the longest I went without washing or showering on my AT thru-hike...

Shoe Replacements

When walking thousands of miles, a fairly common question is: How many shoes will I go through? There is an, "on average" answer to that, but the true answer varies from person to person. On average, the typical thru-hiker will go through three to four shoes while on trail; sometimes less, sometimes more. So, if you know without a doubt in your mind what type of shoe you're going to be wearing for your entire hike, it may be wise of you to have a couple pairs on stand-by. Having said that, some people go through multiple shoes not because they wear them out, but because they can't find the right footwear and have to keep switching. Obviously, a good pair of shoes can be expensive, and not everyone has the budget to keep trying new pairs. If you find the shoes you began with to be inadequate, then utilize the many outfitters you'll find along the way; they have experts who are skilled at getting newbie thru- hikers into the right shoes.

On the Appalachian Trail, I went through three pairs of shoes. My first pair lasted almost 1,300 miles before they completely fell apart. My second pair lasted around 200 miles before I found something I liked better, while my last pair of shoes lasted around 700 miles before I finished with them. On the PCT, my first pair lasted 700 miles. My second pair lasted 300 miles before falling apart, and my third pair went for 400 miles before I found something I liked better. My fourth pair lasted around 1,200 miles before I literally walked right out of them. I only needed my fifth pair for the final 100 or so miles.

Now for the crazy stuff... some people do hike barefoot, and I have also met people who have done the majority of the trail in crocs, or some other form of cheap shoe. Not everything has to be expensive/top of the line. Plenty of people make due with whatever they can find or afford.

Food and Hunger

Food takes on an entirely new meaning to the average thru-hiker. Suddenly there is no such thing as "healthy" or "unhealthy" foods, as the calorie content is all that matters. You can often find thru-hikers comparing similar meals or snacks for the overall calorie content, or the calorie content per serving. Not only is it about calories, but calories versus weight. It's simply not economical to carry foods that don't pull their own weight in calories. That's why you almost never see people packing out vegetables. Some do, but it's not very common. Sometimes your craving for something will outweigh its economic hiking value.

When you're thru-hiking on a budget, life becomes a game of calories. Your body is burning through them so fast that you can hardly eat enough to sustain it. Your only options are to eat copious amounts of more expensive foods that are tough to carry in large quantities, or you can eat the smallest, lightest, more inexpensive foods that have tons of calories. Unfortunately, these inexpensive foods are usually not very healthy for you, causing huge spikes in your insulin levels. Out on the trail, you don't care about any of that; it's simply about putting enough calories into your body to get to the next resupply point where you can indulge in some of your more desired foods.

I was always torn between my Cosmic Brownies and Oatmeal Cream Pies. The Cosmic Brownie was denser and more compact, but had around 100 fewer calories than the Oatmeal Cream Pie per packaged unit. The Oatmeal Cream Pie was fluffier, more fragile, and took up more room, but was lighter. The Oatmeal Cream Pie was lighter in weight and contained more calories than the Cosmic Brownie, making it the most logical choice. On the flip side, you could fit more Cosmic Brownies into your pack than Oatmeal Cream Pies. It was a matter of deciding which quality was more important to you. I almost always went with the Oatmeal Cream Pie when faced with the two of them, but sometimes I chose both.

Most living creatures are driven by hunger, the necessity to obtain food in order to survive. Almost everything a wild and even not so wild creature does is usually a means to an end in the struggle to obtain food in any manner it can. Most humans don't have to worry about this because obtaining food is not really a main concern. It's a secondary concern because in the modern world you need something else before you can get the food. Humans are driven by the desire to obtain money. Obtain money so they can obtain food, as well as all other things we deem important to live and be happy. This is one of the major differences between the majority of modern humans and all other living creatures on this planet.

When you go on a long-distance hike that spans many months, it's safe to say that you're not working, so in most cases you're not making money. In theory, you should already have the money you need in order to complete your thru-hike in whatever amount of time it takes you to complete it. With the acquisition of money removed from the equation, food becomes your main focus. You know you already have the money to buy it, so now you only have to get to where it is. Walking becomes your only means to obtain food. The paradox is that walking all day, every day, really builds an appetite. Therefore, your only means to obtain food becomes the reason why you're craving so much of it in the first place. It's a cruel and vicious cycle.

Food begins to consume your thoughts, as it becomes all you can think about all day, every day. Instead of philosophizing, or trying to solve the major problems of your life and the world, you find yourself in a fierce personal battle over what you want to eat more of when you finally get into town...pizza or wings? The answer is simple, you get both. However, that answer doesn't allay your ravenous, hunger-obsessing mind. You can't stop thinking about it as your brain plays tricks on you by generating smells that aren't even there. I've been in the middle of nowhere, miles from anywhere, when with closed eyes I could've sworn on my life that I smelled Dr. Pepper and pepperoni pizza right under my nose. I could almost feel the bubbles of carbonation popping against my upper lip and nostrils. It's absolute torture!

Food is the only reason that you even HAVE to go into towns. If it was practical and legal to obtain all your food on the trail, then in theory, you would never have to hike into town. However, that's not how it works out there. The food cravings will make you do crazy things; when you look at the map of a town that's ahead of you and see a restaurant or fast food joint you like, it all of a sudden becomes your job to get there. You plan all your days, as well as your miles around it. Case in point, I once completed almost thirty miles just so I could get a frozen, oven baked pizza that I didn't even get to have. Sometimes you might look ahead and see something you like in a town that's hundreds of miles, as well as multiple other town-stops away. You start making plans right away on how to conveniently end up in that town with minimal food stores and an excuse to stay a while. Let me rephrase that, you start making plans to end up there - no matter what.

Yes, food is the driving factor in almost every trip into town, as well as every crazy decision you make out there. Trust me, the obsession with food that drags you into multiple towns doesn't take anything away from the hike or the overall adventure and experience. It's just another part of hiking the trail. If you want to live in the woods, live off the land, not see any people, and never go into any towns while still hiking somewhere new every day, then the Appalachian Trail is not for you. If you are at a level of survival knowledge that allows you to subsist in a nomadic way such as that, then you should trail blaze your own path into the middle of nowhere, and good luck. If that's your thing, then you will be happy and I will be happy for you. If you want to hike a few thousand miles, see the countryside, as well as a plethora of American culture, unique little towns, and meet amazing new people, while at the same time enjoying solitude on an almost daily basis, then the Appalachian Trail is for you.

"Food boredom" is a very real condition on the trail. While you can satisfy most food cravings while in town, the list of "trail-compatible" foods are considerably shorter. You'll have your typical backpacking foods, i.e., tortillas, peanut butter, power bars, pasta sides, instant mashed potatoes, jerky, candy, Ramen, summer sausages, pepperoni, GORP, different nuts, instant oatmeal, instant grits, tuna pouches, Twinkies, etc. This stuff gets old, and it gets old quick, depending on who you are. Coming up with creative ways to keep your food tasting good, while not letting other foods become boring and bland, is an art in itself. Many of the foods I just mentioned are some of the cheapest, lightest, and easiest backpacking foods to find and carry.

However, after eating them every day for weeks or months on end, you may soon want to never look at them again. So please allow me to shed light on a few questions you might have about certain other foods, as well as ways to make your food taste better.

It will amaze you to think about the types of foods/condiments we religiously keep refrigerated or throw away if left out for even just a few hours. Here are some facts about foods we refrigerate. Almost every type of condiment says to "refrigerate" after opening. I think that's more of a disclaimer, because in my opinion, you don't have to refrigerate them at all - do any restaurants? They are fine at room temperature, backpack temperature, outside temperature, whatever. If you leave the ketchup, mayonnaise, or spicy brown mustard out on the counter, don't worry, it didn't go bad.

Another thing people religiously put in their fridge is cheese. An unopened, vacuumed sealed block of cheese is good for weeks in a backpack while being put through a myriad of different temperatures. Yeah, it might get a little soft and sweaty, but the way to combat that is to buy hard and extra sharp cheeses. It will get a little soft, but it's still very good to eat; the sharper the cheese the better. Even once it's been opened, cheese is good for over a week without being in a refrigerator. You leave the cheese out for a day, it starts to sweat and people say "Ewww, its gone bad - I have to throw it away!" The reality is - its cheese, it's already bad. In order for cheese to become cheese, it had to start off as milk and a few other things, then be left out to age and go bad. If your cheese gets mold on it, then simply cut off the moldy parts. Unless your block of cheese becomes a giant block of mold, I guarantee that no matter how sweaty, soft, or moldy it gets, you can still eat it or eat around it.

Hot dogs are good for over a week in your backpack, however, they'll never last that long before you roast them over a fire. They don't have to be in a refrigerator constantly, and the same thing goes for bacon. Bacon will be good in your pack for several days, but I highly doubt it will last that long.

Now let's move on to milk. Yes, milk will go bad and curdle if not kept cool. This posed a problem for me out on the trail because I loved milk with my cereal. I tried a little experiment early on in Southern Virginia and bought some powdered carnation milk, as well as a giant two-and-a-half-pound bag of colossal berry crunch, then packed it out strapped to the outside of my backpack. I must've looked like a real class act with a giant bag of cereal hanging off my pack.

That first night with the cereal and powdered milk was revolutionary as I camped near a spring that offered icy cold water. I filled my pot, dumped in some powdered milk, mixed it all together and added some cereal. BEHOLD! Ice cold milk and cereal atop a mountain in the middle of nowhere. If I thought I'd been living before, I was wrong. You haven't lived until you've enjoyed an ice-cold bowl of cereal in the middle of the woods. To make a short story even shorter, those two and a half pounds of cereal lasted me only that night and the next morning. From the time of my first bowl, it was all gone in less than ten hours; eight hours of which I was asleep. I regret nothing.

Besides the cereal kick that I was on, I was hopelessly addicted to sugary foods. This happens to many, but not all the people who do long distance hiking. As the universe would have it - the lightest, cheapest, and most calorie dense foods are the ones that just so happen to be the worst for you. Since I was not made of money and there were no money trees growing in the Appalachian Mountains, I couldn't afford to eat dehydrated meals every night, or beef jerky and protein bars all day. No, my socioeconomic standings would not allow it, so I made do with what I could afford. What I could afford were foods like Honey Buns, Cosmic Brownies, Whoopee Pies, Oatmeal Cream Cookies, Oreos, M&M's, Skittles, Mini Snickers, Paydays and other candy bars. Yes, sugar was my master and if I didn't have it at least a dozen times a day, I became very "Hangry" (so hungry I became angry).

I've seen and done some crazy things for food while on the trail. "Germs" and "expiration dates" no longer held any meaning and the "five second rule" became law. Actually, it became more of a suggestion. I've dropped things in the dirt and without a second thought, picked them back up and eaten them; sometimes brushing off the dirt, sometimes not. It all depended on how dirty the dirt was at the particular location of the incident.

I've witnessed more extreme cases of this, as I have personally seen people pick food up off the trail and eat it after not knowing where it came from or how long it had been sitting there. I once watched a guy sit down on the side of the trail and pick skittles out of the dirt and eat them one by one. They weren't his, he just happened upon them as he was walking along. This is the kind of tone that life takes on for some people on the trail. I would never go to the extreme of eating food I found lying on the ground, but if it was my food or someone else's I saw fall, I had no reservations in salvaging and eating it.

    The following is a list of lesser known foods that you can take out on the trail, as well as combinations and modifications you can make or add to them in order to make them less boring or taste better. You can take cheese (the harder and sharper the better), hard salami, deli salami, bacon, hot dogs, honey, bacon bits, powdered milk, powdered/instant pudding, summer sausage, pepperoni, quinoa, bagels, bread, condiments, hot sauce, Sriacha, Nova Salmon, pouch tuna, various canned foods (if you don't mind carrying and packing out the can), corn beef hash, etc.

    The above foods are good by themselves, but there are ways to make them even better, or add them to other boring backpack foods to make them more interesting. Roast hard salami, summer sausage, and pepperoni sticks over a fire until they begin to char and drip grease. I can honestly say this never got old. Take your bagels, cheese, whatever deli meats and condiments, and make a sandwich. If you want, toast that sandwich over a fire. Add Sriacha or other hot sauces to your pasta sides, your instant mash potatoes, your tuna, your canned food, anything. Add packets of bacon bits and cheese to your pasta sides, mashed potatoes, and grits. Hydrate your Ramen in cold water (this will take slightly longer), then empty the water and add mayonnaise and/or hot sauce to make cold pasta salad. Take tortillas and put cheese between them, or honey, or chocolate syrup, or Nutella and toast them over a fire to make quesadillas, crepes, or whatever. You can even toast them over your stove in your shelter if it's raining and you can't have a campfire. Make peanut butter and jelly sandwiches/burritos; the possibilities are endless. A few popular combinations you would probably think of on your own eventually are; adding instant mash potatoes, tuna packets or both to your ramen noodles. Adding peanut butter to your ramen noodles. Adding bacon bits and/or tuna to your instant mash potatoes. Honestly...add anything to anything and see what it tastes like, you might be surprised.

Some people try to get super fancy and pack out steaks, or the ingredients for making pizza or bread over an open fire. They pack out vegetables and all the ingredients they need to make whatever elaborate meal they might fancy. The sky is the limit.

In addition to all the creative meals and foods you can make or pack out, there are always going to be more options. Some people freeze dry or dehydrate large quantities of foods before they leave on their hike, then have it sent to them while on trail. You can dehydrate or freeze dry just about anything you want. Searching online will give you more ideas than I ever could about foods you can dehydrate or freeze dry, as well as the process of doing so. You can also buy prepackaged meals from distributors like "Mountain House" and "Backpackers Pantry." While their meals are very light, and very delicious with many options, they can get pricey.

Calories

A question I often hear from people in regards to eating during a thru-hike is: How many calories should I be eating on a daily basis? The very easy and straight forward answer is… as many as you possibly can. For most people, you won't be able to eat enough in order to maintain your body weight, even if that's your goal. The majority of people who go out there don't mind losing a few pounds, but there are some that don't need or want to lose weight. In regards to counting calories on the trail, it usually isn't practical when it comes to weight loss, or even weight maintenance/gain. Depending on how far you're going each day, as well as how hard you're personally pushing yourself, it's incredibly difficult to figure out an average "calories burned" without looking at everyone's individual body composition and daily physical output. There is simply no encompassing answer for everyone. Eat when you're hungry, and eat what you want to eat - that's my best advice. The more time you spend out there, the more you'll learn about your individual needs in regards to calories and the foods related to them.

Weight Loss/Muscular Atrophy

Quite a few people will attempt an Appalachian Trail thru-hike with the goal of getting healthier and losing weight as their main motivation. If there is one thing you lose a lot of when exercising all day, every day, for months on end - it's fat. Unfortunately for some people, not all the weight they lose will be fat; but I'll get into that later.

If you've got weight to lose when you go out there, then you better believe you're gonna lose it. The fastest weight loss occurs during the first several weeks you're out there, then begins to steady and slow down, before picking back up when you reach the White Mountains of New Hampshire, as well as Southern Maine (due to extra physical effort). I myself lost 55 pounds during my thru-hike, but I knew plenty of people who lost quite a bit more or less.

When it comes to body transformations, several observations have been made by many thru-hikers. It's a universal agreement that everyone's legs look better than they ever have during and right after your thru-hike. What also holds true is women's bodies tend to look better overall at the end of a thru-hike, as opposed to men's. It is said that women look like collegiate athletes at the end of their thru-hikes, while men look like refugees. This description is because many men lose so much weight throughout their upper body, they end up taking on an emaciated look. This is due to fat loss, as well as muscular atrophy. Since all you're doing is walking every day, using mostly your lower body instead of your upper body, your metabolism eats away at the muscles you aren't using - chest, arms, shoulders, etc. Since most women don't typically have a lot of upper body muscle, these changes are almost unnoticeable for them. For men, however, it couldn't be more apparent as their arms, chest, and shoulders flatten and shrink from disuse over time; it happened to me. So, fat loss, as well as muscle loss, are two major factors that will happen to both men and women alike while on their thru-hike.

In some cases, people who are extremely lean or fit at the beginning of their hike will sometimes gain weight. This is due to gaining new muscle throughout the legs and butt, which is especially common for women. Oftentimes, some women will start off losing weight, but then gain weight before the end of the hike due to muscular gains in these areas.

What's the best way to combat upper body muscular atrophy on the trail? You simply have to engage those muscles in some way while you're out there. This is easier said than done, because you're always so tired, the thought of doing anything extra is almost painful. The easiest exercises you can perform to help slow or stop the muscular atrophy of your upper body are: Push-ups, pull-ups, planks, and sit-ups/crunches. Pull-ups are the hardest ones to perform on the trail, but some sturdy shelters will have planks, pegs, or giant spikes that are more than capable of supporting a person doing pull-ups. I tried to keep up a regular regiment of push-ups and pull-ups on my thru-hike, but I eventually became too tired and stopped bothering/caring. However, I did know others who kept up with a regular regiment the entire time. Some did them at the end of the day, while others preferred to do them in the morning. There's nothing like a good set of push-ups first thing in the morning to wake your body up and get your blood moving before the hiking starts.

Some argue doing extra exercises out there is detrimental to your weight loss, as well as a waste of calories; this is simply not true. Doing some light upper body exercises at the beginning or end of each day will have almost zero impact on your overall calories burned; perhaps the difference of walking an extra mile that day at the most, but likely much, much, less. Also, the upper body exercises will keep you from losing extra muscle weight and definition. Have you ever heard of the phrase, "If you don't use it, you lose it?" This phrase holds perfectly true for muscles; if you don't use them, you lose them, because your body will simply metabolize them along with any fat for energy. By doing light upper body exercises, it communicates to your body that you're still using them, thus at the very least, you'll maintain what you have, or lose very little; much less than if you were to do nothing. So be ready for lots of physical changes during your long stint on the AT.

Cooking/Eating At the End of the Day

Whether you want to cook or not at the end of the day, as well as what order you cook or set up camp, is totally up to you. I only wanted to touch on one aspect of cooking/eating at the end of the day... Do you do it where you plan to camp, or do it somewhere away from where you plan to camp? On the Appalachian Trail, the majority of people don't worry too much about cooking or eating in camp; creating smells or waste that might attract animals later in the night. If you know you're planning to stay at a shelter, then cooking or eating before you get there in an effort to deter animal visits is for the most part a lost cause. This is because there will most likely be other people there who are eating and cooking. As a courtesy, most people won't cook inside the shelters unless the weather is terrible. Of course, if it's just you or your friends at the shelter, then you'll probably go with the consensus of the majority. The only situation in which cooking or eating your food before or away from camp will be effective in preventing animal visits, is if you know you're going to be camping alone. If you plan to camp alone in an area known to have a high concentration of bears, then it might be more prudent to generate any smells or food waste away from where you will be sleeping. As always, this is a matter of preference, and these are simply suggested strategies to help you do things in a way that's most comfortable for you. Always try to store any packaging/wrappers or waste in a sealed container or bag in an effort to eliminate extra smells.

Hydration

Staying hydrated probably isn't something the average person thinks about on a day to day basis, or even throughout any given day. That is unless you're an athlete or an avid gym enthusiast/runner that's very in tune with their hydration needs. Out on the trail, staying hydrated is your JOB. Even when you're not thirsty, you should take the opportunity to drink as much water as you can, when you can, especially whenever you have the availability to procure more. On another note, during the hot summer months it can be damn near impossible to stay fully hydrated. Even when you're collecting water at every source and drinking like a fish, you'll still feel the effects of dehydration, as well as see them in your urine. The darker your urine, the more dehydrated you are. Ideally you want your urine to be as clear as possible, but at some point, you'll probably get so dehydrated that your urine will turn the color of Pepsi and burn on the way out. You want to try and avoid this at all costs, but odds are, at some point you'll unwittingly allow yourself to reach this point of dehydration. Besides food, shower, laundry, and climate control; forays into town will become the best opportunities to completely rehydrate yourself as well as replenish electrolytes. This is due to the fact that you'll be hardly exerting yourself while in town, if not staying and resting overnight. You might think staying hydrated is one more thing to worry about, but I guarantee you after a little bit of time out there, drinking water at every opportunity will become second nature, even instinctual.

Water sources

Water, the great life giver! Without it you're a dead man- or woman. While staying as hydrated as you possibly can all the time is very important to your health and well-being out on the trail, it's very realistic to be worried about how often you can acquire water. Let me put your mind at ease right now; the Appalachian Trail BLEEDS WATER. There is water oozing out of this trail everywhere you look. Creeks, streams, springs, rivers, lakes, ponds, you name it. Finding water on the trail is not a problem, but being able to recognize the best sources is important. The safest, coldest, cleanest, best tasting water is going to come from springs, straight out of the ground or rocks, right at the source. Springs above 3,000 feet in altitude will be the best of the best. If the water is coming right out of the rocks, you can almost bank on it being safe to drink without filtering; you simply have to be smart about it. Be wary of slow moving or stagnant water sources that reside at low altitude levels, or near farmlands or towns. The longest stretches without water are in Pennsylvania, and even then, they're not far enough to really worry about unless the temperatures are soaring. By that time, you'll know yourself, your water consumption needs, and your hiking style pretty well. You'll be more than capable of making the right decisions.

Foraging

The short answer to foraging food on the trail is - don't do it. It's frowned upon by most, but some people can't resist enjoying the fruits of nature. There are many different things you can forage out there; from vegetables to fruits, berries, mushrooms, and certain other plants. Nobody usually cares if you forage wild edibles, but if those edibles are living, breathing, mobile creatures beforehand, then some might take offense. I did eat some animals while I was out there; animals in the form of a rattlesnake, a squirrel, multiple trout, and multiple mountain stream crawfish. While I would be a hypocrite to tell you not to do it, I will say that if you feel the need to harvest a living creature for food; do not make a habit of it. If the opportunity arises, seize it. Check it off your hiking bucket list and then don't do it again. Also, make sure you don't seize any of these opportunities within the confines of national or state parks, as this is very illegal.

I know the killing and eating of animals is a very sensitive and touchy subject to some people, and it might very well anger you that I condone it in this book. I do not condone it lightly however. I am a realist, and I know there are people out there who are going to do it anyway, so I say unto them; "Do so responsibly, privately, and only once if you feel you must."

Navigation

Getting lost forever, never to be found... and dying of starvation, alone in the wilderness. To those of us who are new to wilderness backpacking or long distance hiking, this seems like an all too real possibility. On the Appalachian Trail, it's extremely difficult to get lost in a way that you can't be found; however, it has happened. Without going into extra details, an elderly thru-hiking female got lost off the trail in 2013 and her remains weren't discovered until the end of 2015, only a mile from the trail. It was concluded she died of starvation after some three weeks of being lost. The chances of this happening to you are slim to none on the Appalachian Trail, and require a set of extraordinary circumstances to come to fruition.

But the question still begs... How do I get around out there without getting lost or losing track of where I am? To begin with, there are several guidebooks and map books you can purchase that will have the lay of the land, elevation profiles, topographical maps, maps of towns, etc. These are easily found if researched online. There are also online apps you can download for the Appalachian Trail specifically (the Guthook App is extremely popular), or general apps that contain maps of all trails from whatever region you decide to search. These apps can come in handy because many of them utilize the GPS on your phone to pin point exactly where you are relative to everything around you. Also, your phone doesn't need service to utilize its GPS function. You can keep your phone in "Airplane Mode" and still navigate or see where you are via any topographical GPS maps that you've already downloaded. Keep in mind; if you don't download the maps while you have service, then you won't be able to utilize them with your phone's GPS function when you don't have service. Although guidebooks and apps are some of the ways you can navigate or figure out where you are, they are hardly an absolute live or die necessity when it comes to finding your way down the trail.

As you may already know, the entire Appalachian Trail is marked with white blazes; tens of thousands of them (possibly more) in both directions. In regards to the AT, a blaze is nothing more than a white rectangle painted on a tree, rock, road, telephone pole, overpass, underpass, guard rail, building, canoe, anything. The white blazes mark the official path of the Appalachian Trail from end to end. You can find them anywhere from several feet apart, to almost a mile apart, but most of them will be no more than a couple hundred yards apart; sometimes closer-sometimes further. The average distance changes throughout different sections. As long as you continue to see white blazes, you are on the Appalachian Trail.

There are also blue blazes that mark side trails to water sources, shelters, alternate routes around bad terrain, loops, bad weather trails, and sometimes paths to towns or roads. A blue blaze can lead you just about anywhere that isn't the AT, but they most commonly mark the routes to shelters and water sources.

When it comes to navigating with the blazes, it's fairly straight forward - follow them. Nevertheless, there are some things you should know ahead of time. When using the white blazes or the blue blazes to navigate, there are directions being communicated through them by the way they are painted. If you see two blazes painted on top of one another, this means the trail is about to make a turn. The top blaze will offset in the direction the trail is about to turn. For example, if you see two blazes painted on top of each other, and the top blaze is slightly offset to the right of the bottom blaze, then the trail is about to make a right turn. The same goes for a left turn; the top blaze will be slightly offset to the left. Many people never make this connection while they're out there, but it comes in handy at night, or in areas where the trail branches off from other trails. Usually it's very easy to figure out where the trail is going without knowing this offset blaze trick, but you'll be more self-assured of where you're going, now that you do.

Zero Days

Zero days can be the difference between being on pace to finish the trail in four to five months, or finishing the trail in six to seven months. Simply put, a zero day is a day in which you hike zero miles. Essentially, you're taking the day off. I've met people who took little to no zero days during their thru-hike, all the way up to anywhere between thirty and sixty zero days. I myself took between 40 and 50 zero days out of a 195 day total thru-hike of the Appalachian Trail. This was due to factors ranging anywhere from being injured, sick, tired, caught in bad weather, or simply wanting to enjoy the area I was in for more than just a passing glance.

In regards to zero days, don't be afraid to take one if you need one, or if you simply want one because you like the area or environment you're currently in. I've seen some people regiment themselves so strictly that they don't allow themselves hardly any zero days, or they plan them out way in advance. Take them and plan them however you wish, but my personal advice is this... do whatever feels right, if you feel like you need one, take it. If you feel like you simply want one, take it. This adventure is about living in the moment and on a whim, it doesn't always have to be about hiking every single day. Some of your greatest memories and experiences will come during zero days; you just have to take the time.

Now having said all that, if you want to finish the trail, you have to hike. Enjoy your zero days and take as many as you'd like, but don't get carried away. There is a window of ideal hiking conditions for this trail, and if you take too many zero days, you can easily shrink that window, forcing yourself to hike bigger days, or skip sections in order to make it.

Blogging/Keeping a Journal on Trail

Do you like to write? I do, as you can probably tell. If there is one thing I am familiar with, its journaling and blogging while on the trail. Most people don't bother with this, but for others, it's their second life, or income. Keeping a detailed daily journal while on the trail was my single greatest advantage when it came to writing a book about my adventure. With a good daily journal, the book practically writes itself. I won't lie to you, it's extremely difficult to stay disciplined, as well as motivated to write every single night; it's easy to fall behind and quit writing altogether. Now, there's nothing I can say that will make you sit down and write at the end of each day, but I can list some advantages that might help with your motivation to do so.

Writing at the end of every day when your experiences, thoughts, memories, and emotions are fresh is imperative. I've gotten behind several days on multiple occasions, and I can tell you, the writing loses something when it's not written down on the day of its occurrence; it's not as raw or authentic. It's simply you writing down a memory, instead of describing the emotions you feel in that immediate moment. That's the best advice I can give you when it comes to motivating you to write EVERY- SINGLE- DAY.

I will also confide my strategy and layout for keeping a detailed and accurate journal. I'm a realist, and I understand that sometimes there is simply too much to a story or experience to write the entire thing down at the end of a long day. Therefore, before I even begin writing my journals, I outline my entire day. I make quick highlights of what happened: names, thoughts, occurrences, times, locations, numbers, miles, dates, revelations, etc. I outline everything just enough that my memory will be instantly jogged when I go back to look at it. Once I have my outline, I begin to write my journal for the day; sometimes including everything from my outline, sometimes leaving details out if it's too much to write, or I'm exceptionally tired. Even though I didn't write it in my journal right away, it's still there in my outline for me to remember and expand upon at a later date.

Aside from the outline, there is a list of things I keep track of every single day in order to catalogue the journey flawlessly. This is basically the secret to my accuracy of recounting the tales, and I'm giving you permission to use it. Before I outline my day, or even begin writing my journal, I log all these following pieces of information; The date, which day of my journey I'm on, the miles I hiked that day, the total miles I've hiked on the journey so far, my current location of where I'm camped, the altitude of my current location, the day's weather, the days temperature's, my morale level, my hunger level and cravings, my pain level, any injuries I might have, and lastly any specific thoughts I might have had. I logged these details every single night, and while it was tedious at times, it eventually became a part of my life that I enjoyed.

You can easily write everything in a notebook, although that can get fairly heavy. Since I blog, it's not practical for me to write in a notebook, then type it up a second time to post it online. I've done all of my writing and blogging on trail from my cell phone or a kindle, however I've permanently switched to my cell phone. The method by which you record your hike is totally up to you, but I prefer to keep it as light and simple as possible. Since I'm going to be carrying my phone either way, I'd prefer to blog from there, instead of carrying an extra device or other equipment. Also, my pictures are on my cell phone, so that makes it easier to upload them with my writing when the time comes. A cell phone may be too small for you to comfortably write with every night, so you may have to look into a larger device, or look into getting a travel keyboard that connects to your device via Bluetooth or USB. Keeping a detailed record and journal of your adventure boils down to one thing - discipline.

Staying Charged

In regards to electronic devices, most people will bring a cell phone at the very least, however, some people bring more. How is one to keep them charged while in the middle of nowhere for days on end? The answer is rechargeable/solar charged power banks/battery packs. Basically, you'll be carrying a battery around that's capable of plugging into your devices and charging them. Some people like to use solar panel batteries that can be charged in the sun and then used to power or recharge their devices. This can be cumbersome and un-economical on the AT, due to the fact that you are mostly in the shade beneath the trees for the vast part of the entire trail. Thus, keeping a solar panel on the back of your pack will be nearly useless. The only times you'll be able to get any kind of steady sun exposure will be during breaks or when you stop for the day. Even then there usually isn't enough time to get enough power to make the device worth its carrying weight. Either way, people still like to carry them for the versatility, and you can also give most of them a full charge by simply plugging them into an outlet when you get to town.

The most popular type of power bank/battery pack is the non-solar type. These can only be charged by plugging them into power outlets. The higher the "milli Amp hour" rating (mAh), the more power the battery can store. Also, the higher the mAh, the heavier the battery will be. The size and power capacity of your battery pack is a matter of personal preference depending on how often and how much you will be charging your devices. You can buy different battery packs that can charge a cell phone anywhere from one time, to between fifteen and twenty times. It's up to you how much weight you're willing to carry.

Carrying Cash

So, you've got all your money saved up, you've got enough to go all the way... but how much cash should you carry on you, if any at all? I can't tell you how much you should carry personally, but I always tried to keep at least a hundred bucks or more in cash on me at all times. The reason for this was mainly emergencies, or if I found myself in a "cash only" situation, or if my debit card got lost or stolen. It really is smart to keep at least some cash on your person throughout the entire journey because I guarantee you will run into situations where you may want to stay at a remote hostel, catch a remote shuttle, or pay for a service or product somewhere that doesn't accept/isn't capable of taking cards. There will almost always be someone who is more than happy to spot you some cash, but depending on who you are, you may not feel comfortable accepting this type of graciousness. Also, if for some reason your card is declined or gets "frozen" due to your traveling, it's nice to have some backup cash so you don't get stuck in an awkward situation;

I've seen it happen. This is why my recommendation is yes, carry cash on you at all times. As far as a maximum amount goes, that should be whatever you're comfortable with carrying. In terms of a minimum amount, between twenty and forty bucks is safe. I personally preferred to carry over a hundred because I wanted enough to be able to travel, eat, lodge, and do whatever else; even if my card wasn't working, or I found myself at a business that only accepted cash. It's also nice to be able to offer money to anyone who gives you a free ride, simply as a nice gesture, or if you feel the situation calls for it.

Hiking With a Dog

You may be considering hiking the trail with your dog. Maybe you're considering this because you think it's a good idea, or because you think it would be nice or fun to have a companion. Perhaps you're considering it because you have nobody to watch your dog when you leave for the hike, therefore you have to bring the dog no matter what. I hiked nearly 2,000 miles of the trail with my Shiba Inu dog, Katana. While taking a dog along seems like an excellent idea, allow me to enlighten you on the responsibility you're undertaking...

The entire time I was on the trail, Katana and I ran into many other dogs and their owners. Out of all the other hikers I met with dogs, Katana and I are the only ones I personally know of (besides one other wolf hybrid) that made it to Maine. I tried to keep tabs on everyone else I met, while taking note of the reasons for why they slowly dropped off. One dog I met early on forced its owner off the trail when it got an infection from the chafing of its doggy backpack. Another dog attacked a bear in the Shenandoah Mountains and was subsequently mauled, having to get off trail. Another dog we met ran away during the night, and when found the next day, had an injured leg and was covered in more than 150 ticks. Another dog fell eighty feet from a cliff in Vermont. I don't remember hearing if it survived or not; I never actually met them, but I heard about the incident. The last dog I heard of getting off trail due to freak occurrences was one that I was actually quite fond of. It was a Husky German Sheppard mix that got bit on the face by a rattlesnake in Pennsylvania. The owner couldn't foot the vet bills without quitting the trail.

There were plenty of other people with dogs who got off the trail due to the stress of hiking with one, or simply because they grew tired of being out there. Anything could happen to a dog on the trail. They could get injured through no fault of their own, get sick, or run away. I even heard about two dogs that were chasing each other in front of a hostel that ended up getting run over right in front of their owners, as they charged across the street.

Another common occurrence along the trail included hikers adopting dogs. We passed through so many small towns and farm areas that we came in contact with stray farm dogs or shelter dogs quite often. I knew of at least four people who adopted dogs while they were out there. While nothing bad (that I'm aware of) happened to their dogs, none of them reached the end of the trail with their adopted dog (as far as I know). The added stress of a dog can be overwhelming, and after hiking with one for months on end, I don't know what would drive someone to adopt one while they were out there. Maybe out of loneliness or a need for companionship, but I can tell you now, the negatives of having a dog on the trail are equal to, if not greater than the positives. This goes for both you and the dog.

If the dog doesn't want to hike, then you're not going to hike; not unless you pick it up and carry it. Depending on the size of the dog, this can be very uncomfortable for you, the dog, or both. Dogs have personalities and get bored or tired just like we do. Your dog didn't sign up for this hike, you did. Not all of them want to go on a walk every day, all day, for months on end. It's a special dog that does, and even when you find that special dog, they'll still have plenty of bad days over the course of a six month walk. Some of those bad days might fall on your good days, subsequently turning them into bad days. Some of those bad days might fall on days when you actually need to be somewhere. A dog doesn't understand the concept of needing to resupply. When you run out of food for you and your dog, but still have twenty miles to the next town when your dog decides it doesn't want to walk, then you're shit out of luck. Even if the dog does want to walk, the terrain might be so difficult that your dog needs your help in order to traverse it. The heat, the cold, rocks, severe inclines, and river crossings are all factors to consider. If I tallied up all the miles I carried Katana during the more than five months that she hiked with me, it would add up to around a hundred miles. There were some days I carried her for more than ten miles straight.

Not only does hiking with a dog present more obstacles on the trail, but just as many off the trail. No doubt you'll want to stay at hotels or hostels along the way. You can say you won't (I did), but I can almost promise that you will. Not all of them allow dogs, and some of the towns are so small, there might be only one hotel or hostel in them. If the establishment doesn't allow pets, then it looks like you'll be camping on the edge of town while your friends live it up in the nice dry room that has showers, cable television, Wi-Fi, and laundry.

If your dog isn't a service dog, then forget about taking it into restaurants, convenience stores, or supermarkets; it will have to wait outside. What if there's no one to watch it or there's a bad storm going on? Too bad; your dog will have to sit next to your pack by itself, possibly in the rain while it waits for you to eat or finish buying groceries; either that or you simply don't go at all. While your dog is used to this kind of weather and independence out on the trail, in the eyes of strangers, you might as well be an animal abuser.

When you have a dog on the trail, you can never make a decision for only yourself. You have to factor in your fur baby. I missed out on a lot of different things while I had my dog. I wouldn't change any of it for the world, but I want people to know the facts. I missed out on train rides into bigger cities, and I was sometimes barred from using public transportation to get from one place to another in certain towns due to the fact that my dog wasn't a service animal. I have been stranded in towns because I couldn't get a ride and certain public transportation wouldn't allow my dog in the vehicle. This left me with the options of hitch hiking, walking, or paying the exorbitant prices for a taxi (granted they allowed dogs). All of those options become more difficult, if not impossible, once nighttime sets in. Those were some of the realities of having a dog on the trail.

The positives are companionship, protection, something to have imaginary conversations with (maybe not that positive or healthy), and something that will keep the creepy crawlies away and stand guard in the night; that's about it. Other than that, a dog is going to cost extra money and extra stress. Plenty of people successfully thru-hike with a dog, but there are even more who don't make it.

You're caring for another living creature besides yourself, 24/7. You have to get yourself, as well as this curious, friendly, playful, sometimes oblivious, happy-go-lucky creature over 2,000 miles through and over mountains, wilderness, towns, roads, weather, and wild animals...in one piece. You constantly have to check and monitor the dog's health and well-being; examining its paws, checking it for ticks every night, making sure it's fed and watered throughout the day, etc. It needs to be on some type of flea and tick prevention, but that will only work to a certain degree. Your dog is going to be exposed to so many ticks, that tick prevention can only repel so many of them, you will have to do the rest. Also, make sure your dog gets vaccinated for Lyme Disease before you go out there, because they are susceptible to it as well.

As far as paw care goes, the best thing you can do is check their paws periodically for blisters, cracks, or cuts. If you notice something doesn't look right, then you need to dial back the dog's activity, or address the issue as soon as you reach the next town. This might mean taking a day or two to rest, or seeking out a veterinarian for a professional opinion. The vast majority of the AT is actually not too bad for dogs, but there are some sections that can get rough on your pup's feet. I'll go into detail on those sections a little further on. "Mush Wax" is a product that can be used on your dog's pads to help provide an extra layer of protection, as well as keep their pad moisturized (it can also help with other little cuts, injuries, and chafes). Putting booties on your dog can also help in certain sections, but don't make them wear them all the time. The booties can end up chafing the sides of the dog's lower leg, causing an entirely new set of issues.

The choice to have your dog carry its own supplies is up to you, as well as if it wears booties or not (if it's even willing to wear booties). It's important to know there are certain national and state parks that don't allow dogs on the Appalachian Trail. Those parks are the Smoky Mountain National Park (around 70 miles of trail) in Tennessee/North Carolina, and Baxter State Park (about 15 miles, as well as your final destination going north) in Maine. Dogs are welcome everywhere else on the trail, although they have to be leashed while in Shenandoah National Park (slightly over a hundred miles long) in northern Virginia. When you reach these "No Dog Zones," your options are to skip them with your dog, or kennel your dog while you hike through them. There are kenneling services, as well as shuttle services that will pick your dog up and drop it off once you're through the park. You can find these services online, or in many of the Appalachian Trail Guide Books. There are also many private residences that will take care of your dog for you, but its luck of the draw whether you meet or run into these types of people. Using social media as a network for information and help is invaluable. Join some of the "Appalachian Trail" or "Hiking with Dogs" groups on Facebook. There will almost always be somewhere near your location who's willing to help you out when you need it.

I know I've brought up a lot of reasons not to hike with a dog, and that may seem very hypocritical on my part. I'm only trying to present the subject as realistically as possible, and the reality is that many people can't do it. Sometimes it's the dog that can't handle the trail, and sometimes it's the person who can't handle the dog on the trail; sometimes it's both. My dog and I have been thoroughly tested by many months and thousands of miles, and we've both discovered we can handle it. That being said, never let someone tell you-you can't do something without first proving to yourself that it's true. The least you can do is give it your best shot and see what happens, then make the best decisions you can. All I ask is that you keep the above information in mind.

Areas of Extra Caution for Dogs

One thing that greatly troubled me while having my dog, pertained to the areas that didn't allow them, as well as areas that might be too difficult or dangerous for them. Obviously, every dog is different, and what may be easy for one, might be nearly impossible for another; hence, do take this advice, but do not take it as absolute fact for your dog.

I'll begin with the areas that do not allow dogs (service dogs are allowed, however). Lucky for you, there are only two "No Dogs Allowed" zones on the entire trail, and they are Smoky Mountains National Park on the border of North Carolina and Tennessee (approx. 70 mile-stretch of trail), and Baxter State Park in Maine (final 15 miles of the trail going north). Some people say dogs are not allowed in Bear Mountain State

Park in New York, but I've never officially heard this, or had anyone say anything to me when I passed through. It's an incredibly short section.

Areas of extra caution for dogs that might be challenging, impossible, or downright dangerous are...

-All of Virginia and Pennsylvania: I add the entirety of these two states in regards to ticks. They seemed to have more of them than anywhere else. Check your dog regularly.

-The final few miles leading down from the Dragon's Tooth monolith in Virginia; just before reaching the town of Catawba. It's an area of rock scrambles that requires the use of your hands pretty often, and might be difficult for certain dogs to traverse. I had to pick mine up to carry or help lower her off certain areas.

-Shenandoah National Park: I mention this 100-mile section which resides in northern Virginia because of the abundance of bears. If you have a dog that likes to chase big animals, you need to watch out here. Also, all dogs are required to be on a leash while within the boundaries of the park; even if they weren't, it would be smart to do so. There is also a TON of ticks in Shenandoah, so be extra vigilant. The trail itself is a breeze.

-Northern Pennsylvania: Once the rocks in Pennsylvania begin to really show up, there are frequent and long stretches of boulder fields that may be difficult or slow going for dogs. I carried mine through many stretches, not because she couldn't do them, but because I moved so much faster over the boulders and didn't want to hike at sub-1 mph.

-Lehigh Gap in northern Pennsylvania: This is a steep and long ascent up from a road that requires quite a bit of hand over hand climbing. Some dogs may have trouble getting up over certain areas on their own.

-New Jersey/New York: The only reason I mention these states is due to the abundance of road crossings. Be cautious if you have your dog off leash.

-New Hampshire: I'm listing the entire state of New Hampshire because a vast majority of the state is riddled with hand over hand climbs and descents that might be very difficult for certain dogs

-Presidential Mountain Range in New Hampshire: This stretch begins at Crawford notch and ends ant Pinkham Notch after a stretch of about 26 miles. I list it as an area of caution due to the abundance of coarse rocks and boulder fields. I carried my dog for a 10 mile stretch through here (starting at the summit of Mt. Washington), and encountered another dog leaving a trail of blood due to cut up paws.

-Southern Maine: From the border of Maine, all the way to the Bigelow Mountain range (a distance of well over 100 miles), you will encounter plenty of areas that require you to use your hands in order to traverse, much like in New Hampshire.

-Mahoosuc Notch: You reach Mahoosuc Notch within the first ten miles of Maine, and while it's only a mile long, it's dubbed the hardest or most fun mile of the trail. Be prepared to pick up your dog multiple times throughout this stretch. Owners with heavy dogs beware.

Besides the "No Dog Zones" - many people, including myself, have taken our dogs (of varying sizes) through and over all of the aforementioned areas. They may be difficult, but it can be done.

Tough Decisions

During your time on the trail, you will be confronted with many tough decisions. Most of them won't be life threatening, but many will be the difference between enduring a lot of misery, and a little bit of misery. Towards the beginning of your hike, when Mother Nature hasn't punished you for all the bad choices you have yet to make and learn from, you will tend to make decisions based on avoiding immediate misery. The only problem with making decisions that avoid immediate misery is they usually result in prolonged misery. For example: In the early days of your hike, when your stamina still leaves much to be desired, climbing tall mountains are going to take a lot out of you. So, let's say it's close to the end of the day and you've just reached the top of a large mountain. You're completely exhausted, your feet hurt, and you don't want to go any further. You'd rather just make camp than have to face several more miles of joint jarring, downhill hiking. Maybe there is a storm coming, or maybe you're simply so high up, and the season is early enough that temperatures will drop well below freezing at that altitude. "Well, the conditions are tolerable right now," you reason. "I'd rather just make camp here and not have to worry about being tired and my feet hurting for another several miles," you decide; wrong choice. Now you're on the top of a mountain, it's below freezing, and a storm at 4,000 feet is much worse than a storm at 1,000, or even 2,000 feet up. You just traded being uncomfortable for another hour or two of hiking for an entire night of misery based on your short sightedness. Perhaps you have everything you need in order to weather such conditions on the top of a mountain, but the potential for misery and mistakes is exponentially higher.

This sort of scenario can be applied to a plethora of situations you'll encounter out there. Try very hard not to make decisions based on your present comfort level; always be thinking ahead. Say you're out of water, it's the end of the day and the next source isn't for a few miles. You decide, "Hey, I'll just camp without water tonight, then get it bright and early in the morning; besides, I'm not that thirsty right now." No, grit it out and get to the water source that day, this way you can start hydrating before you go to sleep, because I promise you will regret not having water in the morning and throughout the night even. Plus, it's going to be a very depressing several miles to that water source the next morning, and you've already given dehydration a head start. Once you let yourself get dehydrated on the trail, especially during the hot months, it's extremely difficult to fully rehydrate yourself without taking a full day off to do it. If you plan to "dry camp" (camp somewhere water isn't available), then you need to make sure you've gathered enough water from the previous source to see you through the night and possibly the morning.

Before you make any decision about camping, stopping, skipping resupply points, or water sources; consider the long- term consequences vs. the short term. While your exhausted brain and beaten body might be telling you one thing, don't immediately give into them until you've examined the bigger picture...

Chapter 6

Gear Accumulation/Information

Talking about gear can be a touchy subject with some people, or an invigorating one for others. I've found "Gear Heads" to be some of the most unbearable people to be around and have a conversation with - usually when conversing about gear. Any other subject and a gear head is usually a pleasure to be around, but unfortunately, gear heads normally only want to talk about "gear." Their gear, your gear, the best gear, the worst gear, gear they don't have, gear YOU NEED, gear that should be invented, and stupid gear that shouldn't even exist. They usually want to recommend all the things they like and use, and most of the time they are good recommendations. The only problem is "THEY" are not "YOU." I am not a gear head, and I do not give "one size fits all" advice. When it comes to gear, it is important to "know thyself." The most important thing to know about thy- self when it comes to selecting gear is your own personal comfort level.

Deciding How Heavy (Or Light) You Want to Go

The first aspect of your comfort level, the majority of people give little to no thought to when first starting out, is how much weight they're going to carry. Most people (myself included) assume they are going to carry however much weight they have to in order to have everything they need, or everything they think they need. Let me be the first to tell ya, you got options when it comes to deciding how heavy your gear will be, and lots of them. So many in fact, that somebody with even the highest, most demanding of comfort needs can end up with a "base pack weight" (BPW) of less than ten pounds, or a base pack weight of close to forty pounds. Your pack weight all depends on your gear selection, manufacturing materials of that gear, as well as the "dual functionality" of that gear. What is your "base pack weight" you ask? It's the weight of everything in your backpack, minus your consumables (water, food, fuel, toiletries, etc.). Your "total pack weight" (TPW) is the weight of your pack with all your gear, plus a full stock of food, water, and fuel.

So, rewind a little bit. People fail to realize that when it comes to long distance hiking, or even section/day hiking, their total pack weight is going to be the first factor in determining their comfort level. Now if you're a big, strong individual, you can obviously carry a little more weight, and still be just as comfortable as a smaller person carrying less weight than you. Disregarding the size of the individual, I'll tell you right now, the less weight you carry; the more comfortable you'll be, as well as the less damage or potential damage you're going to do to your body in the long run. These are just facts, plain and simple. My pack weighed slightly less than 60 pounds when I first began the trail, and while I was strong enough to bear that weight, it got old so fast, I can't even convey to you how depressing it was to pick it up and put it back on after every break, multiple times a day, for months on end. Do yourself a favor, even if you think, or even KNOW you can handle a heavy pack, try and get it as light as you can before going out there; believe me, you will thank yourself later.

When it comes to the different categories of weight out there, they do have names. A base pack weight (BPW) of less than five pounds (this is incredibly difficult to achieve) is known as "Super Ultra-Light" (SUL). A BPW of less than ten pounds is "Ultra-Light" (UL). Anything under twenty pounds, but preferably fewer than fifteen pounds is considered "Light." A base weight of between twenty and thirty pounds is generally considered "heavy." While a base weight of between thirty and forty pounds is considered "Ultra Heavy" (UH). Any base weight beyond that is ludicrous when pertaining to a thru-hike, as well as asking for an injury and endless aches and pains.

So now we know the different weight categories, but which category do most people who thru-hike the AT fall under? The majority fall into the light and heavy categories, but you still encounter plenty in the ultra-heavy and ultra-light groupings too. Your size, weight, strength, gender, etc., are all going to be factors in how much your gear weighs (think clothing sizes, shelter sizes, pack sizes, sleeping bag sizes, etc.); the more materials required to build the gear that fits your body size, the heavier they will be. Regardless of your size, the first step to cutting your base pack weight will start with the "Big Three."

The BIG Three

The "Big Three" are comprised of your backpack, your shelter, and your sleeping bag. These are generally the heaviest, most important of the essential items you will carry. Each one of these items can easily weigh three to four pounds EACH by themselves, or even less than a pound each, depending on where you get them and what they're made of. The factors that decide how much each one of these three items weighs are: the materials and their size. Is your backpack too big for what you need? Is it even a designated hiking backpack? Military packs are notoriously heavy, out of necessity for ruggedness. Is your shelter just the right size for you and your gear, perhaps too big, or made from heavy materials? Is your sleeping bag made of cheap, heavy materials, or light, weight-saving materials? These are all factors that determine the weight of your Big Three.

Backpack: What You Need to Consider When Choosing One

When it comes to choosing a backpack, it never hurts to roughly know what the weight and volume of all your other gear is going to be. Many people will buy their backpack first, then be stuck with something that is too big, too small, or isn't rated to carry as much weight as they intend to load it with. SO, for the inexperienced, it might be a good idea to source all the gear you want to buy before you make your final decision on a pack.

Ideally, once you know "what," and "how much" you want to put inside a backpack, then you can start looking around for the perfect one. The choices out there are dizzying to say the least. So many different styles, sizes, and materials; it will blow your mind that you have so many options. First figure out the "volume" of the pack you need. The volume (how much space it has inside) of backpacks is measured in "liters" and "cubic inches," but liters are the most common form of measurement. Typically, sixty liters or more is a big backpack, with sixty being a "large average." Between forty to sixty liters would be sufficient for someone attempting to go light in most cases. Forty liters and below is when you start getting into ultra- light/super ultra-light territory. Normally, the less volume your pack has, the less weight it can carry; but you will find exceptions.

The next thing to consider after figuring out the size of the pack you need, is the materials it's made from. The materials a backpack is made from will directly influence its total weight, as well as its "load capacity" (the maximum amount of weight it can carry). When you know what the base weight of all your other gear will be, then it becomes easy to estimate the total weight of what's going into your pack when you average in the weight of food and water. To play it safe (and this is very accurate for the AT), we'll say that you'll never carry more than a maximum of twelve pounds of food. This is on the very, very high end of the spectrum for food needs out there at any given time. You might carry a maximum of eight pounds of water (this is a gallon, or four liters) which is about the most water you'll ever need to carry at one time - and in very few situations. It is very rare that you will ever carry that much weight in food or water, but there is always a chance that at some point in the journey you might. So, once you're pretty much positive of your base weight, you can add fifteen to twenty pounds onto that number in order to account for the maximum amount of food and water that you will ever carry; even though it is highly unlikely you will carry those amounts at the same time, or even once throughout the journey. Hey, that's me playing it safe when dealing with the estimations of strangers I'll never meet.

Now you have a very good idea of the total maximum weight of what could potentially go into your backpack. The next step is to simply find a pack with the corresponding volume and load capacity for what you intend to stuff into it. With those numbers and requirements in mind, you are now equipped to browse any backpack that you so wish. You can start considering styles and functions of the different packs, like how many zipper pockets it has, if any. How many mesh pockets does it have? Does it have hip belt pockets? How big are these pockets and where are they located? Do you prefer it to have a back-mesh pocket, side-mesh pockets, or both? Is it water bladder compatible? Does it have a frame (if so what kind), or is it frameless? Does it have an integrated or detachable brain/lid, or does the top close with only a draw string, zipper, or roll top? These are all details that go into different backpacks, and it's your own personal preference as to which of these qualities your backpack will have. With all that being said, almost all hiking backpacks will share similar features/qualities to the ones I've described above. Also, when shopping online, many of these things will be listed in the "specs" and "features" of the pack (including weight and load capacity). When shopping in person, these things should be more than blatantly apparent, but also listed on a removable exterior tag.

Generally, an ultra-light backpack will weigh 2 pounds or less, but some under 3 pounds are advertised as "ultra-light." Your typical "light" pack will weigh between 2 and 3.5 pounds. A super-light backpack will weigh under 20 ounces, and sometimes less than a pound (16 ounces), but those require very specific materials, and even more specific contents. Your typical light to heavy backpack will weigh between 2.5 and 3.5 pounds (sometimes slightly more), and will be able to carry all of your food and gear, no problem. A backpack between three and four pounds will almost always be rated to carry 40 pounds or more. If you're carrying that much weight, then you probably don't care what kind of backpack you're using anyway. Knowing all of this information, the lightest material (of this present day and age) that a backpack can be made from, is "Cuben Fiber." Cuben Fiber has the strongest "strength to weight ratio" of any other material available to the public (or at least the backpacking community). They can make backpacks, shelters, rain-flys, clothing, and a myriad of other items from it (I'll get into those items later). This material is 100% waterproof, as long as any seams where it has been stitched are seam-sealed or taped.

Aside from the materials and various features that packs can have, you need to be aware that some companies make female and male versions of the same packs, while other companies make them gender neutral. Whichever options the company gives you, you should always be aware of your torso, waist, and/or hip measurements. Having a pack that fits your dimensions goes a long way in promoting comfort. Any company worth their salt will have the various dimensions for their packs listed, or sizing charts to go along with them.

Sleeping Bag: What You Need to Know When Choosing One

Besides your shelter, your sleeping bag is probably your single most important item. It's what keeps you warm at night, as well as ALIVE and comfortable during inclement weather and cold temperatures. Once again, this is an item that can give you all the comfort and warmth you'll ever need for several pounds, or less than 20 ounces. The weight of your sleeping bag will be directly related to its temperature rating, and the materials it's made from. We'll focus on temperature rating first.

How do you know how warm your sleeping bag needs to be? Does it need to be rated for zero, ten, twenty, thirty, or forty degrees? The answer totally depends on you. What is your tolerance for cold? If you're from an area where it snows every year, or gets very cold on a regular basis, then you'll probably be more comfortable with cooler temperatures than someone like me who's from Florida. That's the first thing you'll need to consider when choosing your sleeping bag. The second thing is the temperatures on the AT. What time of year will you be on the trail, and what regions at that time? For your typical northbound thru-hike that starts in the spring and ends in the late summer to early fall, a ten-degree bag would be MORE than enough for anybody, especially when you have all your extra clothing layers to wear inside it. For your typical southbound thru-hike that starts in early summer, a ten-degree bag would be more than sufficient as well. If you're afraid that you might get caught in snow (it happens in the early spring down south, and late spring/early summer in some areas up north), then you can go with a warmer, zero-degree bag if you really, really despise the cold. I despise the cold, and I did the entire trail with a forty-degree bag, along with a sleeping bag liner that added an extra ten degrees of warmth. Even then, with all my clothing on, I was still very cold on some nights. So, to be safe, a good average sleeping bag should be rated for twenty degrees (Fahrenheit) for the AT. In most cases, that will be sufficient in keeping you comfortable, as well as alive for an entire thru- hike (especially if layered with all your clothing). Of course, you can always have a "summer bag" for the hotter temperatures during the summer months, when anything warmer than a forty- degree bag might cause you to overheat at night. Besides the White Mountains of New Hampshire, most of the trail is going to get pretty hot during the summer months, so you can safely carry a summer bag, sending your winter bag home. However, you can also simply do the whole trail with one bag like I did, eliminating the logistics and expense of buying two and having them sent to you at different times, or keeping track of a bounce box.

When you've figured out what temperatures you're comfortable with, and know how warm of a sleeping bag you're going to need; then you can start figuring out how heavy that sleeping bag is going to be. Like backpacks, there are countless options for sleeping bags out there. Instead of going over all of the different materials they're made from, and what they can be stuffed with, we're only going to focus on the lightest type of sleeping bag. The absolute lightest, as well as warmest sleeping bags will be made with "down." Duck down, or goose down. Goose down is the higher quality, with the higher "warmth to weight ratio." "Down" is a layer of fine feathers found under the tougher exterior feathers of birds and is prized for its luxurious softness, superior resilience, loft, and insulating properties that are unmatched by modern synthetic materials/fills. There are different "Fill Power" (FP) ratings for the quality of down that affect its overall warmth to weight ratio, but I'll get into those later. For now, we'll just focus on down, as well as sleeping bags in general.

When you decide to get a sleeping bag that has been filled/insulated with down, you have decided on a sleeping bag that is going to give you the most warmth for its insulating weight. The weight of ONLY the down feathers inside of the bag is called the "Fill Weight." The next factors that go into the total weight of your sleeping bag are its size, and the "shell" material. The "shell" refers to the type of material that makes up the outside of your sleeping bag, or what the down is stuffed inside. The thicker, tougher, and heavier the shell material; the heavier the overall weight of the bag. In sleeping bags, the shell is typically made of some form of polyester. Often times, its polyester that has been treated in some way, or blended with something else to make it stronger or more "down-proof." That polyester is measured in "deniers." Denier is a unit of measurement that is used to determine the fiber thickness of individual threads or filaments used in the creation of textiles and fabrics. Fabrics with a high denier count tend to be thick, sturdy, and durable. So, in short, the higher the denier, the heavier the down-filled sleeping bag; the smaller the denier, the lighter the overall weight of the sleeping bag. Typically, 10-denier is the lightest shell material a sleeping bag will be made from.

I'll quickly go into down and it's "Fill Power" (FP) ratings before we move on. Fill power is a measure of the loft or "fluffiness" of a down product that is loosely related to the insulating value of the down. The higher the fill power, the more air an ounce of the down can trap; thus, the more insulating ability an ounce of the down will have. The fill power ratings range from about 300 for feathers, to around 900 for the highest quality of down. The higher the fill power ratings, the larger percentage of down clusters, and larger average down cluster size; the higher the FP, the loftier and more insulating the down. A lofting power of 400–450 is considered medium quality, 500-550 is considered good, 550–750 is considered very good, and 750+ is considered excellent. If you're going to get a down sleeping bag, then you're going to want something with an 800 to 900 FP. Ratings of 950 and 1000 FP do exist, but they are rare, and you are definitely going to pay for them.

There are countless other sleeping bags made from a multitude of different shell materials that are filled with many different types of insulation. Too many to go into individually, but they can all be easily researched. I've only gone into detail on the lightest type of sleeping bag, as well as the most popular on the AT; at least now you'll have an idea of what your options are, as well as what you're looking for. The most important thing is figuring out the temperature rating that suits you, then decide on how light you want your bag to be, as well as how much your budget allows.

Another type of sleeping bag that's quickly gaining popularity isn't really a bag at all. Down "quilts" are becoming more popular amongst thru-hikers every year. There are several different styles that down quilts come in, but their major difference from sleeping bags is they are able to open up completely into a blanket style cover. This comes in handy during warmer months, when a bag style sleep system might be too hot. Many down quilts can be converted from a quilt to a hybrid sleeping bag with zippers or snap button closures that run along the bottom quarter, or sometimes the entire length of the material. Besides the versatility of more easily controlling your temperature with a quilt, they also have several other functions and advantages over your traditional sleeping bag. Your typical quilt will weigh less than your typical bag of the same temperature rating. This is because the quilt is designed to be more economical in the sense that you don't cocoon yourself in a quilt. Since a sleeping bag is designed to completely encase your body, it takes more material to achieve this. However, down is prized not only for its incredible warmth, but for its ability to compress down to a very small size. The only problem is when down gets compressed; it becomes useless in regards to trapping and keeping heat. This means all the down stuffed into your traditional sleeping bag that gets trapped and compressed beneath the weight of your sleeping body is utterly useless; dead weight. In contrast, the quilt solves this problem by draping over you, not wasting any extra material to be uselessly trapped beneath you. The downside? It is possible with the quilts to experience cool drafts throughout the night, especially if you toss and turn... but wait just a minute! Many quilts are being built with special bungee straps that attach the quilt flush to your sleeping pad. So now active sleepers can actually toss, turn, and roll freely beneath the quilt, as well as on top of their sleeping pad without twisting or constricting themselves in the material of a traditional bag. So instead of your body having contact with only the top and bottom of a sleeping bag that's cocooning you; it instead has contact only with the quilt above you, and your sleeping pad below. It is more efficient and economical than a traditional bag, but some people love the cocoon feeling and wouldn't trade a traditional bag for anything else in the world.

Shelter: What You Need to Know When Selecting One

Probably the most important piece of gear you will take with you on your thru-hike will be your shelter. Your shelter is your home. It's what you will be living in for whatever amount of time it takes you to complete your journey; it better meet all of your needs. Your shelter is what keeps you dry in the rain, protected from the wind, cloaked from prying eyes, insulated from the cold, and your first defender from pesky insects and smaller animals that call the wilderness their home. Of course, there are some people that don't even bring a shelter with them, instead sleeping exclusively within the wooden shelters that are set up all along the AT. This is risky, as there is no guarantee there will be room in every shelter when you get there, or that you won't injure yourself, or get caught in weather that doesn't allow you to reach the nearest shelter. For the sake of preparedness (and prudence), let's say you're definitely bringing some type of shelter.

Shelters fall into four major categories when it comes to thru-hiking the AT; tents, tarps, tarp tents, and hammocks (with a few hybrids thrown in). Which one you choose is directly related to your comfort level, as well as what "feels" comfortable for you psychologically and physically. I can't tell you which one to choose, because that is completely up to you. What I can do, however, is give you a sufficient amount of information about each one, which will hopefully make the decision a little easier, based on what you already know about yourself. I'll go over all of them individually; the rest is up to you.

Tarp

A tarp is the simplest, most basic form of shelter you can use while camping. It is quite literally nothing more than a roof over your head. It provides the least insulation, as well as the least protection out of all other shelters. People who "tarp" exclusively are generally considered "hardcore" and/or "crazy." A tarp can be described as a piece of waterproof fabric that you string between two trees, two trekking poles, two tent poles, or two of whatever you can tie your "ridgeline/guy lines" to. The "ridgeline" refers to the "backbone" or center ridge of the tarp, where it folds to either side, creating an "A-frame" shape to shelter you. The "guy lines" refer to the lines that attach to your tarp at different points, pulling it tight and giving it an infrastructure. One end of the guy line is attached to the tarp, while the other is usually attached to a "stake" that goes into the ground; however, a guy line can be tied or attached to anything that will anchor it (think: tree, shrub, rock, log, etc.), not only a stake. There can be as few as two to four guy lines (diamond tarp), or as many as ten guy lines and everything in between, depending on how you set it up. There can be more than that, but then you're getting into some pretty big and elaborate tarps that won't generally be used by a single individual out on the trail. The average number of guy line tie outs is six to eight.

When it comes to your tarp ridgeline, there are two different ways to set it up. You can choose to do what's called a "continuous ridgeline" (CRL), or a "split ridgeline" (SRL). A continuous ridgeline consists of a single piece of line that stretches between your two main anchor points (trees, trekking poles, whatever). The tarp is then draped over this ridgeline and anchored down with guy lines from the tie out points on the sides. A split ridgeline consists of using two different lines; one tied off to the far end of each side of the length of the tarp, then anchored to a tree or whatever you decide to anchor it to.

The main advantage to a continuous ridgeline is it takes quite a bit of pressure off the material of your tarp. It will most likely lengthen the lifespan of your tarp, helping to prevent any potential damage that might occur in stronger winds. The continuous ridgeline also serves as a taught line to hang gear and clothes from without putting extra stress on your actual tarp. The down side to the continuous ridgeline is you will have to carry a long, single piece of line that will inevitably weigh more than two shorter lines used in a split ridgeline configuration. Also, if you don't store that longer line properly, there is a chance it could become tangled, adding a considerable amount of time onto your setup (this can be detrimental in bad weather). It can also be a challenge to get the tarp draped correctly over the continuous ridgeline during times of high wind. The principles of the CRL and the SRL can be used for a hammock's rain fly as well.

Once your tarp is erected, it's going to be open on pretty much all sides. Your only REAL protection will come from straight above you. Unless you have the tarp itself staked down flush with the ground, then wind and cold will be getting in from at least one or two open sides, if not more. Animals, as well as bugs (should they wish), will be able to come and go from your shelter as they please. That is unless you wake up and kick them out or scare them away, but that won't work too well on the bugs. You're only defense from insects when using a tarp will be some form of "bug net," and even that won't keep them from getting under the tarp and crawling all over you. Also, the tarp will protect you from rain falling straight down, but won't fully protect you from driving rain coming in from the sides, or the splash of rain on the ground; and it certainly won't protect you from flooding waters. The size of your tarp, as well as the way you erect it (in regards to the current weather conditions), will have a great effect on how shielded you are from the elements. The lower the tarp edges are to the ground, the more protection you'll have.

To make a tarp shelter work as comfortably and safely as you can, you'll need at least two extra pieces of equipment to go underneath it. Both are completely optional, depending on just how crazy/hardcore you are. Almost undoubtedly, you're going to have a "ground sheet," and a "sleeping pad" underneath the tarp with you. The ground sheet is to provide a barrier between the cold, possibly wet, insect infested ground... and yourself. The pad provides a soft, smooth surface to lie on, as well as insulation from the cold ground. A ground sheet laid upon a surface without a pad, is a ground sheet that has contoured to the shape of the ground, as well as every single pebble, dimple, and twig lying upon it. In short, unless you're a wild person, you need some kind of sleeping pad. There are many different types of ground sheets and sleeping pads, but we'll get into those later.

Yes, the tarp is the lightest, most basic form of shelter, and if you decide to use one as your home while you thru-hike, then you're going to cut a ton of weight as it is, no matter what kind of tarp you choose. BUT, you guessed it! There are many different tarps of different sizes, made from different materials, some lighter than others. The most common material is "Silnylon," but there are many more options. The lightest option (and most expensive) is, you guessed it again...Cuben Fiber. It's completely up to you which type you decide to go with based on your personal needs/preferences/budget.

Tarp Tent

"Tarp Tents" are rapidly growing in popularity, and aside from tarps, they're one of the lightest options available. They offer more protection than your standard tarp, but can be slightly more technical to set up. Usually requiring some form of tent pole to erect, however many are designed to be erected, held up, or given structure by your own trekking poles and a handful of stakes and guy lines. This is another way in which one piece of gear can save you extra weight by having multiple uses. While it may be more technical than an actual tarp to set up, it is normally quicker than your standard tent (once you get the hang of it), as well as more practical to set up during rainy conditions.

A tarp tent is a single walled shelter made from waterproof materials that usually include a "bath tub" ground sheet (we'll get into this later) that is attached, or attachable to the tarp. They also normally come with some form of bug netting that is permanently attached or attachable, as well as a vestibule (tent porch). The biggest difference between a tarp tent and a tent is the fact that a tent usually comes with a detachable waterproof cover. This allows the tent to be vented in the case of higher temperatures accompanied by dry weather. A tarp tent's walls will be waterproof to start with, so you'll have no option of being able to remove them without taking down your shelter altogether; however, the entryway to a tarp tent is usually made of bug netting, allowing for sufficient airflow. Sometimes the bug netting can be set up as a shelter all on its own, with the tarp material being erected over top of it only when the user wishes to do so. Since the tarp tent does not require a separate water proof cover like most conventional tents, setting it up in the rain is quicker and less stressful since a regular tent would normally need to be set-up, then waterproofed with a separate rain cover.

There is a plethora of sizes, options, materials, styles, etc., when it comes to choosing a tarp tent, and many cottage industry type businesses are coming out with fantastically light and functional designs. You simply have to figure out what you like, as well as what works for you.

Tent

"Tenters," or "ground dwellers" as I like to call them, are the most common campers/shelters on the AT. They are the most traditionally modern form of camping and provide the most protection, insulation, and privacy of any other form of shelter (besides some upscale hammocks that are on par with some tents). As with anything else camping related, there are about a billion choices out there regarding tents. Again, you need to pick the one that's best suited for you, but is also suited to your needs. If you're walking 2,000 miles across the United States, then it needs to be suited for quite a bit of diversity. Mostly, it needs to be stable and strong enough to stand up to the wind, rain, as well as any possible flooding issues. I can't tell you how many people I met out there who would wake up in the middle of a heavy rain storm to find themselves floating around their tent on their inflatable sleeping pad. That's not a pleasant way to wake up, so you need to make sure you find a tent that won't allow this to happen.

When deciding the size and style of your tent, there are several factors you need to account for. Is it big enough to accommodate you and your gear comfortably? Also, does it have a "Tent Porch," or an area outside the tent that's somewhat protected from the elements where you can store wet gear without having to keep it inside with you? Is the entire thing waterproof, or does it come with a detachable rain cover? Is it free standing or does it need to be staked down?

If you're hiking the AT with a tent, then you need to go with something that is "just enough" to fit you and your gear comfortably. It needs to be able to be staked down in the case of high winds, and also needs to be waterproof or waterproof-able. You're going to need a ground sheet that's big enough to fit the "footprint" (dimensions) of the tent, that way the bottom doesn't get ripped or damaged, letting in mud and water if you're pitched on rough ground.

Hammock

Last but not least, and my personal favorite, we have the hammock. Are you a hammock person? Do you enjoy versatility? Do you like being suspended/cradled off the ground and rocked to sleep every night? Are you a back sleeper, side sleeper, or stomach sleeper? If you're a hardcore stomach sleeper, then a hammock might not be the best option for you, but there are some out there that can accommodate a stomach sleeper, however they will be quite a bit heavier than your standard hammock. I myself am a "hammocker", and I can't imagine camping any other way. I did the entire AT in a hammock, as well as the PCT, and never once did I awake with sleep related back pain...not once. This is me of course, not you, but I know/met dozens of other hammockers who were in the same boat.

The hammock is the most versatile shelter out there (granted you're in an area full of trees). All you need is two trees, or two of anything that's sturdy enough to hold your weight, and the world is your camping spot. You can thru-hike the entire Appalachian Trail and find a place to hang your hammock every single night, no problem. There are sections of the trail in New Hampshire and Maine that are above tree line, but these are not places you want to camp at any time whatsoever; not in a tent, not under a tarp, not even in a hammock strung between rocks. You'll never want to camp on a ridge above tree line (unless conditions are absolutely 100% optimal), therefore a hammock will work for the entire Appalachian Trail. In a hammock, you never need worry about level ground, rocky ground, tree roots, or even small streams/creeks. All you have to do is find the two trees you want, in the location you want, and BOOM, you're camping. This cannot be said for someone with a tent. Tenters always need level, smooth, ground; if they don't have it, then they either won't be able to set up their shelter correctly, or they're not going to be comfortable. A hammock not only works as a bed, but also as a chair that can cradle/rock you. I've also found that hammocks eliminate any and all pressure points associated with sleeping on the ground, or even a traditional bed.

Once again, you will have choices when it comes to hammocks, and they can range from as cheap as twenty bucks, to over four hundred dollars. It all depends on the features, materials, brands, size, etc. Things to consider when shopping around for a hammock besides its weight, size, and load capacity are... is it double layer or single layer? Is the bug net integrated or does it come separate? Does it come with a weather shield? Does it come with a rain fly? Does it have interior pockets, or pockets underneath? What sort of suspension system are you going to use with it? Do you want to use a pad with it, or an under-quilt? It the end tapered or gathered? What kind of personal customizations do you want to make to the hammock, and can the hammock accommodate them? These are all important questions when it comes to choosing a hammock. It seems overwhelming, but I promise you it's not. With a simple search of popular hammocks for hiking, all of these features can be put into better perspective.

I could quite literally go on for days about the different hammock options, suspension options, pads or under-quilts, double layer or single layer, integrated bug nets, zippers or open style, bottom entry or side entry, the list goes on and on. I'll simply go through some major different style hammocks and list their advantages/disadvantages.

You can't use a hammock by itself and think you're going to use it for months on end without getting freezing cold at some point. There is a condition known as "Cold Butt Syndrome" amongst hammockers. This is when your butt/lower back region becomes very cold during the night due to temperatures dropping and wind chills. This happens because the materials hammocks are made from are never thick enough to completely insulate you from the wind and cold by themselves. If you're going to spend any amount of time in a hammock, you're going to need a sleeping pad, or an under-quilt to insulate you from the open air beneath you. The sleeping pad is without a doubt the cheaper option, but sometimes the more troublesome. If you don't have a double layer hammock, then you'll be lying directly on top of the sleeping pad inside the nest of the hammock. When you begin shifting around at night, the sleeping pad is going to shift too, and at some point, it may slide out of the hammock all together, wind up on top of you, or slide just enough that part of your body is exposed to the cold drafts beneath you. If you plan on getting a sleeping pad with your hammock, then you may want to go with a double layer hammock, this way the pad can be fitted between the layers, thus less susceptible to shifting around when you toss or turn. If you're going to use a sleeping pad in a single layer hammock, then a good trick to keep it from shifting is to put it inside your sleeping bag with you, or use the straps on a quilt to hold it in place. This works wonderfully most of the time, but make sure you have your hammock vented at least a little to keep condensation from building up inside your sleeping bag.

An under-quilt is the more expensive, but more comfortable option when it comes to insulating your hammock. They can come in many different sizes, lengths, widths, temperature ratings, and materials. They can be filled with down, synthetic down, climashield, etc. They suspend snugly beneath your hammock, contouring to the shape of your body once you get in. No shifting, no hassle. You only have to make sure you've hung your under-quilt properly, so it covers the area you'll actually be laying on within your hammock.

The downside to the under-quilt is they usually aren't any lighter than a pad. In fact, they're usually heavier. Also, depending on how large of an under-quilt you decide to use, it can be like carrying a second sleeping bag, taking up a lot of extra room in your pack. Lastly, if the under-quilt is your only form of insulation, then depending on the temperature rating, it could be way too hot to use in the summer months; you'll probably end up getting a sleeping pad to replace it during the warm summer nights that you're sure to encounter.

On a personal note having to do with sleeping pads in hammocks, I used a Thermarest Z-lite, closed cell sleeping pad (these will be explained further on) in my hammock for my entire Pacific Crest Trail thru-hike. I cut it into two separate pieces. One piece was a quarter length of the entire pad, while the second piece was the bottom three quarters of the pad that was left. I laid the quarter length piece horizontally within the hammock to compensate for the wideness of my shoulders, then laid the three-quarter piece parallel (long ways) in the hammock to insulate my torso and thighs. This was incredibly comfortable for me, and the pads were so thin, they never shifted when I tossed and turned. I had some cold nights, but never anything I would deem miserable, or anything that forced me to consider other sleeping pad options. The Z-lite is affordable enough to consider experimenting with before you go out there. It's one of the most popular sleeping pads amongst ground dwellers as well, weighing a mere eight ounces.

The most convenient type of hammock will have an integrated bug net. This means the bug net will be attached to your hammock, usually by a zipper, but sometimes sewed straight on permanently. If the bug net is not integrated, then it's separate, and you'll have to manually attach and remove it every time you set up or break down your hammock. Integrated bug nets will make your hammock weigh more, but if you decide to carry one anyway, then it might as well be integrated. If you plan to use your hammock at a time or location when/where there are no bugs, then you may want to have a separate bug net, that way you can leave it behind completely in order to save weight.

When it comes to hammock suspension, there are several options. The simplest (and heavy) form of suspension is Atlas Straps. Simply wrap them around a tree, then attach your hammock to one of the many loops via a carabineer and voila! One of the lightest forms of suspension is the Whoopi Sling. These are fairly simple to use (after you practice a couple times), and provide a lot of versatility for adjusting the angle of your hang. There are plenty of other suspension systems that do or do not utilize tree straps/tree savers, or that require knots, buckles, or marlin spikes to secure or adjust your hammock, but the two I've described are the most popular and straight forward. Any other forms of suspension techniques can be easily researched on the endless hammock forums that can be found online.

When it comes to the angle of your hang in a hammock, the type of hammock you're using can play a big part. Some require a 35-degree slope between your suspension line and the tree, while others can be hung as tightly between the trees as you can manage. There are yet more hammocks you can hang in a myriad of ways to your own personal liking, but at the end of the day, you're going to lay in your hammock one of two different ways; either diagonally or parallel. When you lay in a hammock diagonally, you are opting for the flattest lay possible, and you'll normally have to sleep on your back in order to achieve this lay. If you go with parallel, then you have chosen a slightly more cradled position that can afford you to sleep on your back, or even your side if you wish. I sleep on my side with one arm above my head, so a slightly larger hammock allows me to do this comfortably. I always hang the foot end of my hammock slightly higher than the head end. I do this to elevate my feet (which feels good at the end of a long day of hiking), but also because the pull of gravity sits me slightly further back in the hammock, allowing me to sleep on my side without too much of a cradle forcing me to bend at my mid-section. It's like sleeping on a very slight decline that I personally find more comfortable.

If you plan to use a hammock, then you'll also need a rain fly, more commonly known as a tarp. I went into detail on different types of tarps earlier on, and many of those same tarps can be used as rain flys for a hammock. You can use flat rectangle tarps, diamond tarps, hex tarps, tarps with folding doors, tarps with tie outs, etc. The same principles for continuous ridgelines and split ridgelines (as mentioned earlier) also apply to the hammock rain fly.

The Essentials

What people personally consider "essential" in regards to long distance hiking can differ quite a bit from person to person. In this book, however, "essential" refers to gear that is more or less required to ensure your safety and basic comfort throughout the duration of your hike, no matter what you may encounter. Some of the essentials are 100% necessary no brainers to survive (certain clothing, dry storage, etc.), while others will simply be imperative to your safety, as well as meeting basic needs, however not necessarily a deal breaker if you don't bring them along.

After you've selected the "Big Three," you next have to select the rest of your gear. The art of getting exactly what you need and nothing more is a matter of streamlining; as much of your gear as possible needs to serve a double purpose on its own, or when paired/layered with another piece of gear. Your gear will fall into categories and subcategories. I will list them out to make it easier.

SHELTER

This category will contain everything having to do with your shelter. Everything from the type of shelter, to all the materials that may or may not come with it in order to erect it, water proof it, bug proof it, stake it down, etc.

-**Type of shelter**

-**Rain fly/rain cover (if separate entity from shelter)**

-**Ground sheet (if tenting or tarping)**

-**Sleeping pad (hammocking/tenting/tarping)**

-**Under-quilt (if hammocking and an under-quilt is your preference)**

-**Stakes/guy lines/poles**

-**Bug netting (if applicable)**

Breaking it all Down (Shelter Category)

Depending on whether you have chosen to hang between the trees or dwell on the ground, there will be some essentials in the shelter category. I'll make this one brief since we've already gone into detail on shelters above. We'll focus more on the ground sheet and sleeping pad.

Your options for sleeping pads are just as endless as anything else on this list. As always, the first thing you need to consider is your personal comfort level, then your application. Pads come in three major categories; Inflating, self-inflating, and closed cell/foam. Inflatable pads/mattresses are on average going to be the thickest, warmest, most comfortable pads you can find. You will have to manually blow them up by mouth more often than not, but some pads come with fancy pumps disguised as dry bags that make the inflation process a snap. If you are a creature of comfort, then an inflatable pad is probably the best option for you. You can use it on the ground or in a hammock, but be aware, if you plan to use one in a hammock, the thicker the pad, the harder it will be to keep underneath you (unless you have a double layered hammock, or you fit the pad into your sleeping bag comfortably). The downside to inflatable pads is they can puncture or tear, and unless you have a repair kit with you (most inflatable pads come with one), then you might be "pad-less" until you can repair it or get a new one. One other drawback to the inflatable pad (in my opinion) is the extra time it takes to deflate, fold, and roll them up. I have a slight OCD problem, so mine have to be folded and rolled up perfectly. The only problem is that I'm terrible at folding and rolling, so the extra air within the pad always gives me trouble when I'm putting it away, or getting out the last pockets of air during the rolling process.

Your next option is self-inflating pads. These are your second-best pads when it comes to warmth and comfort, as well as second best when it comes to ease of use and breakdown. Self-inflating pads are made with open cell foam. When you store the pad, the foam is compressed. When the entire pad is rolled up and compressed with the cap on the air valve, it will not inflate. Once the cap is removed from the valve, and any compression weight/force against the pad is relieved, the foam cells will expand, automatically pulling air in through the valve and inflating the pad. This type of pad is easier to set up and put away than a manually inflating pad, but you won't find them thicker and lighter than your standard inflatable. Sure, you can find a happy medium between the length, width, thickness, and weight that suits your comfort level, while still being lighter than other inflatables, but that's up to you to figure out. Another drawback to the self-inflating pad is that it can also puncture and tear, allowing the air inside to escape once you lay on it and compress the open cell foam. This type of pad is good for all applications.

Our final pad is a closed cell or foam pad, no inflation required. These tend to be the thinnest and lightest of all the sleeping pads, but heavy, thick versions do exist. They will roll or fold up, depending on the brand you get; providing nothing more than a small barrier between you and the ground, or you and the outside air of your hammock. No valves and no air, these are the simplest sleeping pads you can find. They set up and break down in several seconds as opposed to sometimes several minutes or more with inflating pads. You can stab them, rip them, even cut them in half; they'll still work just the same. In fact, some people do cut sections of them off to save weight. If you can sleep on your floor without too much discomfort or trouble, then a closed cell or foam pad may be the pad for you. Their biggest drawbacks are comfort (this may not be an issue for you) and warmth. Depending on who you are, a simple closed cell pad can be more than enough on the ground, or in a hammock, no matter how low the temperatures. The biggest draw back in the hammock will be low temperatures with a high wind chill factor, but if you have your rain fly set up properly, you can block out most, if not all of the wind.

On an ending note about pads, each one of these types of pads will come in a myriad of lengths, widths, thicknesses, shapes, weights, and warmth values. The warmth or insulation of pads is measured by the "R-value." The higher the R-value, the better insulation and warmth the pad will have. The R-value will be most closely tied into how thick the pad is, but the materials and inner chambers will play a huge part as well. It's up to you to find the combination of those qualities that fit your comfort level, as well as your physical dimensions.

Now let's move on to ground sheets, but we won't spend too much time on these either. There are many different types, made from different materials with different shapes and different sizes, with some being more rugged than others. As usual, the toughest and lightest are going to be made of Cuben Fiber. However, there are lighter ground sheets of the same size, simply made from weaker materials. Tyvek is a very popular ground sheet material out on the trail, as it's cheap, tough, and relatively light. If you're hammocking, then you don't need a ground sheet, but some people use one anyway to store their gear on the ground beneath them. If you're tenting, then you need a flat ground sheet beneath your tent. If you're tarping, or tarp tenting, then it would be very wise to look into getting a "bathtub" ground sheet. A bathtub ground sheet will be folded up several inches around the sides, creating a "bathtub" shape. This is practical in the sense that it helps to keep rain splash from getting on top of your groundsheet, as well as keeping any kind of light flooding water from running over your groundsheet, subsequently getting to you and your gear. You can create this same "bathtub" effect with a flat ground sheet by stuffing rocks, sticks (or whatever else you can find), underneath the edges of the sheet so that it doesn't lay flush to the ground, allowing water to flow underneath it, or splash droplets to impact the sides instead of landing on top.

GEAR:

This category contains all the essentials you will need to spend an extended period of time in the woods, while staying relatively comfortable, as well as safe.

-Backpack

*Pack Cover/Pack Liner

-Sleeping Bag

*Sleeping Bag Liner

- Water purification/filtration and storage

- Trekking Polls/Walking Stick

- Storage bags for food, clothing, and gear (preferably waterproof)

-Footwear

Breaking it all down (Gear Category)

Backpack

We've already covered most of the information regarding backpacks, so I will quickly go over the Pack cover and pack liner. For an AT thru-hike, you will undoubtedly want to have a pack cover, a pack liner, or both. A pack cover is nothing more than a waterproof piece of material that fits over top of your pack to keep the rain from soaking the contents inside. It's not 100% effective, but close enough. It can be as simple as a trash bag that's been fit over your pack, to space age materials with stretchy elastic perimeters or drawstrings that ensure a perfectly snug fit. The biggest disadvantages of the pack cover is that it can be blown off by high winds (and possibly not recovered), and that it won't protect your gear if your pack is submerged, or if the panel (the part that goes against your back) is exposed to water (this includes residual water running down your back while you're wearing it, as well as sweat).

A pack liner is also made of waterproof materials. It will be in a circular or rectangular bag shape, and able to fit inside the main part of your pack. All your gear that resides within the main compartment of your pack will also reside inside the pack liner. Once again, the pack liner can be as simple as a trash bag, or as complex as Cuben Fiber, Sil-Nylon; using Velcro, roll top, or snap closures to seal it. The advantage of the pack liner is it will keep the contents within it dry, even in the case of a submersion. The disadvantage is that it won't do anything for the contents of your pack that reside in external pockets that are separate from the main compartment (if there are any).

In the end, your choice to use a pack cover, a pack liner, or both, will depend mostly on the type of backpack you get, as well as which one puts your mind at ease the most. Don't forget, if you opt to go with only a pack liner, allowing the exterior of your pack to get wet, there is always the chance of your pack materials (depending on what they are) absorbing water and making your pack exponentially heavier. For safety, things that could save your life (sleeping bags, warm clothes, etc.), that could be rendered useless by getting wet, should be kept in their own separate dry bags for extra insurance and protection.

Sleeping Bag/Quilt

Since we've already gone over this in great detail already, I'll keep it brief. Depending on what kind of sleeping bag or quilt you've got, as well as its temperature rating, you may or may not want to get a sleeping bag liner. This is like a second sleeping bag (although much, much thinner, and made of different materials) that goes inside your main bag to give you some added degrees of warmth. A sleeping bag liner is completely optional, and adds weight. However, it can be a cheaper alternative to buying an entirely new sleeping bag with a lower temperature rating. The liner can come in handy during the summer if your normal bag is too hot and you want to sleep in something lighter. On the flip side, it can come in handy during the summer for those freak temperature drops, or when camping at higher altitudes where it may get cooler than you anticipated. During the colder months, it can also be helpful when your sleeping bag simply isn't enough on its own. The best way to avoid needing a liner is to know yourself well enough to get the right sleeping bag that already fits all your temperature/comfort needs. Remember, if it's too cold, you can't magically conjure up extra gear; however, if it's too hot, you can always strip down as much as you need to. Don't forget you don't always have to sleep inside your sleeping bag either. In the event that it's too hot, you can simply drape it over yourself like a blanket. It's better to have a sleeping bag that's "too warm" rather than not warm enough. As mentioned earlier on in the sleeping bag/quilt section, a good quilt can solve all of the above overheating issues, or the need for a bag liner all together.

Water Purification/Filtration and Storage

The acquisition, treatment, and storage of water is one of the most important facets of your hike. You can't live very long without water, especially when you're moving and sweating every day, all day. Luckily, there are a multitude of options for treating, purifying, and storing your water while out on the trail; you simply have to find the one that suits your preference. When it comes to the treatment of water, there are quite a few options for thru-hiking. You can opt to "filter" your water, or "treat" your water with chemicals or UV light. They all have their advantages and disadvantages as far as weight, time, and quality of water. Of course, you can always choose to not to filter or treat your water and simply drink it straight from the source. There are people who do that, but the risk of water borne illnesses will be significantly higher. Let's examine and compare several of the more common methods, starting with filtering.

There are several popular ways to filter your water on a thru-hike. You can use a pump filter, a squeeze filter, or a gravity filter. I'll begin with the pump filter. Using a manual pump to filter your water is one of the older ways of doing it. It requires the most physical effort (usually), is made of heavier materials compared to other filters, and also has the most moving parts with the potential to break. They are good filters, but their size, weight, complexity to clean, and potential to break are huge drawbacks. There are many options for pump filters out there, but most people will switch to a squeeze or gravity filter while out on the trail, even if they began with a pump filter.

Squeeze filters are probably tied, if not slightly more popular than gravity filters during a thru-hike of the Appalachian Trail. They require the second most physical effort to operate after pump filters. To use a squeeze filter, you simply attach the filter (which will have a threaded side and a nozzle side) to a water bladder or pliable water bottle, then squeeze (make sure the container has water in it of course). Many squeeze filters will come with water bladders or pouches from the manufacturer that fit them perfectly, however some will easily thread onto and attach to bladders and water bottles made by different manufacturers. The advantage of the squeeze filter is its size and weight. They can come in several sizes with different weights and flow speeds; the smaller the filter, the slower the flow of water; the larger the filter, the faster the flow. Sawyer Squeeze filters are the most popular, and easily fit Platypus water bladders/pouches, as well as "Smart Water" water bottles and many other water bottles. The disadvantage of squeeze filters is they have to be "back flushed" every once in awhile so they don't become too clogged with particulates. Back flushing is when you force water backwards through the filter, pushing all the particulates back out of the way they came in. The longer you wait to back flush, the slower the flow of water, as well as the longer it will take you to filter. Also, you will need clean water to back flush, which means you will need to already be in town, or have clean water already filtered in order to back flush with. Almost all Squeeze filters will come with a back- flushing kit (don't worry - it's not complex or heavy).

The gravity filter is another one of the most popular filters on the trail. It requires the least amount of physical effort on your part, but the most amounts of physics (gravity joke). The gravity filter will comprise of a water bladder, a filter, and tubing. You will fill the water bladder or pouch with water, then hang it (or hold it if there is nothing to hang it from) off the ground. The force of gravity will pull the water down through the tubing, through the filter (which also needs to be suspended high enough that it's off the ground), then through more tubing and into whatever container you intend to store your water in. If you're not holding the bladder, then you can simply set it up and forget it; it will filter the water for you. Simply make sure you're not filtering more than you can hold in your storage container, or you will have to keep an eye on it to make sure it doesn't overflow, thus wasting time and water. You can also opt to not filter water this way, but instead store the full water bladder in your pack with the attached tubing and filter rigged to come over your shoulder when wearing your pack. You can then use the power of suction to suck the water through the filter, down the tubing and into your mouth. I personally do not like drinking water directly through the filter because it's not fast enough for me. I like to take big swigs out of bottles or bladders of already filtered water. So, if you're like me, then you might want to take that into consideration. Gravity filters also have to be periodically back flushed. The biggest disadvantage is the filter possibly clogging, or being unable to find something to hang the bladder/pouch from, causing you to have to hold it up yourself. Other than those drawbacks, the gravity filter is pretty convenient.

After filters, treating water with chemicals/tablets or UV light is the next most common type of water purification. There are many different types of chemical treatment ranging from bleach to other fancy chemicals and tablets, and all of them work. They will kill any and all germs within your water, making it safe to drink. This is the lightest form of water purification to carry, as the chemicals or tablets usually come in very tiny bottles/containers that weigh under an ounce, only requiring several drops or tablets to treat multiple liters of water. The drawback to treating your water with chemicals is they usually alter the taste of your water. Also, there is a specific amount of time you must wait (depending on the chemicals you're using) in order for the chemicals to do their job and make your water safe (usually between 10 and 20 minutes, sometimes less, sometimes more). Yet still, unless you have filtered/strained your water through a bandana or something prior to treating it with chemicals, you are going to be getting any bits of particulate that may have made it into the container you're treating the water in. While the bits of particulate will be rendered harmless by the chemicals, your water may very well have a "texture" to it, which is something some people simply can't deal with. Hence, if you're not impatient, don't mind textured water, and want the lightest option possible, chemically treating your water may be the path for you.

The last method is using UV light. You can buy special battery operated UV light sticks that you put into your water and stir around for about a minute or more. The ultraviolet light creates an invisible radiation that passes through microorganisms, killing them. It doesn't remove them from the water, but renders them incapable of causing you harm. This method is less common on the trail, but you still see people using it. There are several different brands and manufacturers, but it's up to you to decide which one fits your needs. The advantages are that it's relatively quick and easy, while the disadvantages are your water will still have a texture to it, your light will need batteries, and you'll still be ingesting dead microorganisms.

Storing your water for carrying is your next task after acquiring it. The largest volume, most compact containers (especially when empty) will be bladders, pouches, and blivets. The most rigid and easy to drink from will be plastic bottles. Since many backpacks have side pouches for water bottles, most people will carry two generic water bottles (usually a Gatorade, Nalgene, or Smart Water bottle), and one bladder/pouch. The bottles can be stored in the side pockets, while the bladder can be stored inside the pack or a designated bladder pocket (if the pack has one). The bottles will normally have 1 to 1.5-liter capacity, while the bladder will normally have 1 to 2-liter capacity, 3 liters at the most. I drink like a fish, and I never needed to carry more than four liters of water to see me through to the next water source, and that was only once or twice. I very seldom carried more than two liters at a time throughout my entire hike of the AT.

Trekking Polls/Walking Stick

Having a pair of trekking polls or a walking stick can be a life saver on a thru hike, especially for your joints. Even still, there are plenty of people who do the entire trail hands free, without any assistance. I used a large walking stick for my entire thru hike, and I'll freely admit it saved my ass more times than I can count. My walking stick was especially useful on steep down hills that required large step downs off rocks. I got a lot of use out of my walking stick, but I still paired it up with a second walking stick, as well as another trekking pole several times throughout my thru hike. This was to add to my pushing power on the steep climbs, and many times I found myself wishing for the efficiency of two trekking poles.

Trekking poles come in many different styles and materials for a wide range of prices. They all perform pretty much the same tasks, but it's up to you to decide what other features you want out of them; grip style, weight, folding, non-folding, shock absorbers in the tips, etc. I'll list some of the advantages of having trekking poles or a walking stick, as well as some disadvantages.

They can increase your speed by helping to propel you forward, reduce impact on your joints, reduce the weight on your knees by up to 25 percent, help to maintain a consistent rhythm, provide extra balance and stability on uneven or slippery surfaces, act as a probe, can be used to help erect shelters, and can be used for protection if you really need it. The disadvantages are they can get caught on things like bushes or rocks, causing you to lose balance anyways. They leave your hands occupied, which can be a pain if you need them to catch yourself or grab onto something. Also, depending on what features your trekking poles have, you may not be able to store them conveniently when you're not using them (you definitely can't store a walking stick).

Trekking poles are a personal preference, and should be a fairly easy decision based on what you know about yourself at this current moment. I will say that way more people use trekking poles on the AT than those who don't. Their advantages vastly outweigh their disadvantages, and your body will probably thank you in the long run.

Storage Bags/Sacks/Pouches for Gear

Storage bags are an important yet often overlooked aspect of gear for a thru-hike. They are what keep all your gear organized, protected, dry, and easy to find within your pack. There are many different materials used to make storage bags, as well as many different styles. Some are compression, draw string, snap buckle, Velcro, zipper, or roll top; sometimes a combination of several of those. They can be waterproof, water resistant, or even mesh. When it comes to selecting your storage bags and pouches, in order to make the most economical choice possible, you need to know what's going into each bag, as well as what level of protection those items need. You will definitely need a waterproof bag for your sleeping bag/quilt, and clothing; that goes without saying. Whether you want to separate your sleeping bag from your clothing in different storage sacks is up to you, but they need to be protected from moisture. Your food needs to be protected from moisture as well, but that's a matter of personal preference. Since electronics are not usually very water compatible, you'll probably want to store them inside a Ziploc bag or waterproof pouch/sack as well. Anything else that isn't water sensitive can be stored in whatever kind of bag you want, or no bag at all depending on your personal level of organization. As usual, the material your storage vessels are made from will affect their weight. Depending on the size of the bag and the materials it's made from, they can weigh anywhere from multiple ounces, to fractions of an ounce.

Footwear

When it comes to comfort and the level of misery you can tolerate out on the trail, footwear is going to be the first thing you take notice of. Maybe you've always been in tune with your feet's needs and know what works for you, as well as what's right for you. Nonetheless, many people buy shoes based on what looks good, or from reviews they've read or heard by other people. Well, guess what? Those people aren't you, and they don't have your feet. The best thing you can do is try the shoes on before you buy them; preferably under the supervision of someone who knows the product, knows the different foot types, and knows what to recommend for them. The wrong shoe can be disastrous! It can be disastrous in the sense that you can become more prone to blisters, hot spots, stumbles and falls, as well as deeper rooted issues that can arise from using improper footwear for prolonged periods of time. Issues like ankle problems-that turn into knee problems-that turn into hip problems-that turn into back problems. It's a chain reaction that all starts in your feet, so you need to make sure you make the right choice. I can't make the choice for you, and I can't tell you what kind of feet you have (pronation, over pronation, supination, over supination, flat, or neutral). It's up to you to find the help and do the research to determine that for yourself. Trust me, there is a lot of information and help to be found regarding those subjects on the internet, as well as at your local shoe/running store.

What I can do is give you some options on types of footwear to look into based on what your needs might require. First off, it's almost never a good idea to get a waterproof shoe or boot for long distance hiking. It might seem like a good idea, especially when you begin trudging through puddles of mud and water, but they will do nothing for you when it rains, and I guarantee you will spend plenty of days walking in the rain. Waterproof shoes take FOREVER to dry. Once they do get wet, they're going to stay wet for quite some time, even after the conditions have long since turned dry. Your waterproof footwear will keep your poor feet suffocating and soggy for hours, sometimes days after the rain has stopped. Also, they will turn into ovens in the summer time because they don't vent well. You will literally feel your feet cooking inside your shoes. Wear them if you really want to, but ye' have been warned!

So, what kind of style is right for you? Would you prefer a below the ankle cut shoe, an above the ankle boot, a light and vented trail runner, or an active type sandal/open shoe? If you're very worried about ankle support and have a history of injury or ankle rolls, then you'll probably want to go with something that comes up over your ankle. This type of shoe/boot will be very heavy and cumbersome, but at least you'll have the extra support. If you need the support, but don't want the clunky boot/shoe, then you can always opt for some form of ankle wrap/brace to be worn inside a smaller, lighter, more minimalist shoe (this is what I do).

If you want something with more protection, cushion, as well as ruggedness, but without the extra ankle support, then you'll probably opt for a below the ankle type hiking shoe. They will normally be heavier than a regular shoe, and much heavier than a running or trail running shoe, but they will have that added support and protection from stubs and bumps.

If you want light and fast, then you'll be looking for a trail running shoe. Trail running shoes are often built a little more rugged, and with more traction than a simple road running shoe. A normal road running shoe can work for hiking, but it most likely won't last as long as a trail runner, and may not offer some of the traction, protection, or cushion that a modern trail runner can offer. The advantage of using running/trail running shoes, is they are much lighter than hiking boots/shoes -YES, you can feel the difference! They also dry much quicker. A disadvantage is they don't offer as much foot protection, and may not last as long as tougher boots/shoes that are designed for hiking. One last thing that goes overlooked regarding trail running shoes; their light weight can sometimes offer you more control over the stability of your foot. This is because you are allowing more muscles to be engaged with a lighter shoe, thus making your joint naturally stronger, more stable, and attuned to rough/uneven terrain. Sometimes the human body does it better than anything technology can try to simulate. However, if you've had multiple ankle injuries or surgeries, sometimes nothing will ever restore your ankle to its natural levels of stability; time to opt for some extra man-made support.

Sandals and open type shoes are another option. In today's world of outdoor footwear merchandisers, you can find almost any type of footwear for any type of application. Yes, they have created sandals for hiking. There are many different styles you can wear many different ways. Some are nothing more than straps that go around your feet, toes, or ankles in various ways/combinations, while others can be in more of a shoe style, but with open vents or slats that allow for air flow and exposure of your feet. The biggest advantage of various sandals/open shoes is they don't absorb or hold water. You can walk through a creek or stream and they're dry after several minutes of walking. They can also be fairly light compared to other shoes, allowing your feet to breathe without getting sweaty or clammy like they would inside a regular shoe. Disadvantages can be support and foot protection. You are more vulnerable to foot stubs and trips, as well as sticks/vegetation poking your feet as you walk, or small pebbles getting between your feet and the sole. Some of the vent type shoes/sandals have raised lips or protected bumpers on the front of the shoe to protect your toes.

Many hikers will carry "camp shoes" with them. These are extremely light shoes that can be worn to protect your feet around camp, without having to wear whatever heavier footwear you wore while hiking. This allows your hiking footwear to air out and dry while you're still able to walk around in your camp shoes without having to worry about injuring your feet. The most popular camp shoes are "crocs," but many people use "shower shoes," or very light/cheap thong sandals. Crocs are also very handy for creek/river crossings. If you're already hiking in sandals or a vented shoe, they can eliminate your need for any kind of camp shoe.

As with everything in this book, your footwear will be a personal choice regarding your comfort level, as well as whatever you need to get out of the footwear itself. Simply make sure you try them on first, and if you have no experience in finding the right active footwear, make sure you have someone help you.

CLOTHING

Clothing is a category in which you can save a lot of extra weight by being practical, as well as not going overboard. This category represents everything you will wear throughout all and any temperatures and weather conditions. Not every single thing listed is a necessity, I've simply listed the most popular/basic options.

-Cold Weather

    *Down Jacket

    *Base Layers (top and bottom)

    *Wind Shell

    *Gloves

    *Hoodie

    *Socks (sleeping)

-Warm Weather

    *Shorts

    *Shirt

    *Compression Underwear

    *Socks

-Rain

    *Rain Shell Jacket

    *Rain Shell Pants

    *Poncho

    *Rain Kilt

    *Rain Mitts

    *Umbrella

-Worn

    *What you wear on a daily basis usually falls into the category of "warm weather clothing."

Breaking It All Down (Clothing Category)

As mentioned above, clothing is a category where you can save a lot of extra weight if you do your research. It's easy to bring along too many clothes or garments that are much heavier than they need to be. This is a result of over thinking your clothing options. Everything you bring regarding clothing should have a stand-alone use, as well as a layering use. I'll go through the different clothing categories, as well as the options within them. The information should give you the knowledge and confidence to be able to make the right selections.

-Kyle S. Rohrig-

Cold Weather Clothing - Upper Body Layers

When we think of cold weather clothing, we think of protecting our arms, torso, heads, hands, legs, and feet. That's a lot of garments that have the potential to get very heavy if we overdo it. We're talking jackets, long pants, gloves, hoodies, thick socks, long underwear, and possibly more if you're over-compensating. The key to making the correct cold weather garment selections is "layers." You need to be able to layer everything; we'll start with upper body layers. It's smart to have a base layer, an insulating down/fleece layer, and a wind/rain shell layer. That's three layers for your upper body. Each one by itself can be worn comfortably on its own, depending on the climate. The colder or worse the climate, the more layers you can put on. The base layer (which can be worn under a T-shirt) is your first defense against the cold and elements. It's normally very form fitting, acting as a thin insulator to keep your body heat on your body, as well as wicking away moisture from your skin.

The next layer over top of that would be a fleece or down jacket/pullover (down being the lightest and most popular on the AT). This layer's job is to further insulate your own body heat and trap warmth within your garments. Your down/fleece layer will be the warmest article of clothing you take with you. Features like hoods, zippers, drawstrings, and pockets are all things to consider when you factor in how heavy and functional you want this layer to be.

The most exterior layer is the wind/rain shell jacket. This layer can simply be a windbreaker shell jacket (lightest option), or a waterproof shell jacket (also works as a windbreaker), but normally slightly heavier than a windbreaker due to its waterproof properties. The job of this final third layer is to block out any wind chill or water that could possibly get through, making the job of the other two layers more difficult. Keep in mind they don't always have to be worn all together. The sequence I've just described is simply the warmest most protective way of layering them. You can wear any of those garments by themselves (depending on the conditions), or layer them two at a time. For example, just the base layer and the down jacket; the base layer and the shell jacket; or just the down jacket and the shell jacket, etc. By using the layering method, you can eliminate the need of going overboard by buying something that could possibly be too heavy or warm by itself during most conditions, or worse... not enough.

Let's go over options for those three individual garments. Base layer tops come in many different thicknesses for different temperatures. Based on your own individual comfort levels, you should be able to select how heavy a base layer you need in order to layer it with your other garments and be comfortable. Many base layers are made from synthetic materials, but some are made from wool or a combination of wool and synthetic materials. Wool has the advantage of maintaining its insulating properties even when wet, but at the expense of being a little bit heavier. Base layers made from synthetic materials tend to be lighter than wool and wick away moister better, but don't share the same insulating properties. The ones that are blended with both materials have a little bit of the best of both worlds. It's up to you to decide which is more important to you.

The insulating layer that goes over top of your base layer will usually be a down jacket/pullover, or a fleece jacket/pull over. Almost everyone you run into will have a down jacket on them, also referred to as a "puffy." The warmth, comfort, as well as warmth to weight ratio of down is simply superior to anything else out there. Choosing a down/fleece jacket is another personal comfort choice. They can be as light as four to six ounces, to as much as almost two pounds and everything in between. The deciding factor in how much your down jacket weighs will come down to how much "down" it's stuffed with, what the outer and inner materials are made of, how many pockets and zippers it has, and whether it has a built-in hood. The warmth of your down jacket should depend on your own comfort level with the cold, as well as the heaviness/warmth of your base layer, and the heaviness/warmth of your shell layer.

Your shell layer has the potential to be the lightest of all your upper body layers. If you opt for just a wind shell, you can find them as light as an ounce to only a few ounces. If you're opting for something waterproof, then you're looking at around four to six ounces at the very lightest and up (if you're a smaller individual, then you might be able to find lighter). How do you decide whether you want to go waterproof or not? It all depends on your comfort level with the rain. Some people (myself included) choose to go with as few clothes as possible when it rains. This is done in an effort to spare any layers getting wet from rain, or sweat. The only time some people wear a wind shell is to protect them from cold wind chills penetrating their other layers. If I was to wear a rain shell, I would only wear it by itself when it rained, in an effort to give myself a little more insulation/protection from the water (if it was particularly cold). Remember, no matter how waterproof a garment is, if it rains hard enough, the water will find a way to soak through. At some point, you have to decide if you want to hike in the rain wearing as little as possible (to safeguard any extra layers from potentially getting wet and becoming useless), or if the rain is way too cold/strong to hike in while wearing the bare minimum...learn when to call it a day, in an effort to avoid accidents or unnecessary misery.

Lower Body Layers

Just as there are layering options for your upper body, there are layering options for your lower body. They are roughly the same types of options as mentioned above, so I won't spend as much time going over them. Like your upper body layers, you can choose to wear a long underwear base layer of varying thicknesses, lengths (above the calf/below the calf), weights, styles, and materials. You can then choose an insulating down layer to wear over top of that, or wind/rain shell pants as the outer most layer. Rain or wind shell pants are decidedly more popular and functional than wearing "down impregnated" pants.

When it comes to layers on the lower extremities, they're nowhere near as important as layers on your torso. This is because your legs do not contain any vital organs that need to be insulated and protected from the cold. Most people hiking the trail will have fantastic circulation in their legs, and you will see many people still hiking in shorts, even if the conditions are freezing. At the very most, some hikers may carry a base layer of long underwear in addition to a rain/wind shell layer of pants. More often than not, you will be able to get by with either the base layer or a wind shell by themselves. If you are particularly sensitive to the cold, then it would be smart to go with light base layer underwear and a wind/rain shell, this way they can be used in the event of strong freezing winds or an exceptionally cold night in your shelter.

Gloves

If you're hiking through the early spring, fall, or winter months, then you'll probably want to carry a pair of gloves, especially if you're sensitive to the cold. If you're hiking through New Hampshire during any time of the year, then you will certainly want all your cold weather gear, just to be on the safe side. Gloves are another item that can weigh many ounces, or next to nothing at all; there are plenty of options for windproof, snow proof, and waterproof gloves of varying weights, thicknesses, and materials. The best thing you can do is keep it simple and apply the layering method to your gloves as well. Before we get into layering methods for gloves, let me enlighten you on a streamlining technique. Some people will carry a pair of thick, long wool socks for sleeping in (not hiking); these socks can double as a long glove that can stretch as far up as your elbow. This is one way to have a double use for one piece of gear while saving weight and space in your pack. I've even heard of some people using only a down vest instead of a jacket, then using a large pair of wool socks as their sleeves; this is streamlining at its finest.

When layering gloves, the best way to do this will be to have a very light and thin insulating layer made of wool, "possum down" or some other type of synthetic materials. It's not really too important what they're made of, as long as it's warm enough for you, but not overdoing it. Then you can layer a waterproof/windproof mitten shell over top of the glove. There is nothing worse than hiking in freezing cold wind and rain while wearing a glove that does nothing to protect you against either. Numb fingers that don't work can be a serious problem out there. Take the steps to insulate and protect your hands, but do it smartly, without overdoing it. A cheap and useful technique for waterproofing and wind-proofing your gloves/ hands is to buy a cheap pair of rubber gardening gloves to go over top of them.

Socks

When I go to sleep at night on the trail, my most prized piece of gear for sleeping (besides my sleeping bag) is a pair of long wool socks. Much of your body heat can be lost through your feet and your head. Therefore, on exceptionally cold nights you should take measures to insulate both. As mentioned above, a good pair of thick wool socks can double as sleeping socks and hiking mitts. How thick and warm the sock you choose is totally up to your personal preference. Since a good pair of warm socks can split the hairs between a perfect night's sleep and an uncomfortable night's sleep in the cold for me, I tend to lean on the thicker side.

Hoodies/Beanies

When it comes to protecting, and insulating your head while hiking and sleeping, there are many options in which to do so. Some people may prefer an integrated hood on their down jacket or shell jacket. Others may prefer to have a standalone hoodie/cap to add and remove as they please. They can be as simple as a cap that covers only the top of your head and your ears, to a full-on balaclava that covers your head, face, and neck, allowing only your eyes to see and your mouth to breathe. As you probably guessed, there are many styles of each, made from different materials of different weights, thicknesses, and warmth ratings. Anything made of down will be the warmest/lightest/most expensive for your money, but you can also find them in all styles made from wool, fleece, synthetics, and synthetic blends. Decide what fits you best and make the most informed decision you can.

Final Word on Cold Weather Clothing

An important thing to remember about your cold weather clothing is you will mostly be wearing it at night, or during periods of rest or leisurely walking. When you are strenuously hiking non-stop, putting forth a good effort, you will normally be able to wear surprisingly few garments, even in freezing weather without too much discomfort. Of course, there are exceptions when it's exceptionally freezing, or the wind chill is exceptionally high, but for the most part, you will only wear all your layers at the same time when you're sleeping in your shelter, at rest during a break, or doing leisurely activities around camp, like collecting water.

Warm Weather Clothing

You may not realize it, but it's very easy to go overboard with your warm weather clothing. This is clothing you will be wearing and hiking in the most frequently. Where some people tend to go overboard, is when they bring multiples of the same types of garments. For example, multiple t-shirts, multiple shorts, multiple pairs of compression underwear and undergarments, and multiple socks. While having at least two pairs of socks and compression underwear is perfectly reasonable; carrying multiple t-shirts and shorts is completely optional. The reason for why it's safe to carry two pairs of socks and compression underwear is simply because if one pair rips or becomes wet, the results can be very painful. Hiking in wet underwear during dry or humid conditions can sometimes cause serious chafing. Wet socks are just plain miserable and can make your feet soggy, causing calluses to peel and skin to tear, while torn socks can cause serious blisters. It's simply safe to have a back- up of each of these items in case one is compromised. Some people like to use sock liners as well. They're normally made from a thin polyester material, worn underneath your main sock and used to wick away moisture from your feet and into your thicker, outer sock. They are a personal choice, and depending on your footwear (as well as your proneness for sweaty feet), may be a good option for you.

Some people like to have extra shirts and shorts in case one pair gets too wet or stinky, they can have a clean, dry pair to put on; usually around camp, in their shelter, or in towns. This is advantageous in all those instances, but also a personal decision. Some people keep one shirt, one pair of shorts, and hike in them/wear them around town no matter how stinky, dirty, or wet they get. This is a personal decision you can make before you go out there, or make once you get out there and figure out what works for you. In the event that you decide to take multiple types of the same clothing, make sure you opt for the lightest, most comfortable, moisture wicking kind you can find. Polyester and other synthetic materials are always better than cotton because "cotton kills." Cotton has zero insulating properties when it becomes wet; so in my opinion, it really has no place out in the woods for months on end. Maybe take one pair of super light running shorts, as well as one pair of hiking shorts with pockets and zippers in them. This ensures a nice balance, as well as the best of both worlds when it comes to active-wear shorts. You can do the same for shirts, although many people will opt for as simple and light as possible. Others may choose a very light button down shirt they can open up and vent in case of hot temperatures without having to go shirtless. Your options are endless.

Final Word on Warm Weather Clothing:

In the end, you could be wearing all of your warm weather clothing while you hike, or include an extra set in your pack that you're always carrying around, not matter what. On the flip side, you could also be wearing some of your cold weather clothing, while carrying two sets of warm weather clothing in your pack (think about it). It's up to you to decide what will work best for your comfort level and psyche; try to make efficient choices.

Rain Shell Garments

Since we have already covered almost everything pertaining to rain shell garments in the "cold weather" section, I'll make this extra brief. In an effort to keep any "shell" layers extremely light and only windproof, some hikers will opt to use a "hiking umbrella." These can be extremely useful in blocking rain, wind, and sunlight. It can also be used as an extra layer of protection in tarp shelters if you set it up to block out extra wind and rain. Special hiking umbrellas are becoming increasingly popular out on the trails and can help to eliminate some of the need for heavier waterproof garments, while also serving multiple uses that simple waterproof garments aren't able to fill. They are also extremely useful when it's snowing, hailing, sleeting, or the sun is particularly strong - with shade at a premium.

You can also choose to use a poncho. Ponchos are your original rain garment, as they have been used for many, many decades. They can be incredibly versatile, serving multiple uses, but some people simply can't stand them. A good poncho can double as a pack cover, a ground sheet, and even a shelter. There are companies out there who make ponchos specifically to serve these multiple functions. If you're savvy, you can make your own poncho out of whatever materials you want, even a trash bag. Lastly, "Frog Toggs" can be a very effective option that is relatively light and cheap. You can find them at pretty much any Wal-Mart, and I've seen plenty of hikers who make them work wonderfully. Not to mention, they're extremely warm.

MISCELLANEOUS

This category is the most flexible; it contains a few essentials, but a good portion will be made up of items you personally decided you can't live without and needed to bring with you.

-Cooking

* Cook pot/hydration container

*Stove (alcohol or gas)

*Fuel/fuel container

*Utensils

-Hygiene

*Toothbrush/toothpaste/toothpowder/floss

*Nail clippers

*Toilet paper/wet wipes

*Feminine products (if applicable)

*Comb

-Medical

*Pain killers/anti-inflammatory

*Athletic tape/medical tape/moleskin/band-aids

*Neosporin

*Anti-chaffing powder/body powder/ body glide/ Vaseline

*Sun block

-Electronics/Battery Operated Gear

*Cell phone

*Headlamp/light

*Portable backup battery charger

*Spare batteries

*Wall charger

*Watch

*Respective charging cords/outlets

-Survival

*Knife

*Cordage (550 paracord is most common)

* Duct tape

*Super glue

*Sewing supplies

*Bug spray

Breaking It All Down (Miscellaneous Category)

Nearly everything that falls into the miscellaneous category is optional. A vast majority of it you will want to bring along no matter what, but plenty of hardcore individuals get by with very little of it.

Cooking

Cooking on the trail is a personal preference. Some people prefer to cook and eat most of their meals (especially dinner) hot. Others could care less if their food is hot, or even if they eat foods that require cooking in the first place. If you're not cooking your food, or it doesn't require cooking to prepare, it's referred to as eating a "cold meal." You can have a cold breakfast, cold lunch, cold dinner; just as you can have a hot breakfast, lunch, and dinner. Let's go over some of the supplies/gear involved in cooking.

Cooking Pot/Mug/Mugpot/Hydration Container

Your first choice when it comes to cooking is deciding what you want to do your cooking in. If you have no desire to cook (I usually don't), then a cooking pot is not that important. There are a multitude of different cooking pots of various sizes, shapes, materials, and weights; it's your personal choice. Titanium pots tend to be the lightest/strongest pots you can carry, but there are plenty of other options to choose from (too many to go into). Some decide not to bring a pot, but instead bring a small Tupperware or plastic pouch to rehydrate food in. You can easily rehydrate grits, instant mash potatoes, ramen, some lentils, couscous, anything freeze dried, and other grains/starches with cold water; this avoids boiling all together, while eating these items cold. It will take longer to hydrate them, but it does work. Freeze Dried meals that you can buy pre-packaged online, as well as at the store and many outfitters along the trail (think: Mountain House or Backpackers Pantry) can also be rehydrated with cold water; however, it will take longer than it would with hot or boiling water, but not much. The preference is yours.

Some will opt to take a hydration container and a very small titanium mug/mugpot. The mug can be used to boil water which is then poured into the hydration container to rehydrate, cook, or warm up whatever food you're preparing. However, many people who decide to bring some kind of mug or pot, usually opt to hydrate or eat the food directly out of it, eliminating the hassle of having two different containers. People normally have just a pot, or just a rehydrating container; find the balance that works for you. The rehydrating container can be nothing more than a plastic Ziploc bag, but slightly more durable options are available.

<u>Fuel/Stoves</u>

If you decide you're going to cook on a regular basis, then you're going to need some form of reliable fuel and a stove for cooking. Some people choose to go with gas stoves, of which there are many styles and sizes. While others decide to go with alcohol stoves, of which there are also many styles and sizes. Without spending an inordinate amount of time going into the different styles and types of gas and alcohol stoves (which you can research on your own), I will give you the general breakdown, as well as the pros and cons of both.

Before I get into the details of gas vs. alcohol stoves, let me tell you that some people manage to cook without them. These people opt to cook/boil their pots of water and food over open campfires. This is all well and good, but you may not always have one available to you when you're in the mood for something hot. This is due to rain, fire bans, or the availability of natural fuel for that fire. Decide how important hot food is to you; whenever and wherever you want it.

While there are incredibly light options for gas stoves that screw on and attach to gas canisters (under two ounces in some cases), alcohol stoves will always be the simplest and lightest option. However, simple and light is not always the best when it comes to cooking. If you decide to go with an alcohol stove (homemade or otherwise) you will need to carry rubbing alcohol or the automotive anti-freeze/water remover- "Heet." Both are very cheap, but Heet will burn hotter and faster than your standard isopropyl or ethyl rubbing alcohol. You will also have to carry both in a separate container, adding them and removing them to your alcohol stove as needed. While the alcohol stove can be an excellent and simple stove to carry with you, it does have its drawbacks.

The flames that alcohol stoves produce, are much weaker compared to gas stoves. They can be put out fairly easily by a gust of wind, requiring you to keep a small wind screen in place every time you cook. In addition to being easily extinguished, waiting for your alcohol stove to boil a pot of water can be likened to watching grass grow. It can take twice the amount of time to boil water than a gas stove, sometimes more, sometimes less, but never equal to or faster. You will also have to carry a wind screen for your alcohol stove, and it will take longer to cook with.

Gas stoves are quicker and easier than alcohol stoves, but on the heavier/more expensive side. They can range from under two ounces to close to a pound, and you cannot choose how much fuel to carry. The gas canisters come with specific amounts of fuel in each one, and they can be heavier/more expensive than rubbing alcohol and Heet (possibly harder to find in some cases). A super light gas stove will run you over forty to fifty bucks most of the time, and the fuel canisters will usually start around six bucks or more. The advantages to gas stoves are that you can control the size of the flame, the flame is very resistant to the wind, and boiling your water is much faster than an alcohol stove.

These are the pros and cons to having a gas, alcohol, or no stove at all. Based on your wants, needs, and preferences, you should be able to make an informed decision about which will suit you best. If you plan to cook as often as possible, then a gas stove may be the most efficient and economical overall choice. If your cooking is going to be erratic and random, then perhaps a superlight alcohol stove with a small plastic container of fuel will be best. Being out on the trail requires constant adaptation and evolution of routines and tactics, so there is no telling if what you think works for you now, will work for you throughout your entire hike. The best thing is to be flexible and open minded.

Utensils

This piece of gear requires very little explaining. I'll go ahead and say it, whether you bring a pot, a bowl, any type of container, or nothing at all, it's safe to have some kind of lightweight titanium or plastic SPORK. Having a spork will cover all the bases if you find yourself trying to eat peanut butter, Nutella, pouch tuna, soup, canned foods, etc.

General Hygiene Items

Your hygiene on the trail is one thing that takes a major beating out there. You'll be going for long periods without showers. You're going to get dirty. You're going to smell bad. You're going to have to come to terms with all of it. There are essentials in your daily life away from the trail that are going to have no place on the trail. Conversely, there are essentials in your daily life now that will be daily essentials out there. I'll tell you right now, forget about deodorant, body spray, or any kind of fragrances. You're going to stink along with everyone else, and everybody learns not to care or even notice; so just forget about it. Besides a few feminine products (if applicable), your main hygiene products are going to be toilet paper, toothpaste, floss, toothbrush, nail clippers, and a comb or brush if you so wish.

Toilet Paper

Out in the woods, toilet paper can take on the form of real toilet paper, or squares of paper towels. One square of high quality paper towel goes much further than one square of toilet paper. Toilet paper is thinner and lighter, but you will require more of it to get the same job done with a lesser amount of quality paper towel. It's totally your call based on what's available, and what you prefer to wipe your bottom with. In addition to toilet paper/paper towels, many people will also carry baby wipes, or wet wipes. They certainly help with extra maintenance down below, but also double as a way to wash your hands. You can also have a "wet wipe bath" should you feel the urge to clean up a little bit. The choice is yours.

Toothbrush/Toothpaste/Floss

These are a couple more hygiene essentials. While all of these options are completely up to your own personal preference, some outfitters do offer special ultra-light tooth brushes that fit into special cases, as well as tooth powder to replace toothpaste. Many people will simply cut part of the handle off their toothbrush to save weight, while opting for a small tube of toothpaste and roll of floss.

Nail Clippers

This is an easily overlooked aspect of hygiene that can also be easily borrowed, found, or purchased in town. There is nothing worse than letting your toenails grow too long for your shoes, then not having a safe method of managing them. Same goes for chipping/tearing finger nails while climbing, gathering, or assembling whatever. It's just a good idea to have a small, reliable pair of nail clippers; that is unless you're wild and crazy enough to file them down on rocks while you're out there.

Comb/Light Brush

While it's not a "must," it's very nice to have a comb on you. Since the majority of thru-hikers let their body hair grow wild while they're out there, it's nice to tame it every once in a while. When you go into town, it helps to have a somewhat groomed appearance. Also, when beards and mustaches start to get long, you'll want to comb them so they don't become scraggly and tangled. Not only does this look bad, but upon your return to the civilized world, you may not be able to remove certain kinks and tangles that might have become permanent in your hair.

Medical Supplies

This is another subcategory of miscellaneous gear that can contain a large number of items, or a very small number of items. After several weeks, my medical kit contained nothing more than medical tape and body glide. When it comes to what type of medical supplies you bring, it all boils down to what you're comfortable with having or not having in the face of potential pain, injury, or emergency.

Pain Killers/Anti-inflammatory

A great deal of people on the trail will carry some kind of pain killer or anti-inflammatory. If you have a personal preference, then use that. The most common form you will find on the trail is Ibuprofen in a multitude of different milligram dosages. Also referred to as "Vitamin i," many people wouldn't be caught dead without it. It certainly helps with swelling, as well as various aches and pains, but I would just as well not take it, for fear of becoming dependent on it (believe me, some people find themselves unable to hike without it). Pain killers and anti-Inflammatory supplies are your call.

Duct Tape/Athletic Tape/Medical Tape/Moleskin/Band-Aids

These are all items you might find in a person's medical/repair kit, and while they all have their uses, I've found that one of them can substitute all of them. I find that athletic tape and medical tape by themselves can replace or do the same job as Moleskin or Band Aids, just as well - if not better. Athletic tape can also be handy in gear repair. If you're worried about the sticky part of athletic tape or medical tape touching a wound and pulling off any scab upon its removal, simply place a piece of paper towel or toilet paper over the affected area and tape over it. You might lose a little more hair than a band-aid upon removal, but suck it up; you're hiking the Appalachian Trail! Moleskins help to prevent and protect blisters, but I've found athletic/medical tape can get the same job done for half the price. In my opinion, athletic/medical tape is the only "must" out of this subcategory. I've used it to tape blisters, hot spots, deep cuts, as well as taped my ankle with it for extra support.

Neosporin +Pain

This is completely optional. Some people wouldn't be caught without something to prevent infection of a wound, while others don't worry about it in the slightest. Personal choice whether you carry it or not, as it won't be the difference between life or death in a pinch, or the prevention of immediate pain and misery.

Anti-Chaffing Powder/Body Glide/Body Powder

Some people may never have an issue with chaffing, but for others it's a constant risk if they don't take proper measures to prevent it. Anti-chaffing powder, body glide, Vaseline, and Talcum Powder can help to prevent chaffing of the thighs, butt, genitals, and other areas; you really only need one of those to get the job done, so it's up to your personal preference. Body powder is nice to put on at night, or during a long break; this is to dry and heal areas that may start to chafe or stay sweaty long after you've stopped hiking. These are all optional items based on what you know about your body. What I will say is if you forget or neglect to bring one or all of these items when you really need them, you are in for a world of discomfort and pain until you can get your hands on some.

Sun Block

While most of your time will be spent beneath trees, out of direct sunlight, save for treks across balds, fields, and barren ridgelines; some people may want to consider sun block. During the early spring and late fall, the trees will be devoid of most of their leaves, allowing sunlight to pour through to the forest floor. If you are of fair complexion or burn easily, you may want to consider carrying a small amount of sun block if you plan to be hiking during those times of the year.

Electronics

You're trying to get away from the modern world while simultaneously trying to get in touch with nature; but you can't completely unplug yourself from some of your electronics/battery operated devices. We'll go over some of the more common electronics found on trail, as well as some optional ones.

Cell Phone

The cell phone is the most common electronic device. It's a method of staying in touch with loved ones, making emergency calls, blogging, and taking pictures; almost everyone will have one. You can choose to take your current cell phone, or you can pick one more suited for the task of hiking. Find the lightest cell phone with a high-quality camera that's also water resistant or waterproof. This will ensure the greatest chances of its survival and usefulness on the trail.

Chargers/Battery Packs

If you're taking electronic devices, then you're going to need a means of charging them in between town stops. Some people will take nothing more than a simple wall charger with a detachable USB to charge their phone, or whatever electronic devices they take. Bare minimum, you will need a wall charger that plugs into an outlet. On top of wall chargers, many people will bring battery packs/battery cells that hold multiple charges on their own. You can plug them into an outlet, and once full, you can plug them into your electronic devices using a USB cord, charging them on trail. There are many different battery chargers of different sizes, charge capacities, and weights. It's up to you to decide which will meet your charging/weight needs. "Anker" chargers are popular, reliable, as well as affordable, but there are plenty of other brands of higher and lesser quality.

Solar chargers can also be effective out there, but slightly less common; they do have drawbacks. You'll see people with them in the beginning, but most will get rid of them further on. To be practical, solar chargers need to be of a fairly decent size in order to absorb the energy they require to charge your devices. The extra weight usually isn't worth the hassle of leaving them in the sunlight for prolonged periods of time. They are largely ineffective on the back of your pack while hiking due to the fact that you're mostly in the shade for the majority of the trail. It's normally easier to wait until you're in town to use an outlet to charge any battery packs.

Headlamp/Light

You'll probably want some form of illumination for when it gets dark. Whether you are night hiking, reading, going to the bathroom at night, or rummaging for gear in the dark, you're going to need some illumination. It's completely up to you how big or powerful a light you choose. Most people will have some kind of headlamp, but others will get by with nothing more than a small photon light that clips onto a hat, or can be worn on a thin line around their neck. It's best to choose something that's waterproof or water resistant. Don't forget to carry a couple sets of the corresponding spare batteries.

Watch

I never go anywhere without my watch. Watches can vary in function, features, and price, but regardless of what kind you get, it's always important to be able to tell time. Being able to keep track of time will help with estimating your distance in regards to your pace, which in turn keeps you from always guessing how far you've gone and checking your maps. Depending on the watch you get, they can also contain thermometers, altimeters, barometers, depth meters, compasses, GPS, plus many other functions. At the very least you should be able to keep track of time out there without relying on your cell phone. As always, it's completely a matter of personal preference.

Final Word on Electronics

The aforementioned are the most common electronic essentials, but many people will take extra or less. Those extras may come in the form of Kindles, tablets, cameras, GPS's, IPods, portable speakers, portable radios, etc. Take whatever you want, but remember... you will be carrying it.

Survival/Repair

This category contains items you might request if you were stranded on a desert island. While you're not really "surviving" on the Appalachian Trail, there are some survival type items that can make life much easier, or save you some headache while you're out there.

Knife

It's always smart to carry a knife when you go into the woods. Some people go overboard, carrying enormous survival/defense knives with them. These are for the most part unnecessary, and you'll never get your full use out of them. You can get by with a small knife, or multi tool Swiss Army Knife just fine. You'll only need it for opening things, shaving bark, cutting certain foods, or cutting cordage. If your knife is three to four ounces or less, (including the sheath if applicable), then you're in good shape. Neck Knives are always a practical choice.

Lighter/Flint

Having a lighter is a "must." If you plan to cook, you'll need it to light your stoves, or start fires. In the case that your lighter gets wet or runs out of fuel, you could carry a small flint as well. While I never carried a flint, and took very good care of my lighter, it's a good idea to carry two small lighters, just in case something happens to one of them. A flint is a fun option for people who really want to test their fire making skills, plus it comes in handy in the event of an absolute emergency. Having said all that, you will be perfectly fine out there without a flint. It's more of a fun novelty on the trail than anything else. Always store your lighter someplace dry, where water and moisture cannot get to it; preferably in a dry storage bag.

Cordage/Rope

It's always good to have some form of light but strong cordage on you. The most common type you'll find is 550 Paracord. It's cheap, strong, easy to find, and its uses are endless. You can hang food away from animals, hang gear away from animals, hang your laundry, strap things to your pack, you name it. Most people get by with twenty feet of 550 cord, but some bring between twenty and fifty feet. Still, many people do the hike without any kind of cordage, or a much smaller amount; it's totally up to you.

Duct Tape

Duct tape is rugged. It's tried and tested and has proved its usefulness again and again. Nobody carries a full roll, but instead carefully unwind several feet (or however much) around a trekking pole or other cylindrical object; this way you'll have some in case you need it for whatever reason. Athletic tape can fill the same need, but duct tape is wider, stronger, and can be used for both injures, repairs, as well as reinforcements with great results. It is heavy, so don't go overboard with how much you take, if any.

Super Glue

Super Glue isn't a must, but it does come in handy with some repairs and injuries. If you get cracks in your feet, small blisters, cuts, or punctures, Super Glue helps to fill them, sealing the wound from outside bacteria and preventing further bleeding. I found it particularly helpful when my feet began to crack. Don't worry about any kind of poisoning; believe it or not, super glue was originally invented for sealing wounds.

Sewing Supplies

These are completely optional, depending on whether you even know how to sew, or if you even want to sew. They come in handy for various gear repairs and reinforcements, but if you were desperate, you could also use it to stitch yourself.

Bug Spray

Bug spray will help up to a point out there. I gave up on it because most of the situations where I found myself needing it, it was practically useless. While it may stave off some of the bugs, it won't keep all of them away. Plus, hiking for days on end with a mixture of dirt, sweat, and bug spray chemicals caked on your body is less than pleasant. Take some if this is a big issue, but I found it to be almost useless when the bugs get really bad; sometimes you simply have to grit it out.

Final Word on Any and All Gear

Due to the fact that I intended this book to have a very nonpartisan stance regarding gear, you may find some of this information very overwhelming. I've given you a lot of general information on a multitude of different types of gear without giving specific brands or models. This is because the world of backpacking gear, as well as the companies who make it, are constantly changing and evolving. Gear becomes obsolete or modified, while some companies may disappear, or better companies may rise to take other's places as the leading manufacturers of certain products. The world of backpacking is ever changing, so to throw out specific names, brands, or models would be a disservice to you, the reader. Also, I am not endorsed by any backpacking companies; therefore, my recommendations are neutral, and for the most part unbiased.

Having read all of the information I've provided, without really knowing where to begin applying it, may seem frustrating and/or daunting. In an effort to keep this book somewhat brief, while not saturating it with an abundance of mind boggling name brands and opinions, I will leave that part up to the Internet. There are countless excellent blogs and websites specifically dedicated to the Appalachian Trail, long distance hiking, gear reviews, etc.; you simply have to type in what you're looking for and you will immediately be swamped with information. Use some of the general knowledge I've provided to narrow your searches, weed through information, as well as the options you'll encounter everywhere else; then make the perfect choice for you.

-Hear the Challenge-

Chapter 7

Appalachian Trail Thru-Hiker Slang/Jargon

While you're out there, you're going to be hearing a lot of words and terms you've never heard before, or are unfamiliar with. I've compiled a list of some of the most common and not so common hiking/thru-hiking terms and jargon you might hear or use while on the trail. I don't have absolutely everything listed here, but I've got most of it (in no particular order). Many people end up creating their own terms for certain things. Enjoy.

-Trail magic: Kind deeds from thoughtful strangers in the form of food, rides, favors, or anything that impacts your hike positively.
-Thru-hike(r): The official spelling and term that describes completing the entire length of a long trail in a single attempt. To be considered a single attempt, the hike must be completed the same year it was started. Some believe in order to be a thru-hike, you cannot leave the trail for an extended period of time, regardless of whether you complete the entire thing in a year or not.
-Thorough Hike: This is a term that refers to completing a "thru-hike" in a slightly slower than average time, due to intentionally taking your time to "smell the roses" and enjoy yourself.
Aqua blazing: This refers to traveling by water while on your thru-hike. The most popular aqua blazing area is in Virginia on the Shenandoah River, just west of the Shenandoah National Park. You will miss the entire 100 or so miles of the National Park if you Aqua Blaze here.
Brown blazing: This refers to hiking off the trail in search of a place to defecate.
Yellow blazing/ Yellow blazer: This refers to an individual that skips portions of the trail by driving around or past them.
Blue blazing: This is the act of hiking the blue blazed trails. These are trails that branch off of the AT, but aren't the AT. They lead to

shelters, water sources, towns, privies, roads, around mountains, and bypass dangerous terrain sometimes.

Pink blazing: This refers to a male or female following their partner on the trail. Sometimes (most of the time) this term refers to a guy that follows a girl down the trail in hopes of getting lucky. It can also refer to a guy "getting lucky" out on the trail.

Green blazing: This has two meanings. It can refer to cutting straight through the forest in an attempt to bypass switchbacks or bends in the trail. It can also refer to hiking while simultaneously smoking marijuana, or hiking while "high."

Deli blazing: This term mostly applies to the New York section of the trail. There are so many delis near the trail in New York that it's called "Deli Blazing" when you stop at each one of them to eat or resupply.

Stump bear: A large tree stump, or uprooted tree that you momentarily mistake for a bear when you first see it. This is usually accompanied by a slight heart attack, depending on who you are and how close the stump bear is when you notice it.

Stick snake: Simply put, it's a stick that looks like a snake when you first see it, or notice it in your peripheral vision. Depending on who you are, this can give you a bigger heart attack than a stump bear.

Zero: Also, referred to as a "Zero Day," hikers say "Zero" for short. It refers to a day in which you hike zero miles. Zero basically means you took the day off for whatever reason.

Nero: Pronounced "Near-O," this is a shortened term for "Nero Day," or a day in which you hike almost zero miles. Depending on who you are, a Nero Day will usually constitute hiking less than five or ten miles.

Vitamin "i": This is what "Ibuprofen" is referred to out on the trail. This is the go to medicine for most people when they are "hurting" or in pain.

Vitamin M: The "M" stands for Marijuana. When people smoke marijuana in attempt to dull any hiking related pain, or in an

attempt to relax at night, it's referred to as "Vitamin M."
Hiker Medicine: This is a broad term that can refer to anything that makes you feel better, dulls any pain, or improves your hiking (in your own opinion) in one form or another. Ibuprofen, Marijuana, alcohol, and most other substances are sometimes referred to as Hiker/Hiking Medicine.
Pack in: This term refers to hiking an item into a town, shelter, or campsite. It could be food, trash, alcohol, anything.
Pack out/Packing out: This refers to hiking an item out of a town, shelter, campsite, or the wilderness in general. It could be food, trash, alcohol, anything.
Blazes: Rectangular shapes painted on trees, rocks, roads, posts, buildings, etc., to mark trails and paths. They can come in all different colors, but the blazes marking the AT are white.
Bald: A low elevation mountain surrounded by forest, yet devoid of trees on the crown. They're often covered in meadows, and offer great views of the surrounding landscape.
Baseball bat shelter: Old style shelter construction in Maine where the floor is constructed of parallel logs, each with the diameters not much greater than a baseball bat.
Bear bag: A bag that hikers use to hang their food out of reach of bears and other wilderness critters.
Bear burrito: This is a term that refers to people that sleep in a hammock. The hammock being the tortilla of the burrito, and the hiker being its tasty contents. Sometimes sleeping bags are also referred to as bear burritos.
Blow down: A tree that falls across the trail as a result of being "blown down" in a storm.
Bog Bridge: A narrow wooden walkway that has been placed to protect sensitive wetlands. You encounter most of these in New Hampshire and Maine.
Bounce box: A mail drop type box containing seldom used necessities that is "bounced" ahead to a town where you think you might need the contents.

Bush whack: To hike where there is no marked trail
Trail-blaze: To "blaze" or make your own trail.
Cat hole: The hole you dig to burry your feces.
Caretaker: A person that maintains, as well as collects fees at certain shelter and campsites. Most common in New Hampshire and Maine.
Camel up/Cameling-up: The act of drinking lots of water, carrying extra water (or both), in anticipation of a long dry stretch of trail without water. This can also be done when you're in a hurry and don't want to take the time to stop and filter/collect water while on the way to wherever you're going.
Cairn: An easy to spot, manmade pile of rocks that serves as a trail marker. They are usually found above tree line. They are normally close enough to see the next one in heavy fog, and high enough to see above fallen snow.
Cowboy camp: This refers to camping out in the open without a shelter. Usually with nothing more than a pad and sleeping bag.
Double blaze: Two blazes, one above the other are an indication of an imminent turn or intersection in the trail. Offset double blazes indicate the direction of the turn by the offset of the top blaze. If the top blaze is offset to the right of the bottom blaze, then the trail is about to make a right turn.
Fence stiles: A set of wooden steps, or a ladder that helps you to climb over the fences of pastures and private lands the trail passes through.
Flip flop: A term used to signify a hiker that begins hiking in one direction, then at a later point decides to jump ahead and hike back in the opposite direction.
Gear head: A hiker that likes to talk about gear all the time, or a hiker that's very knowledgeable about different gear.
Gap: A low spot along a ridgeline.
Giardia: Officially known as Giardiasis, it's an infection of the lower intestines caused by an amoebic cyst, Giardia Lamblia. Giardia resides in water, so it's smart to always filter or treat any water you

collect. Symptoms include; stomach cramps, diarrhea, bloating, loss of appetite, and vomiting.
Food bag: A bag that you keep in your backpack that is specifically for storing your food.
Gorp: Acronym for "Good Ole Raisins and Peanuts, or anything similar.
Hicker: A person who is still trying to figure out the whole hiker/gear aspect, while out on the trail.
Hiker box: A box or cabinet that can be found at hostels, some hotels, and many other places where hikers can leave unwanted food and gear for anybody hiking behind them.
Hiker trash: This is an endearing term that thru-hikers use to describe themselves, as well as other thru-hikers out on the trail.
HYOH: An acronym for "Hike Your Own Hike." Simply meaning, do your own thing, don't worry about what others are doing, and don't let other people try to influence/affect the way that you hike the trail.
Knob: A prominent rounded hill or mountain.
LNT: Acronym for "Leave No Trace." Refers to leaving only footprints, and taking only photographs.

Lyme disease: A debilitating illness carried by small ticks.
Mail drop: A method of resupply while hiking. The boxes they are packaged in are usually prepared ahead of time, then mailed to the individual later on by relatives or friends. Usually timed to arrive in a town before the hiker gets there. They can be received at post offices, hotels, or hostels.
Maintainer: A volunteer that helps to maintain sections of the trail through organized trail maintenance programs of the ATC (Appalachian Trail Club).
Mountain money: Simply put...toilet paper.
Privy: A wooden outhouse usually found around shelters, except in Tennessee.

Purist: A hiker that wants to pass every single white blaze on the trail.

Ultra-Purist: A hiker that won't take bypasses or even walk around blown down trees if it means leaving the trail. A true ultra-purist can claim to have walked every single inch of the trail without ever having left it or missed even a miniscule section the size of the width of a tree.

Ridge runner: A person paid by a trail maintaining club or governmental organization to hike back and forth along a certain section of trail to educate hikers, enforce regulations, monitor trail and campsite use, as well as sometimes performing trail maintenance or construction duties.

Shelter: There are more than 200 shelters set up along the Appalachian Trail. They are usually nothing more than a three-sided wooden or stone building that's open to the elements on one side. Usually spaced out no more than a day's hike from each other, they normally reside near a reliable water source and will have a privy.

Shuttle: A ride from town to the trail head, or the trail head to town, usually for a fee.

Slack packing: This refers to hiking without a backpack, or hiking with a nearly empty or "slack pack."

NOBO: The name used to describe a Northbound Thru-Hiker.

SOBO: The name used to describe a Southbound Thru-Hiker.

Silk Blazing: This is what early risers tend to do. If you're the first person to begin hiking from a certain location in the morning, you'll be the first person to knock down all the spider webs that were strung across the trail the night before.

Switchback: A turn in the trail that takes a hiker 180-degrees in the opposite direction. They can usually be found on long climbs south of New England, in an effort to lessen the steepness of the climb.

Stealth camp: This refers to camping off the trail in areas that are

not shelters or designated campsites.
Trail Angel: A person that provides trail magic, or does any kind deed for a hiker.
Trail candy: A good looking man or woman.
Trailhead: Where the trail leaves a road crossing or parking lot.
Tree line: The point of elevation on a mountain above which the climate will no longer support tree growth.
Widow-maker: Limbs or whole trees that have partially fallen, but remain hung up overhead, posing a danger to anybody below.
Work for stay: Hostels, AMC huts, personal residences, and sometimes other places will allow hikers to do chores or work, in place of a fee for lodging.
Yogi-ing: The art of getting things (food, services, anything) for free, without directly asking for them.
Yoyo: Finishing a thru-hike, then immediately turning around and completing another in the opposite direction.
Trail name: A nickname given to you by your peers (or chosen by you), that you go by while hiking the trail.
Active hitch hiking: The art of hitchhiking while simultaneously walking in the direction of wherever you are trying to hitchhike to.
Register: A log book normally found at a shelter or trail head. Originally intended for rescuers to use for figuring out lost hikers last known location.

Chapter 8

Topographical - State and Regional Insight

This chapter pertains to each of the individual states. I will provide the approximate miles of trail that reside in each state, as well as my own personal impression of each state, in addition to some insight into the terrain, conditions, and other noteworthy tips. Remember, the length of the trail changes every year due to reroutes, added switchbacks, repurposing of land, etc. As a result, the miles per state will not always be exact.

All locations, miles, landmarks, or anything that I reference in this following chapter can be found or corroborated in what is called the "AWOL Guide." The official name of this guidebook is "The AT Guide," by David "AWOL" Miller, and serves as a handbook for hiking the Appalachian Trail. This is the most popular and detailed guide used by thru- hikers while on the trail, not including any online apps. The AWOL Guide contains elevations, distances, profiles of the terrain, maps of towns, phone numbers for businesses, addresses, GPS coordinates, and much more; it's an invaluable asset to hiking the trail.

If you are someone who would prefer to have no insight into the terrain that lies ahead of you, then I would suggest skipping this chapter altogether. Reading it will take nothing away from the journey itself, but once you're out there and familiar names pop up, you will be reminded of what you read in this chapter. If you were to skip this chapter, then you will essentially have a "clean slate" when it comes to having any kind of opinion or "heads up" regarding any terrain, hostels, landmarks, side trips, etc., that I include; this is just the way some people prefer it. If you do decide to read this chapter, then allow me to add this disclaimer. I wrote this based on my own perspective, my own experiences, and my own travels. I didn't see everything there was to see in regards to what lies around the trail and within the towns; I don't think anyone has. Some of what you will find in this chapter is fact, while other information is simply a matter of my own personal opinion which could be of use to someone who might value it. I urge you to explore as much as possible, create your own adventures, and find as much as there is to possibly be found out there...

Georgia:

Miles of trail: 76

My impression: Since I hiked northbound, Georgia was the first state I hiked through. This meant the learning curve was at its steepest while I was in this state. I associate Georgia with mountains of pain and frustration, as I'm sure many other hiker newbies do too. Although Georgia is a relatively short state, it felt like I was there forever. Once I got my trail legs and confronted more terrain throughout other states, I realized in hindsight that Georgia wasn't so bad...

Insights: If you start the trail in Georgia, you'll be starting in Amicalola State Park, around 50 miles north of Atlanta. You'll have the option to start near the top of Springer Mountain (about 1 mile away), or you can begin at the approach trail. The approach trail starts directly behind the Amicalola Welcome Center and stretches 8.5 miles before reaching the summit of Springer Mountain and the start of the official AT. While there are plenty of people who don't do the approach trail, there are just as many people who claim you're not a "real" thru-hiker if you don't complete the approach (since it was originally part of the AT back in the 1930's).

The approach trail will kick off with a set of 600 stairs climbing directly up the face of the Amicalola Waterfall before meandering through the woods, up and down various moderate climbs. It then ends with your final, longest climb of the approach trail up Springer Mountain and the start of the AT. Roots and rocks will abound in Georgia, and if starting in the early spring, you can be sure to encounter no shortage of mud and chilly nights.

Your first option to go into town will come at a road crossing called "Woody Gap," about 21 miles into the official trail (not including the approach). This road leads into the town of Suchess. The majority of hikers will bypass this town and continue on to a road crossing on the far side of Blood Mountain, called "Neels Gap," where an outfitter/hostel called "Mountain Crossings" can be found. The trail passes straight through Mountain Crossings, which is situated approximately 31 miles into the official trail from the summit of Springer Mountain. This outfitter is normally the first sign of civilization people see when first beginning the trail, and is a very popular area for thru hikers to quit the trail permanently (enjoy the tree of lost shoes). You will see a lot of people quit the trail in Georgia. The rest of the trail throughout this state has its ups and downs, as well as its fair share of challenging climbs, but nothing that stands out, or that is worth mentioning or warning you about. Having said that, for a first timer there will be plenty of climbs and areas you think are ridiculously challenging, but after finishing the whole trail, you'll look back on Georgia as gravy train.

North Carolina:

Miles of trail: 95

My impression: North Carolina was a huge morale boost, as it was the first of many state line crossings. You'll feel elated to cross into North Carolina, but the steepest climb of the trail thus far will come about a mile from the state line in the form of a mountain named Court House Bald. I found North Carolina to be more challenging terrain wise than Georgia, as the climbs were much longer.

Insights: While the condition of the trail in North Carolina is about the same as Georgia, the climbs are undoubtedly longer and the altitudes consistently higher. You will spend a longer time at higher altitudes in North Carolina/Tennessee than any other states. Since you will frequently spend prolonged periods above 4,000 and 5,000 feet, you'll encounter some very cold temperatures through both of these states in the spring time.

Nantahala Outdoor Center or "The NOC," will quite possibly be the most unique area that you pass through on the trail up to this point going north. Situated on the swift Nantahala River, it resides approximately 137 miles into the trail and contains an amazing outfitter, as well as picnic areas, a post office, a restaurant, lodgings, kayak - canoe and rafting excursions. The Smoky Mountains National Park is in North Carolina, and requires thru-hikers to purchase and carry a $20 permit.

The permit can only be filled out and purchased online, but you will also have to print it out. Nantahala Outdoor Center (the outfitter) has a computer upstairs just for this specific purpose. To avoid headaches, it's smart to get your permit taken care of while you're there.

After the NOC, Fontana Dam is normally the next town hikers come to. This town is the southern gateway into the Smoky Mountains. The resupply here is very expensive and limited; so many people have food mailed to them at this resort town. If you forgot to print out your Smokies permit at the NOC, you can call a shuttle to the Fontana Lodge and print one out there. There is a shelter right next to the trail called the "Fontana Hilton." It's a large shelter, situated on the shores of Fontana Lake, and has the first "on-trail" showers you will encounter going north.

The Smoky Mountains will be some of the most challenging climbs you'll encounter thus far, and the trail through the Smoky Mountain National Park itself will stretch for 71 miles. You'll climb the tallest mountain of the entire trail, Clingmans Dome. While in the Smoky Mountains, you'll also have the option to hitchhike into the famous town of Gatlinburg, TN.

After exiting Smoky Mountains National Park, you'll hike 30 more miles before the trail passes directly through the town of Hot Springs, NC. While the trail has passed through some seemingly populated areas before this, Hot Springs will be the first legitimate town the trail passes completely through. You'll literally walk straight down their main street full of different businesses, outfitters, restaurants, and stores where you can resupply. Shortly after the Smokies, but before reaching Hot Springs, you'll get to climb a mountain called Max Patch. The summit of this mountain is a "bald" (see Appalachian Trail terms in Chap. 7), and provides you with a 360- degree view of everything around you. On a clear day, you can see the entire Smoky Mountain range stretching back to the south, and Unaka Mountain far to the north. Max Patch is nicknamed the "crown jewel" of the AT.

You'll spend a decent time crossing between North Carolina and Tennessee throughout the main bulk of North Carolina. At many times, you may not be completely sure which state you're in. You'll continue to bounce between states until you cross another border into Tennessee, several miles before the town of Roan Mountain, TN. After you cross into Tennessee this final time, you'll stay there until you reach Virginia.

Tennessee:

***Miles of trail:* 287**

My impression: For me, Tennessee represented the "good ole' days" from the trail. Tennessee is the last state where you'll see the largest groups of thru-hikers. For some reason, a lot of people quit the trail at the first town in Virginia called Damascus. There were some challenging areas, but this is the state where people start coming into their own and really adapting to the trail. Tennessee really stuck out to me for its exceptionally lush forests, as well as an increased presence of Rhododendrons. I suppose this could have been unique to Tennessee, or simply a by-product of the time of year I passed through there. Overall, Tennessee left a good enough impression on me that if I had to choose any land locked state to live in - Tennessee would be my first choice.

Insights: While you're bouncing between North Carolina and Tennessee, there are a few highlights that fall definitively within Tennessee. Aside from Gatlinburg in the Smokies, the next noteworthy Tennessee town that you'll come to is Erwin. The trail doesn't pass through the heart of town, but right by a residential type area and a hostel situated on the banks of the Nolichucky River; right before crossing a bridge spanning the river and continuing north. The hostel does provide some food, but they also provide shuttles into downtown, where a Wal-Mart can be found. The Nolichucky River offers some great opportunities for sunbathing, as well as swimming. There are also some amazing stealth campsites along the river, on the far north side of the bridge, on the right side along the shoreline.

The terrain is no worse than what you'll encounter earlier in the trail, but has its fair share of unique ups and downs. After Erwin, the next major climb is the famous Roan Mountain. However, Unaka Mountain may prove a slight challenge before you reach Roan. Roan Mountain, at more than 6,000 feet in altitude requires a more than

2,000 foot climb to reach the summit. The first half of that climb is relatively easy, while the second half is quite steep and rocky. I heard they may have added more switchbacks since I passed through, making it easier, but I'm not sure. Roan Mountain is also home to the highest shelter on the AT, at 6,194 feet above sea level. The climb down the north side of Roan Mountain is relatively easy and unchallenging.

About seven miles after the summit of Roan Mountain is a shelter called Overmountain Shelter. It's a large barn that's been converted to a shelter, and while I never stayed there, it's many people's favorite shelter on the AT.

You'll later make the long climbs up Little Hump Mountain, and Hump Mountain before crossing one more border that will keep you in Tennessee until you reach Virginia. You'll descend Hump Mountain to a road that will take you into the towns of Roan Mountain, TN, or Elk City, NC. I personally would recommend not missing the Town of Roan Mountain, due to the presence of a restaurant called "Bob's Dairyland." They serve an enormous burger here called the "Holy Cow Burger" that I couldn't get enough of. It's a starving thru-hiker's dream come true.

The remainder of Tennessee after the Town of Roan Mountain is relatively unchallenging, but beautiful terrain. There are a couple good climbs and descents, one of them being the joint jarring descent down to Laurel Falls (very big waterfall!), and the climb up Pond Flats Mountain. After climbing over Pond Flats, you'll reach the huge Watauga Lake, near a road that leads into Hampton, TN. If the weather is nice, the Watauga Lake shore is an amazingly beautiful location to hang out, swim, and spend a day. The next 40 miles to Virginia, after Pond Flats Mountain are relatively easy and unchallenging. During this 40-mile stretch you'll get to experience your first crossing of a cow pasture. Whether there will be cows in it when you pass thru, you're guess is as good as mine.

Virginia:

Miles of trail: 550

My impression: Virginia seemed to never end, and took a toll on my morale due to the feeling of not getting anywhere (Virginia Blues). I remember everyone gossiping about how easy Virginia was, and I bought into that hype. The southern half of Virginia was extremely easy by comparison to the states south and north of it. Not quite as easy as it was made out to be, but much easier than other places. While most people say that all of Virginia is easy, you'll find the northern half of this state to be quite challenging and arduous in many areas, especially in the heat of the summer. There are plenty of big climbs with a good mix of different types of terrain. As much as I began to resent Virginia towards the end of my foray there; looking back on it, it was much easier and enjoyable than the majority of the terrain encountered in further states. I even recall missing Virginia not long after leaving. It's a state that most people become very frustrated with, and in that cloud of frustration, you take many unique things about Virginia for granted while there. In hindsight, you realize Virginia was absolutely wonderful.

Insights: Out of all the other states, Virginia seemed to have the most ticks, the most snakes, the most bears, deer, as well as other forms of wildlife. Perhaps it was due to the fact that I was there in the late spring and early summer, but Virginia seemed to be teeming with more wildlife than any other state.

Damascus is a town you'll reach only three miles into Virginia. The trail will wind its way all through the town before following the Virginia Creeper Trail (famous bike path made from an old railroad bed) and branching back up into the mountains. Damascus is billed as "Trail Town USA," and boasts more thru-hiking permanent residents than any other town. The locals here take excellent care of thru-hikers, and there is no shortage of outfitters, restaurants, hostels, and friendly people willing to do you favors or help you out. In mid to late May, a huge festival known as "Trail Days" takes place over the course of three days; normally Friday, Saturday, and Sunday. Thousands of people attend this event; current thru-hikers, previous thru-hikers, hopeful thru-hikers, hiking enthusiasts, regular people, and gear distributers/companies. There will be merrymaking, food, drink, dancing, bonfires, shows, live music, and a plethora of free stuff and raffle prizes. Lots of different gear distributors/manufacturers (many of them cottage industry) attend trail days to give away thousands of dollars-worth of free gear. Many thru-hikers, no matter where they are on the trail when the festival begins, hitch rides forward or backwards to Damascus in order to attend. With so many people there, finding a ride back to wherever you left off is relatively easy.

Virginia is such a long state for the trail, I couldn't possibly cover everything about it without writing a second book. I'm going to limit this section to the major highlights of Virginia, as well as some of my own personal highlights that I feel are worth mentioning or recommending.

Throughout Virginia, you'll walk through more cattle pastures, farm lands, and private properties than any other state; frequently having to climb fence stiles and ladders that take you in and out of pastures. The livestock regard you with a curious indifference most of the time, but some of the younger cows will occasionally approach you to investigate.

Not long after leaving Damascus, you'll reach a famous stretch of trail known as the Grayson Highlands. This section is home to a large population of wild ponies. The ponies are wild in the sense that nobody takes care of them as they range freely throughout the highlands; however, they seem tame at times due to their friendly curiosity and willingness to approach humans. Most of the time the interactions are docile, but people do sometimes get bit by the ponies, especially if the pony gets frustrated with you for not providing food. The terrain through parts of the highlands is quite rocky, so be very vigilant; the highlands are where I fractured my ankle. You will also cross the 500- mile mark of the trail while passing through this section.

Not too far outside of the Grayson Highlands is a shelter called "Partnership Shelter." It's near a road leading into the towns of Marion and Sugar Grove. There is a shower at this shelter, and you can have pizzas delivered here as well.

My own personal highlight that I found worthy of mentioning is a spot called Dismal Falls. It requires a short three tenths of a mile trek off the AT, and is situated about twenty miles north up the trail from the town of Bland. Dismal Falls is a camping utopia. There's a beautiful waterfall, smooth limestone rock everywhere to lie out on, or cowboy camp on, tons of amazing camp spots, as well as a huge population of crawfish that can be gathered up and boiled (if you're savvy enough). You can camp above or below the falls, or you can also find a small dirt road nearby. If you follow this dirt road down the mountain, it will lead you to a small convenience store that sells hot food, as well as a plethora of other things.

There is a hostel that many people agree is one of the best hostels on the entire trail. It's called Woods Hole Hostel, and I greatly enjoyed the atmosphere and layout of the entire place. It's basically a self-sufficient little farm, with all the food grown and harvested at the farm; even the meats. Woods Hole resides about thirteen miles north of Dismal Falls, or 33 miles north of Bland.

Dragon's Tooth is another cool highlight you'll encounter just before the town of Catawba. It requires a very short trek off the main trail to get to, but you won't regret going to see it, or possibly climb it. After leaving Dragon's Tooth, you'll encounter the most treacherous, technical rocky descent of the entire trail up until this point, as well as until you reach New Hampshire. You'll reach a road crossing shortly after, which can take you to such places as "Four Pines Hostel;" which is a free hostel, as well as one of my top three favorites of the entire trail. You will also find a restaurant called "The Home Place." It's an all you can eat southern style restaurant with perhaps the best "AYCE" (All You Can Eat) style food you'll encounter on the entire trail. Both of these places are within walking distance of where the trail passes over this road, but you can always call the shuttle at Four Pines.

The terrain is "so-so" from Catawba on, but you'll soon encounter MacAfee's Knob, the most photographed spot on the entire AT. It's a cliff at the top of a mountain that gives you one of the most spectacular views of the entire southern section of the trail. Six miles from MacAfee is a spot called the "Tinker Cliffs." There is a gorgeous view here, as well as an ideal spot to camp, provided the weather is good.

Up until a shelter named "Bryant Ridge," Virginia has been mostly pleasant and not too terrible - terrain wise. This shelter resides approximately 756 miles into the total trail and would mark the starting point for what I would deem the most challenging section of Virginia. From Bryant Ridge shelter until the town of Waynesboro (a span of about a hundred miles), I can honestly say is the hardest stretch in all of this state. This is due to the seemingly never ending stream of long climbs and descents, as well as the fact that it's usually the middle of summer when the majority of people pass through here. Besides a short stretch prior to Waynesboro, this section will be a collection of long and short steep climbs.

You'll enter Shenandoah National Park directly after Waynesboro. Many people call Shenandoah the "Disney Land" of the trail. The trail travels through the park for just over a hundred miles, and comprises the most leisurely hiking you'll encounter so far of the journey; it almost feels like a vacation. There are restaurants/souvenir shops called "Waysides" throughout the park, as well as camp stores and camp sites for RVs and car camping. You can resupply at these locations, but it's fairly expensive.

Shenandoah has more black bears per square mile than any other national or state park in the country. I saw eighteen bears while I was there, and nearly every other hiker saw their fair share as well. Besides bears, there are abundant deer, rattlesnakes, black rat snakes, and ticks; more so than many other parts of Virginia. There are a couple good climbs, but the entire trail through Shenandoah is well graded and smooth.

With the completion of Shenandoah, you'll be nearly done with Virginia, save for one last extra challenging section. This section is called the Virginia Rollercoaster, and I would say it's probably the most physically challenging short section of all Virginia. The Rollercoaster stretches about thirteen miles and is comprised of about twelve different climbs, each one directly after the other. The climbs are short and steep, normally never more than several hundred feet each (sometimes a little more), but their frequency and steepness make them all the more challenging. The final leg of the rollercoaster will dump you right onto the 1,000-mile mark of the trail. Completing the entire rollercoaster in a day is a fun, but very doable challenge. I did them as the last half of a twenty-nine-mile day. There is an impressive hostel called "Bear's Den Hostel" towards the end of the rollercoaster. A little less than 20 miles past Bear's Den is West Virginia, as well as the end of your Virginia Blues.

West Virginia:

Miles of trail: 4

My impression: With only four miles of the entire trail residing in West Virginia, there really isn't too much to talk about. Despite how short this state is, I spent the better part of three days here, in and around the town of "Harpers Ferry." During this time, I was able to sleep under an apocalyptic train bridge (by accident), sleep on the shores of the Potomac River, shelter from a horrendous storm in a train station, be discriminated against for looking like a bum-by some locals in a neighboring town, and met the manager of a restaurant who believed in dark magic and claimed to be an ordained priest of Satan. Little West Virginia packed quite a punch for me.

Insights: When people who thru-hike the Appalachian Trail think of West Virginia, they think of the historical town of Harpers Ferry. That's pretty much all there is to the trail in West Virginia, besides an awesomely huge bridge that crosses the Shenandoah River, and a long footbridge that crosses the Potomac into Maryland. Harpers Ferry is the unofficial halfway point of the trail, but is also home to the Appalachian Trail Conservancy (ATC) - official headquarters. You can sign in here, get your picture taken, and register your starting date, as well as the date you reached Harpers Ferry with the ATC. This information will go into a giant binder for the year that you thru- hiked, along with everyone else who made it there.

Harpers Ferry doesn't have much in the way of resupply, and what they do have costs an arm and a leg; many people have food mail-dropped to them here. There are plenty of old buildings to look at, as well as an excellent selection of different restaurants and vendors. Since Harpers Ferry is really more of a tourist town, the prices for everything are exorbitant. I will admit, the BBQ and ice cream in Harper's Ferry is second to none anywhere else on the trail.

West Virginia is also a crucial part to a thru-hiking challenge/tradition. That challenge is called the "Four State Challenge," which consists of hiking in, as well as through four different states within a 24-hour period. It starts at the border of Virginia and West Virginia, stretching across West Virginia, then Maryland, and ending at the border of Maryland and Pennsylvania. If accomplished, you will have hiked in or through all four states, which amounts to a 44 mile stretch of trail, in less than 24 hours. Many people accomplish this challenge, but it's not for everyone.

Maryland:

Miles of trail: 40

My impression: Out of all of the states on the Appalachian Trail, I would have to say that Maryland had the smallest impact/ impression on me overall. I never went into any towns in Maryland, and the terrain was never challenging enough to really take note of. It was simply just a short stretch that seemed to fly by with nothing overly notable besides a few really good views and one short but tough section towards the end. To many thru-hikers, Maryland is simply the prelude to the dreaded Pennsylvania.

Insights: Maryland is a very short state, so you won't be here very long. Unlike West Virginia's Harpers Ferry, Maryland doesn't really have anything to distract and hold you in one place. The terrain is relatively easy, with a few decent but not very difficult climbs, as well as several stretches of moderately challenging boulder fields. The most difficult stretch of Maryland comes a couple miles from the border of Pennsylvania. This stretch is nothing more than a jumble of large rocks and a steep climb that you'll have to ascend and descend. The worst of the rocks is on the descent, but upon completion you'll have a smooth trek into Pennsylvania.

The border for Maryland and Pennsylvania lies within the vicinity of PenMar Park. This is a huge park full of gazebos, picnic areas, jungle gyms, stages for live music, and kiosks for foods vendors. In the summer time (usually on the weekends) you can find the park thriving with activity and live music. This state crossing also signifies your crossing of the Mason Dixon Line. The Mason Dixon line is what separates the southern half of the country from the northern half of the country. Say goodbye to sweet tea.

Pennsylvania:

Miles of trail: 230

My impression: Pennsylvania is perhaps the most infamous state of the entire trail, if not infamously equal to New Hampshire. You learn to fear the rocks in Pennsylvania long before you get there, or perhaps before you even start the trail, depending on how much research you've done into the different states or books you've read. I dreaded Pennsylvania with a sort of nervous anticipation. I was excited for the potential challenges of the Pennsylvania terrain, but nervous of their equally potential consequences. In the end, I found this state to have some of the friendliest, most generous people of the entire trail. I also found it to have the worst, most painful types of rocks, out of any other state on the trail. I would certainly have to say that Pennsylvania was my least favorite state to hike through, but I wouldn't have it any other way.

Insights: While the whole of Pennsylvania tends to get a bad rap, it's a classic case of several rotten apples spoiling the bunch. Southern Pennsylvania is an absolute breeze. Much like Shenandoah, you'll feel like you're taking a vacation from your vacation. There are little to no climbs, and the infamous rocks have yet to show themselves. There are a couple climbs here and there, but for the most part, you're walking along ridges. The only time you have bigger ups and downs are when you're descending towards gaps and roads that lead into towns; even then they're nothing to squawk about. The information about the climbs holds true for the vast majority of Pennsylvania, with the exception of a few spots that I'll mention, along with where the worst of the rocks begin.

About nineteen miles into Pennsylvania you'll hit Caledonia State Park. Within view, but a short distance off the trail, is a pool area with a concession stand that makes for an awesome spot to: go for a swim, order some hot food, as well as mingle with car campers and other state park visitors. Between Caledonia State Park and the town of Boiling Springs, you'll pass the numerical halfway point of the trail, as well as Pine Grove Furnace State Park. There is a convenience store in Pine Grove Furnace that is home to the "Half Gallon Challenge." The challenge is to eat a half gallon of ice cream as fast you can with only a tiny wooden paddle spoon.

Not far after Pine Furnace, you'll hike directly through the beautiful quaint town of Boiling Springs approximately 57 miles into Pennsylvania. Right before you hit Boiling Springs, you'll enjoy a challenging six-mile section of small, rollercoaster type climbs that are strewn with large boulders that you'll weave between, and stride across. This area is called the "Rock Maze," and is most challenging towards the beginning of the rollercoaster stretch. The last mile and a half into Boiling Springs will be a completely flat walk through fields and along small roads. If I recommended anything in Boiling Springs, it would be "Anile's Pizza." This was the best pizza I found on the trail up until this point. You can also find the ATC's Mid Atlantic Regional Office here (the trail will go right by it).

There will be a 25 mile stretch between the towns of Boiling Springs and Duncannon that might possibly be the easiest stretch of the entire Appalachian Trail. There are two easy climbs spaced out throughout this stretch, but other than that, it's almost completely flat with grass or hard packed dirt and gently rolling hills at the steepest. Between the last climb of this 25-mile section and your descent into Duncannon, there are a few rocky spots that might get your attention, as well as a few more on the descent; these are nothing worth fretting about.

The greatest Highlight of Duncannon is a hotel called "The Doyle." This hotel is famous for being bad, and it's a tradition for thru-hikers to stay there when passing through. It's bad in the sense that the accommodations are terrible; it's dirty, full of bugs/spider webs; each floor shares a bathroom, paint is cracking and peeling, etc. Bottom line is... as a thru-hiker, you'll love this place. They love hikers, and the food in the downstairs bar is to die for. Across the street from The Doyle is a little breakfast joint called "Goodies," which is home to a pancake eating challenge. I don't know what the challenge is up to now, but when I passed through, all you had to do was finish six of their monster pancakes to win it. Duncannon also marks one of the longest road walks you'll ever have on the trail. You'll walk along roads through the town for over three miles before crossing the great Susquehanna Bridge, then cross a highway before tackling a decent climb back onto a ridge.

After Duncannon, I found most of the rest of Pennsylvania to be very overgrown in many sections. I don't know if it was simply the nature of the trail from that point on, or if trail maintenance crews hadn't been by in a while; either way, the vegetation was often thick on all sides. Myself and many other hikers got poison ivy between Duncannon and the Pennsylvania/New Jersey border.

Pennsylvania continues its mostly easy terrain up until a shelter called the "501 Shelter." As a side note, this shelter resides near a road where you can have food delivered to you. On a more important note, directly after this shelter is where the infamous rocks of Pennsylvania rear their ugly faces, not letting up until further into New Jersey. The rocks will mostly take on the form of sharp, jagged protuberances, rising out of the dirt as parts of larger rocks buried underneath. There will be every type of rock you can imagine throughout the rest of Pennsylvania, but it's the partially buried ones that cause the most pain and grief for your feet. Every now and then you'll get stretches of smooth ground, but they will be short lived. Many of the ascents and descents you make from here on will be over jumbles of rocks.

Going north, the descent into the town of Port Clinton is easily the steepest and most challenging descent in all of Pennsylvania. Separated by a river and bridge, the towns of Port Clinton and Hamburg are practically touching each other. Hamburg has an enormous selection of restaurants and other businesses, as well as an enormous Cabellas Outfitter store.

The most significant attractions of the trail in all of Pennsylvania are "The Pinnacle," and an area called "Knife's Edge." The Pinnacle requires about a tenth of a mile side hike to reach, and offers what is considered the best view in all of Pennsylvania. Since Pennsylvania is mostly ridge walking with the trail almost never reaching an altitude of two thousand feet; there aren't many spectacular views. There certainly is a fair share of beautiful views and sights, but nowhere near the frequency in other states, adding to the monotony.

The trail will pass directly over the Knifes Edge, and although some parts are daunting and challenging, it's so unique to anything else you've seen up until now, you will enjoy it. The Knifes Edge only stretches for a couple hundred yards at most, but is comprised of a naturally formed, narrow wall of jumbled boulders and rocks that you pick your way across. My best advice, "Don't fall!"

The final and most challenging climb in Pennsylvania is the ascent out of Lehigh Gap where you cross a road that gives you the option to go into the towns of Palmerton or Walnutport. For a northbound hiker, this will be the steepest climb you've encountered on the trail to date, requiring quite a bit of hand over hand scrambling, as well as pulling yourself up and over rocks. While challenging, this is a nice change of pace from what you've been dealing with before. At the top of this climb is a pleasant stretch of smooth trail that last for several miles before turning rocky again. The rocks will continue in all of their forms until you reach the town of Delaware Water Gap, on the shores of Delaware River, near the New Jersey border.

New Jersey:

Miles of trail: **72**

My impression: Overall, I hold a fairly neutral stance on New Jersey. I didn't love it, I didn't hate it, and I didn't see anything that really made me go "WOW!" The best part of New Jersey was simply knowing that you were no longer in Pennsylvania.

Insights: Terrain wise, New Jersey isn't too difficult. The rocks from Pennsylvania sporadically continue until you're finished with High Point

State Park, around forty-five miles into the state. The rocks are nowhere near as bad as they were in Pennsylvania, but there are a few short stretches that get you thinking.

One of the most leisurely miles of the entire trail takes place on a wooden boardwalk that crosses over top of a swamp within the final 11 miles of New Jersey. While there are almost zero big climbs in New Jersey, the two biggest and most challenging take place on either side of this boardwalk. Prior to the boardwalk is a moderately challenging series of small climbs over Pochuck Mountain. After the boardwalk, there is a decently challenging climb up Wawayanda Mountain. After Wawayanda, the rest of New Jersey is a mall walk until you reach New York.

New York:

Miles of trail: 88

My impression: When most people think of New York, they think of New York City. They don't think of a state full of waterfalls, lakes, and some of the most beautifully challenging terrain our country has to offer. I didn't know what to expect from New York, but after having completed it, this state solidified itself as one of my top favorites of the entire trail. Far more challenging and beautiful than you'd think it would be, I found this state to be a pleasant surprise.

Insights: While I would consider the entire state of New York to be filled with its fair share of challenging terrain, there is no doubt the most challenging of that terrain comes within the first thirty-five miles, ending with the completion of West Mountain.

Going north, within the first six miles of New York, you'll reach a road leading into the towns of Bellvale and Greenwood Lake. If your turn west on this road towards Bellvale, within half a mile you will reach an amazingly delicious ice cream shop called "Bellvale Farms." On a hot day, I highly recommend it; hell, I recommend it on any day.

The terrain throughout the first thirty-five miles or so of New York is very rocky. It's not a jagged type rock, but more of giant boulders and coarse granite climbs. The climbs themselves are not big at all, but their frequency and steepness are enough to keep you from maintaining any kind of quick pace. The challenging nature of this terrain is almost certain to catch you off guard. After dealing with long stretches of relatively flattish terrain since Maryland, the curve ball thrown at you by New York is sure to have you huffing and puffing once again.

My favorite stretch of New York would undoubtedly be everything within the confines of Harriman State Park; which starts about eighteen miles into the state itself. My best advice; take your time through here, enjoy it, and camp wherever you get the urge to camp. Harriman was one of the most beautiful stretches of trail I ever saw, and gorgeous locations to camp or take breaks seemed to be endless. Not far into Harriman you will encounter a stretch of trail called the "Lemon Squeezer." It's a narrow crevice of rock that stretches for approximately thirty yards; it's so tight, many have to take their packs off in order to "squeeze through," or avoid damaging them.

The closest the trail passes from New York City is thirty miles. At the end of Harriman State Park, you'll make a challenging climb up West Mountain. On the summit of this mountain is a shelter called "West Mountain Shelter" that requires a half mile hike down a side trail. The location of West Mountain Shelter affords a perfect view of the Hudson River, as well as the New York City sky line, thirty miles away. It's absolutely gorgeous, especially at night.

Directly after West Mountain is Bear Mountain, and while it's a long climb, it's not nearly as steep as the one up West Mountain. I kid you not, but at the top of Bear Mountain there are snack and drink machines - enjoy! After getting over Bear Mountain, the trail will pass directly through a small zoo (admission is free for thru-hikers), then pass over the Bear Mountain Bridge that spans the Hudson River. After Bear Mountain, Bear Mountain State Park, and Bear Mountain Bridge, the rest of New York is still challenging (but not nearly as challenging as those first thirty-five miles). The terrain is mostly the same as what you have already gone through earlier in NY, just not as severe.

One thing you will notice about New York, besides the frequency of short but steep climbs, is the frequency of road crossings. You cross a road or multiple roads at least every ten miles or less. The upside to these road crossings is they're usually within the vicinity of establishments where you can get something to eat. These establishments tend to be delis more often than not, and you will encounter them near the trail throughout New York, but mostly in the second half.

Connecticut:

Miles of trail: 52

My impression: Connecticut was a state that I looked forward to with an optimistic curiosity. Rumors swirled around this state, mostly about the people who called it home. Those rumors were a mixture of positive and negative experiences. Connecticut is branded as somewhat of a "snobby" state, filled with rich, arrogant, Connecticans. Some people told stories of being snubbed or unwelcome at certain establishments throughout the few towns you encounter in this section. Others told stories of immeasurable hospitalities showered upon them in the form of stays in private, multimillion dollar mansions that resided on mountainsides or the shores of lakes; all the while given free run of the premises and fun toys such as jet skis, boats, golf carts, four wheelers, and swimming pools. Yes, the intrigue with Connecticut swirls around its people, not its terrain.

I had no negative experiences in Connecticut. I was treated kindly and respectfully, and although I never stayed in any mansions, I personally found the people to be more than friendly, charitable, and likeable. The terrain was nothing to write home about; however, there are a handful of climbs that work up a good sweat, but nothing harder or as hard as what you encountered early on in New York. Connecticut will fly by in a few days or less; many even attempt the entire state in twenty- four hours. The most negative aspect of Connecticut was undoubtedly their mosquito problem throughout the summer. To compound the problem of the mosquitoes, campfires are not allowed on the trail in Connecticut. Fires are about the only way to keep bugs away at night, so with the absence of fire, most will go straight to bed when it gets dark in an effort to get away from the biting insects.

Insights: The trail throughout Connecticut is for the most part very well graded and well maintained. There is very little rocky terrain to deal with overall, and the climbs are not overly steep or long.

Easily the most challenging part in all of Connecticut is the descent down St. Johns Ledges to the Housatonic River. This is the rockiest part in all of Connecticut, with a very sheer, bone jarring descent over large rocky steps. You encounter this descent around sixteen miles into the state.

All the towns in Connecticut are in close proximity to the trail, or have the trail skirting through, or right by them. You can visit almost every town here without ever really needing to hitchhike. The town of Falls Village is one of the towns the trail will wind straight through for a couple miles. Towards the end of your walk through the town, just before climbing back into the mountains, you'll pass the waterfall - "Great Falls" on your right. This will be the biggest waterfall you'll see since Virginia or earlier, and it's surrounded by smooth limestone. The falls themselves are in tiers, and there are many calm pools in which to submerge yourself and bathe. The smooth rock makes for an amazing spot to lie down and sun or take a nap.

The rest of the terrain isn't bad after Falls Village. You'll walk through the residential outskirts of the town of Salisbury before your last (biggest set of climbs) up Lions Head and Bear Mountain; the tallest mountain in Connecticut. There are a few steep spots on these two climbs, but nothing bad. The summit of Bear Mountain will be a pile of old rocks that used to be the base of a fire tower. The view is wonderful, and the altitude is above the "bug zone," affording you a nice spot to rest while not constantly swatting the air and yourself.

You will cross into Massachusetts about halfway down the descent from Bear Mountain. In my opinion, the descent down Bear Mountain and the crossing into Massachusetts is the most beautiful border crossing of the trail; streams, creeks, and little waterfalls abound everywhere.

Massachusetts:

Miles of trail: 90

My impression: Again, in my personal opinion, Massachusetts is the first challenging state in which every subsequent state gets progressively harder until you finish the entire trail. A few areas in the first half of Massachusetts gave me the impression of southern New York, due to the collection of steep but short climbs in rapid succession. Another personal observation of mine was that biting insects and mud increased about ten-fold in this state. I never endured more torture from mosquitoes anywhere else on the trail than I did in Massachusetts. Amongst thru-hikers it was dubbed "Mosquito-chusetts." Aside from the bugs, you'll encounter some of the longest climbs and descents since probably Virginia. Overall, I found the terrain more challenging than Connecticut, less challenging than southern New York, but psychologically tougher than both; mostly due to the increased mud and bugs. Of course, the mud and bugs could be relative to the time of year I passed through this state (July). That's all I have to go on as far as my personal impression.

Insights: Upon the gorgeous border crossing into Massachusetts, you will finish the rest of the mostly unchallenging descent of Bear Mountain before a long sloping climb up Mount Race. After a small descent down Race, you'll climb Mt. Everett, and while not a terribly long climb, it's the steepest climb you'll encounter since coming out of Lehigh Gap in Pennsylvania. The descent down Everett and the subsequent Mt. Bushnell is a fairly long one. I did it at night, which made it more challenging than it really is, but there was no shortage of rocks on this descent. After you reach the bottom, you will have about six miles of almost completely flat, grassy terrain. This is the easiest stretch in Massachusetts.

After the six-mile flat stretch, the following twenty miles after that is what I would consider the toughest stretch in all of Massachusetts, most akin to southern New York. Lots of short but steep climbs, with a few longer arduous climbs thrown in; no shortage of mud pits too. These harsher climbs stop at the town of Tyringham, and are then replaced with somewhat milder climbs (again, no shortage of mud), until you reach Mt. Greylock towards the end of Massachusetts.

Some of the greater highlights of Massachusetts, as well as some little pit stops that enrich the journey can be found not long after Tyringham. About seven miles after the road that leads into Tyringham, you'll reach a side trail that leads to a location called "Upper Goose Pond Cabin." The trail requires a half mile detour, but is well worth it. Besides the cabin, which always has a crew of caretakers, there is the beautiful Upper Goose Pond itself, which has an island in the middle that is reachable by available canoes. The water is crystal clear, as well as an excellent location for swimming, should the weather permit. You can stay in the cabin for a fee, or camp around it. Regardless of whether you stay in the cabin or not, you have the option to pay for any meals they might serve. It's a beautiful pit stop.

Approximately eleven miles after Upper Goose Pond, you'll cross a paved road called Washington Road. If you take a right on this road and walk about one hundred yards, you'll see a house on the left. This house is home to a woman called the "Cookie Lady." A sweet older couple lives here and the woman provides fresh cookies to any thru-hikers that stop by. You can get water from a spigot here, and also pick countless blue berries to pack out. The couple also allows you to camp overnight on their property, which is beautiful to say the least. They are quite advanced in age, so I have no idea how much longer they will remain a pit stop on the Appalachian Trail. At the very least, their property will become a landmark.

The trail will pass directly through the next town of Dalton about ten miles after Washington Road. There is a private residence that takes in hikers on Depot Street (first road you walk on when coming into town), but I found the best highlight of Dalton to be Mill Town Tavern. This little tavern had the best Buffalo wings I've ever had in my life; and some damn good pizza as well. Eight miles, as well as some moderate climbs and descents after Dalton, you'll walk straight through the town of Cheshire. Cheshire has a lot to offer, but I found the free hostel at St. Mary's Church to be the biggest highlight. Dunkin Doughnuts on the northern outskirts of town is also a nice stop.

When you finally leave Cheshire, you'll immediately begin climbing Mt. Greylock, the tallest mountain in Massachusetts. The climb itself is not too bad, but the descent is the longest one you've done since Virginia. On the summit of Greylock is an expensive lodge where you can stay or order food from. There is also an enormous memorial tower erected on the summit, as well as the most spectacular view across the Berkshires I believe you'll ever see in recent memory.

After the three-thousand-foot descent from Greylock, you'll enter a residential neighborhood and walk down a street before coming to a slightly busy road crossing. The town of Williamstown is to the left, while the town of North Adams is to the right. Both are within walking distance, but there is so much traffic that hitchhiking is a breeze. There are places to eat -galore; Williamstown has a Mexican restaurant called "Desperados" that offers free meals to thru hikers. The top of the somewhat challenging 1,600 foot climb out of these two towns will put you across the border into Vermont, as well as into more challenging terrain.

Vermont:

Miles of trail: 150

My impression: For me, Vermont was psychologically the toughest state, second only to Pennsylvania. I would say that Vermont is the state where you consistently begin climbing real mountains again on a daily basis. Due to the higher altitudes, you are consistently hiking. Vermont wasn't too bad when it came to bugs. However, Vermont was extremely bad with mud. Thru-hikers referred to this state as "VerMUD," and for good reason. Whatever mud was to be found in Massachusetts, Vermont had it beat by a country mile. There was no shortage of long, steep climbs that were mixtures of rocky steps or smooth dirt. It rained for a good portion of the time I was in Vermont, so it made the mud that much worse.

Other than the reintroduction of large, challenging climbs, you will notice something else about Vermont. The overall terrain and fauna will seem different to anywhere else. The dirt will seem different, and the abundance of small ponds all around the trail will increase. It's tough to pin down exactly what all the differences are, but not too far into Vermont, you will get the impression you have truly moved into a different region. Although very challenging in many areas, Vermont is merely a warm up to New Hampshire.

<u>Insights:</u> When you first get into Vermont, something you're going to become very familiar with is "bog bridges." You will have seen these before, but they start to show up in great abundance in Vermont, then even more in New Hampshire and Maine. A bog bridge is nothing more than one or two wooden planks or logs that have been nailed or bolted onto fallen logs, or bigger sections of treated wood. Their purpose is to protect sensitive wetlands, but I think the greater purpose is to prevent you from being swallowed up by the mud, never to be heard from again.

The first fourteen miles of Vermont aren't too bad in regards to climbs, as there really aren't many of them. It's mostly bog bridges, mud pits, and thick vegetation. After those fourteen-miles you'll reach a descent to a road that leads into your first Vermont town of Bennington. That descent is nothing more than a giant staircase made of slippery moss covered rocks, so be careful. I did it in the rain, so it was probably much worse in the wet conditions than I'm making it out to be. If it's dry for you, then you're lucky.

I recommend going into Bennington. It's a very neat town that has a cozy, small town - old timey feel, but with a very modern twist on all of it. I found it to be one of the more unique towns I encountered on the trail. The Catamount Inn Motel has some excellent prices for thru-hikers.

The climb on the other side of the road into Bennington is a good one. It's got a little bit of everything in regards to rocky steps, mud, and smooth incline. It won't rattle you, but you'll probably take your fair share of breathers before reaching the pinnacle of that series of climbs called Glastenbury Mountain, ten miles from the road.

You'll have some easy trail for another thirteen miles or so after Glastenbury Mountain, until you reach Mt. Stratton (birthplace of the concept for the AT). Mt. Stratton is a long 1,800- foot climb that honestly isn't too steep in most places; it's not a tough climb, just a long one. The summit is a rocky clearing with a caretaker's booth/cabin and a large fire tower you can climb and take in the views from. The descent down Stratton isn't much different from the climb, and the terrain for the next eleven miles or so isn't tough either.

Bromley Mountain will come after those eleven miles, also not a terribly difficult climb...unless it's raining. This mountain is used for skiing in the winter and the trail makes its way up some of these ski slopes. The slopes are made up of smooth grass or smooth dirt, and when they become wet, there is no traction for your shoes - creating a very slippery climb. There is a nice shelter a little more than half way up Bromley, but there is also a Ski Patrol cabin on the summit that is normally open to hikers. The cabin provides a very nice place to sleep out of any wind, rain, or cold temperatures.

After you complete Bromley, I have to admit the rest of Vermont is pretty challenging. There are a few level stretches thrown in there, but for the most part you'll be doing a lot of steep climbs and descents, one after the other. Starting about ten miles before Mt. Killington (the tallest mountain in Vermont), you're going to get hit with a few good climbs and descents. They're mostly short, but a couple will require a good bit of scrambling to navigate. When you hit the road "VT 103" that leads into the towns of Rutland or North Clarendon, you can take a left and be at a road side restaurant called "The Whistle Stop" in about half a mile. Good prices, good food, good atmosphere, and outlets to charge any devices outside. The climbs on the other side of "VT 103" are STEEP, and the prelude to the seemingly endless climb up Mt. Killington.

The climb up Mt. Killington isn't a physically tough climb. It's got a few steep areas, but mostly it's just very, very long. The climb itself is about 2,500 feet, and I'd have to say the hardest part of the climb is the multiple sections of washed out tree roots. Other than slick tree roots and some really washed out sections that require very large steps, it's not a very steep climb. There is a nice big shelter at the top which can accommodate a lot of people, and also a side trail that leads to some great views, as well as a ski lift. The descent from Killington is a breeze; you could probably jog most of it if you really wanted to.

The terrain is for the most part agreeable and relatively unchallenging for the next five miles after descending Killington. Those five miles will find you at the base of Quimby Mountain, as well as the beginning of the toughest stretch in all of Vermont. The next thirty-seven miles to New Hampshire are nothing more than a collection of short but steep climbs, one after the next. Quimby is an exception, because it's a long steep climb of mostly smooth dirt, thus burning your calves more than anything. This last section of Vermont was where I began to see Moose droppings for the first time, so keep your eyes peeled.

Approximately ten miles from the summit of Quimby is a side trail that leads to a lookout tower. It's labeled as "The Lookout" in your guide, but I assure you it's much more than a simple lookout. This is a four-walled building with a door, a loft, windows, and a fire place. There is also a front porch and a platform on the roof with benches. The view at sunrise and sunset from this location is utterly breathtaking and easily ranks as my favorite spot in all of Vermont. You can see Killington to the south, and even the White Mountains of New Hampshire way to the north. If you can make it so you end up staying here over night, you won't be disappointed.

The rest of Vermont will be short and steep climbs. These climbs will be different from other climbs in the sense they are completely smooth and free of rocks for the most part. This means nothing to step onto, which in turn means you'll have to lean into these climbs, subsequently setting your calves ablaze with lactic acid.

My last tip for Vermont comes in the town of West Hartford, about nine miles before the New Hampshire border. You'll road walk through a residential neighborhood here, then cross the White River Bridge spanning the White River. You can jump from this bridge if you want. There is paint on the rails near the center of the bridge, marking where the water is deepest on both sides; it's a very fun jump. Also, on the far side of the bridge, at the first house across the street on your right; there's a woman who has served thru-hikers breakfast, lunch, and dinner for years. She also allows you to camp in her yard if you wish. You won't find her listed in any guidebooks, so your meeting will have to be of your own design.

New Hampshire:

Miles of trail: 162

My impression: New Hampshire was a state I greatly looked forward to with a nervous excitement. You will hear throughout your entire time on the trail that New Hampshire has the toughest terrain there is. All of these rumors and descriptions of New Hampshire are going to build a pretty intimidating picture in your mind; I know it did for me. Overall, New Hampshire certainly has the longest, steepest, rockiest, most challenging climbs of the entire trail, no doubt. The bright side is you mostly won't care because the views afforded to you are unlike anything you've seen up until this point. The most fantastic, dramatically beautiful sunrises and sunsets you'll probably ever see will take place on a daily basis. I was blown away by the difficulty of this state, as well as the beauty. You begin to feel truly remote the further you push into New Hampshire.

Insights: The crossing into New Hampshire from Vermont will consist of the longest road walk of the entire trail at just over three miles. You'll cross into New Hampshire while on a bridge spanning the Connecticut River before making your way into the city of Hanover. Hanover is the home of the Ivy League Dartmouth College, so it's basically a big college town. It's extremely modern, hiker friendly, and has a myriad of great places to eat. The trail snakes through the heart of downtown, as well as several athletic fields and academic facilities. If you want to stay near the town (but not pay for a hotel), you can camp on the northern outskirts behind a soccer field, right where the trail picks back up from a road.

When you first leave Hannover, about forty-three miles will be separating you from the beginning of the White Mountains, the most infamous mountain range of the entire trail. These forty-three miles are going to be a major gut check, as well as a prelude to what the Whites have in store for you. You'll encounter quite a few big climbs, three of which are going to be exceptionally challenging. The order you will encounter them is as follows: Holts Ledge, Smarts Mountain, and Mt.

Cube. There are other climbs, but those are the only three really worth mentioning. If I mentioned every good climb in New Hampshire, I could write another book. Holts Ledge isn't a terribly long climb, but it's steep on both sides and will kick your ass. There is a road crossing at the bottom, and if you continue to follow the trail you'll see a sign pointing you in the direction of a private residence. The man at this house will allow you to play crochet, and give you ice cream; you can fill up on water and rest as well. *Update note: the owner of that property passed away after my thru- hike; I have no idea if anyone is carrying on his legacy.* Smarts Mountain is directly next; it's the first tall and steep mountain you'll encounter on this part of the trail. It's more than a 2,000- foot climb, and it's so steep in some places, they've sunk rebar and steps for you to hold onto or get footing. The summit has an old fire tower and an old fire warden's cabin. If the timing is right, I recommend camping here. Off a small side trail that's impossible to miss, there's a small grassy knoll with a fire ring surrounded by small pine trees. The view and location is gorgeous, especially at sunset. The descent down Smarts Mountain is long but relatively easy. Mt. Cube is a good climb, but it's made difficult by the many rocks that make up a large portion of the ascent. Many of the rocks are large, slanted chunks of granite that are easy to slip on, so be careful.

    The first forty-three-mile stretch will end at a road crossing in the residential neighborhood of the town of Glencliff. There is a hostel within walking distance of this road crossing where you can charter a shuttle for resupply, do laundry, get a shower, watch movies, etc. As soon as you depart this town, you'll be making your way into the Whites…

    For this next section, you'll have more than a hundred miles of the White Mountain range to cross. I'll get way too long winded trying to describe this entire section, so I'll list each noteworthy, larger mountain, as well as a brief description of what to expect; all in the order you will encounter them going north. I devoted a section earlier to the White Mountains regarding weather, hiking strategy, the huts, etc., so I'm going to keep this one specifically about the terrain.

Mt. Moosilauke: This is the first mountain you climb in the White Mountain range, and it'll find you ascending nearly four thousand feet to the summit, the longest continuous climb you'll encounter on the trail to date. The climb up Moosilauke is nothing short of monotonous, but not overly challenging. It never gets that steep, but it feels like it never ends. It's mostly rocky stairs on the way up, but the climb down is another story; it's a treacherous descent full of scrambles, foot holds, and rebar to grab onto. There is a narrow cascading waterfall that parallels the trail for a good portion of the way down. The descent of Moosilauke is the steepest one you'll encounter to date.

Mt. Kinsman: This Mountain has two peaks, and easily ranks as one of the toughest mountains of the trail. It's about a two-thousand-foot climb, and while the first half of that climb isn't too bad, the second half is nearly all hand over hand scrambling until the summit. Then you'll make a small descent before a short climb up to the second, lower summit. The climb down Kinsman is just as tough as the second half of the climb up; lots of scrambling, holding onto rocks and trees, as well as sliding down short but steep rock faces.

Mt. Lafayette: On paper, this three and a half-thousand- foot climb looks pretty daunting. In real life, it's not too terribly bad. Mt. Lafayette is actually a culmination of a couple different mountains, but they're all ascending towards the highest point, which is Lafayette. The first initial big climb is a lot like the climb up Moosilauke; it's a never ending rocky staircase. No real scrambles, just lots of stair steppers. The stairs will end near a short side trail that leads to the summit of Liberty Mountain. The summit of Liberty quite literally comes to a point, and serves as an absolutely amazing location to watch the sunset or take in an incredible view of the entire White Mountain Range. Continuing on the AT, you'll encounter a few little scrambles before emerging onto a famous section called Franconia Ridge. The ridge itself is not difficult to traverse, but the openness and views provided are staggering. Franconia will lead you to the summit of Lafayette. The climb down Lafayette isn't too bad for the most part, but there is a good mix of small scrambles here and there until you reach the climb up Mt. Garfield.

Mt. Garfield & South Twin Mountain: The climb up Garfield is steep and filled with a few scrambles here and there, but the climb down is harder. It's a lot of jagged rocks and big step-downs. You'll find yourself holding onto rocks in order to balance quite a few times; the going is very slow. The climb up South Twin is another climb that I would describe as fast and furious. It's over pretty quickly, but it's incredibly steep and filled with lots of rocky steps. The next fourteen miles from the summit of South Twin down into Crawford Notch is a mixture of small scrambling climbs and descents, mixed in with some bigger descents. There is also a seven mile stretch on an old railroad bed that accounts for the easiest flat stretch of the entire Whites. After the railroad bed is a relatively unchallenging, but long descent into Crawford Notch. You can get to the Appalachian Mountain Club (AMC) from the road in Crawford Notch.

Presidential Mountain Range: Between Crawford Notch and Pinkham Notch is a twenty-six mile stretch of mountains known as the Presidential Mountain Range. This is the most dangerous, unpredictable stretch of the entire White Mountain Range. A vast majority of these twenty-six miles will reside above tree line, leaving you exposed to any wind and weather. You'll first climb nearly three thousand feet straight up Mt. Webster. This mountain has a little bit of everything, and is an extremely challenging climb that feels like it never ends. You'll have rock scrambles of varying degrees, smooth inclines, little flat areas, and large humps of rock to climb up and over. After Webster, you'll encounter (in ascending order): Mt. Jackson, Mt. Pierce, Mt. Eisenhower, Mt. Monroe, and then the tallest mountain of the Whites (as well as the entire northeastern United States) - Mt. Washington. After you finish climbing Webster, the going will be a little slow while you're still under the trees. Once you break through the tree line and get up on the ridge, you'll be able to move a little quicker. The terrain isn't too bad, but the distractions are mesmerizing. You'll make your way up and down short climbs and descents while slowly making your way to the final climb up Mt. Washington. You won't find hardly any scrambles, just a rocky path. The final climb to the summit of Mt. Washington will be a rocky staircase ascent of about 1,200 feet. Upon reaching the summit, you'll find a gift shop, snack bar, restaurant, observatory, post office, a train station, plus a few other small buildings. You don't get the solitude you might desperately crave up there, but you'll welcome the food happily.

Coming down the Presidential Range is decidedly more difficult than going up. From the summit of Mt. Washington onward (for the next nine miles) you'll be walking on very coarse, sometimes jagged rocks. This section is torture for most dogs, as I had to carry mine the entire way. I also encountered the blood trail from a large white lab that was too big for its owner to carry. So, doggy hikers beware! After descending Washington for more than a thousand feet, you'll climb and descend Mt. Jefferson, Mt. Adams, and Mt. Madison. This is a grueling section that's tough on your feet; it was made all the more grueling for me by carrying my dog. The last climb up Madison is a rocky hell, right before a three-thousand-foot descent towards Osgood Cutoff. That three-thousand-foot descent from Madison is quite literally nothing but boulder hopping on jagged and steep rocks the entire way. I would personally say it's the most challenging descent of the entire trail, with the exception of one other in Maine. After you finish the descent down Madison, you'll have a relative easy five-mile stretch to reach Pinkham Notch where you can catch a ride into the town of Gorham.

The next twenty-three mile stretch of the White Mountains between Pinkham Notch and the "US-2" road is, in my opinion, the most physically challenging section of the Whites; it's also the final section of the Whites. Once you exit the northern boundary of the White Mountains National Park, you only have sixteen miles before you reach Maine. The combination of the "longest, steepest" climb of the entire trail will kick off that twenty-three-mile stretch in the form of Wildcat Mountain; two thousand feet straight up, vertical stair cases, long scrambles, hand over hand. The rest of that twenty- three miles will be a never-ending barrage of steep climbs and descents, with a rapid fire of small up and down scrambles until you reach a rather sloping descent that takes you to "US-2," as well as the northern boundary of the White Mountains. You can hitch a ride back into Gorham from this road if you wish.

The last sixteen miles out of New Hampshire are a series of large to medium climbs and descents, with more scrambles thrown in than you can count. The going is slow and grueling, and it's tough to keep up a good pace with all the short hand over hand climbs. Within a quarter mile of the Maine border, you'll slide down an enormous, smooth rock face. I recommend hugging the edge and grabbing onto whatever trees and vegetation you can. Congratulations, you survived New Hampshire!

Maine:

Miles of trail: 282

My impression: Maine is the grand finale that lives up to every expectation you've conceived prior to reaching it. The majesty of Maine is unrivaled to anywhere else on the trail (in my own humble opinion). Whatever the rest of the trail had to offer, Maine outdid it in every way possible - good and bad. When I crossed into Maine, the realization of "I am a thru-hiker," finally set in. I never felt more isolated and remote than I did when I was in Maine; I couldn't get enough of it. Most people say New Hampshire is home to the toughest terrain, but for me personally, southern Maine easily holds that title. If long, endless climbs are what you consider torture, then New Hampshire might seem harder to you. If a medley of constant rock scrambles, mud pits, and no shortage of steep, challenging climbs that never let you maintain any kind of regular pace are your bane, then southern Maine will undoubtedly be harder. Even though Maine was the most physically grueling state, I found it the most beautiful. I also found myself never wanting it to end...

Insights: I would describe the first 110 miles of Maine as the nearest thing to being put through a grinder as physically possible. You truly don't catch a break throughout this section, and if you have any injuries, aches, or pains - they're definitely going to be exploited to the full extent. You'll never cross more rivers, streams, and creeks than you do in Maine. You'll find yourself wading across bodies of water throughout this entire state. Most of the time they're very shallow, but after a good rain they can become swift and deep. Always use proper judgment before you ford a river in Maine, especially after a hard rain.

The first six and a half miles of Maine are nothing but an up and down slough of short rock scrambles and mud pits. The going is incredibly slow, and the potential for injury high. At the end of those six and a half miles you will reach Mahoosuc Notch, an area dubbed the "hardest or most fun mile of the entire trail." Mahoosuc Notch is nothing more than a mile-long jumble of boulders that come in every shape and size imaginable. You'll climb, slide, leap, crawl, squeeze, shimmy, and stride your way through this section. Even though it's only a mile long, most people take an hour and a half to two hours to complete it. It's totally up to your perspective whether this is the "hardest or "most fun" mile of the trail. I had a blast in Mahoosuc Notch, but I could easily see how this mile could be an absolute nightmare for some people. Once again, doggie hikers beware!

Directly after Mahoosuc Notch, you'll climb 1,800 feet straight up Mahoosuc Arm Mountain. This is a brutally steep ascent filled with lots of smooth rock faces that force you to lean hard into the climb. The summit is a crater with a body of water called Speck Pond. The camping around there is beautiful, but depending on when you pass through, it could be exceptionally cold.

I could go on and on about the next hundred miles of Maine, but I would repeat myself often. The terrain is going to be a constant mixture of big climbs, scrambles, mud, washed out roots, and rock for the entire time. There will be some milder areas thrown in, but they will be mostly short lived. I would have to say the easiest stretch of southern Maine would be the fourteen miles leading into the town of Rangeley, about sixty miles in.

You'll stop in nearly every town in Maine due to the fact they're further apart than the towns anywhere else on the trail; resupply options aren't very good in those towns either. The town of Rangeley is the last conveniently reached town in Maine that has an actual supermarket. A very good strategy is to buy two or three resupplies worth of food in Rangeley, then mail two of them ahead to yourself. Send one to the post office in Caratunk, and one to the post office in Monson. These are the last two towns you'll visit before you finish the trail; neither of them have very good resupply options (and are also pricey). That being said, you can always make-due with what you do find; that's part of the fun and challenge of this adventure.

The last string of exceptionally challenging mountains in southern Maine will end with the completion of the Bigelow Mountains. The Bigelow Mountains stretch for about fourteen miles, and upon their completion, you will have finished the worst of what Maine has to offer. There will be virtually no more scrambles after the Bigelow Mountains. Only a couple miles after these mountains is a huge body of water called Flagstaff Lake. If you can camp here, do it. The call of the loons around this lake in the evenings, nighttime, and early morning is absolutely staggering!

From Flagstaff to the next town of Caratunk, a distance of about nineteen miles, the trail is what I can only describe as mostly leisurely. A couple very easy ups and downs, with some mud and root beds thrown in there, but for the most part it's a cake walk compared to what you have gone through. Throughout this nineteen-mile stretch, there are a few exceptionally beautiful locations worth your time to stop or even camp at. The first is a spot called East Carry Pond. The water is shallow, crystal clear, and there is a sandy little beach that offers an amazing camping or hang-out spot to relax. Carry Pond is about nine miles past Flagstaff Lake. Around six miles past Carry Pond is a shelter called Pierce Pond Lean-To; this is another stunning location that offers some exceptional swimming if you're up for it (a hiker has drowned here due to cramping in the cold water, so beware).

Half a mile before you reach Caratunk, you'll reach the Kennebec River. During the height of hiking season, there is a man that ferries people across in a canoe for free. He usually has specific hours that he's available at different times of the year (you'll find these out while on trail). It's smart to utilize the canoe, but some people ford the river on their own. It's several hundred feet across, but if you can find the right spot, it's shallow enough to wade the entire thing; you cross at your own risk, as some people have been swept away and drowned in the past.

From the towns of Caratunk to Monson is a distance of about thirty-seven miles. This is a fairly easy stretch, aside from two moderately challenging climbs up Pleasant Pond Mountain and Moxie Bald Mountain. Again, there will be some rocky terrain through here, as well as no shortage of mud, roots, and small river crossings, but for the most part it's not overly difficult.

The town of Monson is the last town you'll visit while thru-hiking the Appalachian Trail. This town also marks the southern boundary of the 100-Mile Wilderness. The 100-Mile Wilderness is the longest stretch without resupply on the entire trail. You will need to pack a minimum of five days of food; six days if you want to play it safe. This stretch is actually slightly over a hundred miles long, ending at Abol Bridge, right on the border of Baxter State Park. There is a camp store just past the bridge where you can get a modest resupply for the remainder of the time it takes you to reach Katahdin, climb up, climb down, then hitchhike to the nearest town of Millinocket some twenty miles away. From the camp store, most people will resupply about two days-worth of food with some extra snacks thrown in.

The Hundred-Mile Wilderness is what I would call the grand finale of the trail. To me it was the most beautiful stretch of trail in all of Maine; I only wished I could have spent more time there. For this final hundred-miles you can expect a little bit of everything; river crossings, rocks, roots, mud, waterfalls, ponds, large to small climbs, you name it. It could be said the washed-out root beds in the Hundred-Mile Wilderness are synonymous with the volume of rocks in northern Pennsylvania. The first 47 miles of the Hundred-Mile Wilderness are the most physically challenging and slow going. They will be filled with a constant onslaught of short but steep climbs and descents covered in rocks, roots, moss, and mud; with a few longer climbs thrown in.

The last big obstacles you'll face in this first 47-mile stretch is a string of mountains by the names of Gulf Hagas Mountain, West Peak, Hay Mountain, then finally climaxing at White Cap Mountain before a long descent back down. These climbs are challenging, but you will have faced much tougher. On a clear day, you'll get your first good glimpse of Mt. Katahdin from the summit of White Cap Mountain.

A little over ten miles after your descent from White Cap Mountain, you'll reach Cooper Brook Falls Lean-To. The cascading waterfall here is breathtaking, and the swimming hole it empties into is one of the best I've seen on the entire trail. If it's a hot day when you pass through here, keep this information in mind.

The rest of the Hundred-Mile Wilderness after White Cap Mountain is for the most part a mall walk. There will be a few little ups and downs, as well as no shortage of mud and washed out roots, but you're basically home free until Katahdin. You can look forward to an excellent view of your final destination from a small climb called the Rainbow Ledges; you'll reach them about six miles before Abol Bridge.

When you enter Baxter State Park, you'll have to register your presence at a small booth that lies directly on the trail. You'll simply sign in, and a park employee/volunteer will go over a few policies and ground rules before allowing you to continue on. It's only a ten mile stretch from Abol Bridge to the campgrounds at the base of Katahdin. That ten-mile stretch is an absolute breeze, although you will have to ford two rivers before you finish it. There is a side trail that bypasses those river crossings, but this trail is not recognized officially as the AT.

From the "Katahdin Stream Campground" at the base of Katahdin, you'll have five miles to reach the summit. The first mile is a cake walk, while the next couple miles after that are the hardest miles of the entire trail (in my opinion, and many others). You'll start off with some easy scrambles, but once you break through the tree line, you'll encounter a scene that resembles a vertical Mahoosuc Notch. You will be climbing over rocks for more than a mile before you reach The Tablelands. The Tablelands will be a flat walk over rocks for a short distance before the trail begins to gradually slope up towards the summit. Once you hit The Tableland, the rest of the way to the summit sign is extremely easy. Depending on the time of year, it could be a beautifully clear day, or a fogged-over, icy wonderland. Either way, nothing will dampen your spirits as the feeling of momentous accomplishment washes over your entire being. CONGRATULATIONS Thru-Hiker, you just completed the entire Appalachian Trail.

Post Completion

Once you've reached the summit sign and basked in all your glory, you have to then make that grueling climb back down. Some people have family meet them in Baxter, but many don't have anyone meet them. The plan after you climb back down is to find your way into the nearest town of Millinocket. It'll be easy to find a ride with park visitors, another thru hiker's family, or simply pay for a shuttle. From Millinocket, you can find a ride to the city of Bangor (about fifty miles away), where there will be an international airport ready to fly you home, or onto your next adventure. Of course, you can always rent a car and make a road trip out of the journey home, stopping at as many familiar places along the trail as possible. Some people even choose to hitchhike back home.

Final Words

Phew! That was a lot of information, but I think I've covered just about anything you'd need or want to know in regards to thru-hiking the AT, and maybe a little bit more. A lot of this information may seem like basic, common sense stuff, but if I didn't put it in here, I promise somebody might be wondering or asking about it. I've done my best not to be too biased, get too preachy, or make you feel like I'm telling you how to hike. If you felt that way at any point, I sincerely apologize, as it was not my intention. This adventure is about freedom and self-discovery; figuring things out on your own - sometimes the hard way. Although I may have suggested a certain way of doing things; always go with your gut instinct. The worst that can happen is you learn something… by trial and error, perhaps.

Let me confide something in you… If you are reading this, having never done any long-distance hiking, and are currently preparing to embark on your first thru-hike… I envy you. You have no idea what an incredible experience you are about to have, as there is nothing in the world like your first thru-hike. So, I say unto you this – ENJOY IT! Enjoy every single wonderful, miserable second of it. Keep your sense of humor at all times, keep yourself open to new things, leave no stone unturned, and embrace every experience that comes your way - while laughing at all the bad things that happen to you. It doesn't matter how many bad days you have, because when the day comes that you look back on them all… they're going to feel like the best days of your life!

So now that you've heard the challenge…

Are you ready to answer the call?

-Kyle S. Rohrig-

If you would like to read the full story of the author's Appalachian Trail thru-hike, check out his other book...

"Lost on the Appalachian Trail"

Made in the USA
Lexington, KY
07 February 2017